Lipstick & High Heels

Compliments of / Gracieuseté du
Canadian Forces College / Collége des Forces canadiennes
Information Centre / Centre d'information
215 Yonge Blvd.
Toronto, Ontario
M5M 3H9

Lipstick and High Heels:

WAR, GENDER AND POPULAR CULTURE

Emily Spencer

CANADIAN DEFENCE ACADEMY PRESS

Canadian Defence Academy Press
PO Box 17000 Stn Forces
Kingston, Ontario   K7K 7B4

Produced for the Canadian Defence Academy Press
by 17 Wing Winnipeg Publishing Office.
WPO30285

Front Cover Photo: "Welcome Home – VE Day" by Silvia Pecota
                    Courtesy Silvia Pecota
Back Cover Photo: "The Bren Gun Girl" Photographer unknown,
                    National Film Board of Canda,
                    WRM 768, DAPDCAP562468

Library and Archives Canada Cataloguing in Publication

Spencer, Emily
Lipstick and high heels : war, gender and popular culture / Emily Spencer.

Issued by Canadian Defence Academy.
Includes bibliographical references: p.
ISBN 978-0-662-46283-5 (bound).--ISBN 978-0-662-46284-2 (pbk)
Cat. no.: D2-208/1-2007E (bound) -- Cat. no.: D2-208/2-2007E (pbk)

1. Women--Press coverage--Canada--History--20th century.
2. Gender identity--Press coverage--Canada--History--20th century.
3. Sex roles--Press coverage--Canada--History--20th century. 4. World War,
1939-1945--Press coverage--Canada.   5. Chatelaine (Toronto, Ont. : 1928).
I. Canadian Defence Academy II. Title.

PN4914.W6S63 2007   070.4'83470971   C2007-980227-3

Printed in Canada.

1 3 5 7 9 10 8 6 4 2

For my mother,
Claudia

Acknowledgement

Any work of this magnitude owes its completion to a host of individuals who directly or indirectly assisted in its production. As such, I would be remiss if I did not sincerely thank Dr. E. Jane Errington for all of her tireless efforts in helping me write this book. This volume would not be what it is today without the continuous inspiration and insight that she provided. I owe her my deepest gratitude for all the attention that she paid to the seemingly endless number of drafts that I provided.

Colonel Bernd Horn also deserves special recognition. Without his motivation, endless encouragement and (gentle) prodding there was the real danger that this manuscript would have sat for a lengthy period before being put on the shelf to add to literature on gender, war and society. Colonel Horn deserves thanks for insisting that I "get on with it."

Additionally, I would like to thank the staff at both the Royal Military College of Canada's Massey Library and Queen's University Stauffer Library for their professional and responsive assistance. My research was greatly facilitated by the kind staffs at each institution.

Last, but certainly not least, I must acknowledge all the support, guidance and encouragement that I received from family and friends. This network was invaluable in keeping me focused and inspired. To all of them I owe a great debt of gratitude.

Like the stories of the women and men that are retold in *Lipstick and High Heels*, the process of writing this book is not reflective of the acts of a singular person; rather, it was the combination of certain instrumental people that allowed me to put pen to paper or, more precisely, finger to keyboard. I sincerely thank all of you and humbly recognize that what is good is reflective of this group dynamic and what is lacking is my sole responsibility.

Table of Contents

Foreword

I am delighted to have been asked to write this foreword to *Lipstick and High Heels: War, Gender and Popular Culture*. This book has been written by a new scholar who I have had the privilege of watching develop over the past few years. And the result is a study that provides fresh insight into the field of gender, war and society.

The interplay of gender, war and popular culture has received little scholarly attention, particularly in the Canadian context. Yet, popular culture – magazines, television, and today, the internet – has been and continues to be an important vehicle through which gendered relationships have been shaped. Certainly many things, including the ways that women and men are viewed in contemporary Canadian society, have changed since the Second World War; at the same time, gendered relationships today continue to be shaped by those of the past. Moreover, such issues as balancing career and family are as relevant today for both men and women as they were in the mid twentieth century. The insights provided by this examination of *Chatelaine* magazine between the end of the 1920s and the mid 1950s provide a critical lens through which to understand the present.

Understanding how war can and does affect culture is particularly relevant to Canadian Forces personnel today. In a world that is increasingly complex and that requires all the unique skills of those engaged in the profession of arms, military history of the kind offered by this study helps to fill an important niche in continuing education so vital to the development of the first-class army. *Lipstick and High Heels* makes an important contribution to our understanding of ourselves, one that should reach beyond the traditional scholarly audience to include those women and men who are actually engaged in conflict and directly implicated in forging those dynamic relationships between gender and war.

E. Jane Errington
Professor
History Department
Royal Military College of Canada

Preface

The Canadian Forces Leadership Institute (CFLI) is proud to release *Lipstick and High Heels: War, Gender and Popular Culture* under the auspices of the Canadian Defence Academy (CDA) Press. This title adds another important work to our ongoing effort to create a distinct body of Canadian literature on conflict, war and society. For too long, the Canadian Forces has relied on foreign examples, case studies and research to address issues important to our own distinct professional development. Through the seminal CFLI Strategic Leadership Writing Project, we have started to correct this imbalance. After all, we have a rich military heritage and moreover, Canadian examples are more pertinent and relevant to our own military culture, temperament and character.

Lipstick and High Heels is a significant addition to the project. Written by Dr. Emily Spencer, it provides an excellent account of how war affects perceptions of gender in the popular media. Although *Lipstick and High Heels* is an examination of how the Second World War affected images of women and men in *Chatelaine* magazine, the conclusions underscore relationships that are particularly relevant today given the current defence environment. The interplay of gender, war and popular culture is an often neglected subject, yet one that arguably shapes many facets of our lives as Canadians.

I believe you will find this book of great interest and value whether you are a military professional, a scholar or simply interested in the study of conflict and war. As always, we at CFLI and the CDA Press invite your comment and discussion.

Colonel Bernd Horn
Chairman, CDA Press

Chapter One

Introduction:
Studying Gender, War and Society

To the women of Canada,

Wherever we turn to day [sic], we see and hear the oft repeated phrase "this is total war." If we, the women of the Western World, accept this as literally true, we must fight for victory just as valiantly as our gallant soldiers, sailors and airmen.

Our weapons on the spiritual side are courage, faith and inspiration. On the mental plane, we must cultivate clear, forceful minds. From the physical standpoint, we must keep our bodies healthy, strong. On the material side, we must look to our budgets and find new economies in every sphere, in the kitchen, in our wardrobes, in our daily beauty routine.

…Our men are fighting for the preservation of good things of life – beauty is certainly one of them – beauty of character, of expression, beauty of self-sacrifice. Let us preserve these ideals while the battle rages.

Helena Rubinstein
Chatelaine, March 1942[1]

In November 1942, an advertisement for the Canada Starch Company appeared in *Chatelaine*, a popular magazine for middle-class Canadian women.[2] It encouraged Canadians to pay tribute "to those mothers and wives who are exerting every effort to keep the workers of Canada fit

[and] vigorous...." The advertisement continued, "*They are Canada's housesoldiers.* They are doing their part by devoting their skill and knowledge to providing appetizing and nourishing meals that protect and preserve the health of those carrying on the war work of the nation."[3] The Department of Munitions and Supply for Canada also ran an advertisement in *Chatelaine* that suggested women could best contribute to the war effort as "good" wives and homemakers. The advertisement observed that "Men produce more when their minds are at ease, when they are not worried by domestic problems." It advised women that "If you shoulder these worries and help your men to relax, you are playing a real part in winning the war." It encouraged women to "do [their] part cheerfully for [their] country's sake. Keep that man of yours fit and happy for his job." The advertisement provided women with the slogan, "Brave men shall not die because I faltered."[4]

According to *Chatelaine*, women also supported the war effort by symbolizing a democratic ideal. As *Chatelaine* contributor Helena Rubinstein noted to the women of Canada in the epigraph, among other things, Canadian men were fighting to preserve the beautiful housewife heroine. "He's fighting for you – so it's up to you to look the part!" stated a January 1943 advertisement for Woodbury Cold Cream.[5] A November 1942 advertisement for Palmolive Beauty Oils upheld the image of a beautiful woman supplying the motivation for men to fight. A blonde starlet declared, "I pledge myself to guard every bit of beauty that he [soldiers, sailors and airmen] cherishes in me."[6] For women who wished to support the war effort through their femininity, the Don Juan Lipstick Company created the new colour "Military Red" to help them express their patriotism.[7] Tangee, a competitor of Don Juan's, acknowledged in 1943 that "No lipstick – ours or anyone else's – will win the war." "But," the advertisement continued, "it symbolizes one of the reasons why we are fighting ... the precious right of women to be feminine and lovely – under any circumstance."[8]

Chatelaine did recognize and applaud the growing number of women who were working in factories to support the war effort and the women who donned the uniforms of the three women's military services. But, even among these women who performed "double duty"[9] during the war years, femininity was not to be neglected. The Tangee advertisement noted of Canadian and American women that "It's a reflection of the free democratic way of life that you have succeeded in keeping your femininity – even though you are doing man's work!"[10] To encourage women to keep up their beauty routine, Palmolive sponsored a "Miss War Worker" beauty contest.[11] Other beauty pageants were also organized for women working in factories. In August 1944 *Chatelaine* correspondent Adele White observed about one contest that, "The winner was no breath-taking blonde, no dashing brunette nor flashing redhead. She was the all-Canadian type with chestnut hair, fair skin and grey eyes. It was her attention to detail, her carriage, her complexion, her hands, smile and trim, straight figure – all as perfect as possible."[12] *Chatelaine's* wartime message was clear: Canadian women should look their best while supporting their men.

The wartime images of modern Canadian womanhood that appeared in *Chatelaine* are perhaps not surprising. As a number of authors have noted, in Canada and other parts of the western world, war afforded women unprecedented opportunities both for work and for play; at the same time many of the images of women presented by the popular presses emphasized their femininity and physical appearance.

Lipstick and High Heels explores some of the continuities and changes to the images of middle-class Canadian womanhood expressed in *Chatelaine* throughout the depression, the war years, a postwar economic boom and into the Cold War. Of particular interest is how World War Two may have affected these images. This examination of one of Canada's principal women's magazines during the thirty years surrounding the

Second World War suggests that the relationship of gender, war and society is more complicated than the historical record suggests. This is partially because most historians who have explored this issue have concentrated their attention on the war itself, generally to the neglect of the pre- and postwar periods.

Notably, *Chatelaine's* wartime images of modern Canadian womanhood were not simply a continuation of those published in the early 1930s. *Chatelaine's* modern woman of the 1920s and early 1930s was capable in both the public and private spheres[13] and her competence was not a direct measure of her femininity.[14] Examining the images of middle-class Canadian womanhood within the broader time frame from 1928 to 1956 reveals that the images of women presented in *Chatelaine* did not just change with the coming of war in 1939. Rather, it was when the survival of democracy seemed to be in serious peril, starting in 1936/37, that the capable, competent woman began to give way to the "lovely," feminine woman who existed largely in the shadows of her husband and children.

For example, in March 1930 author C.B. Robertson described to *Chatelaine* readers how Mary Ellen Smith, a member of the British Columbia Legislature, had in 1918 been able to accommodate a group of returning World War One soldiers gathered in Victoria to secure certain rights from their provincial government. The group had been largely successful in achieving its goals. Nonetheless, the returning soldiers remained "anti-government." Robertson observed, "How that antagonism, that discord, was overcome by the lone woman on the platform was a fine example of physical capacity – poise. Of mental capacity – stored up power to think and speak clearly in an emergency which would have put the average man's ideas to flight. Of spiritual power existing by virtue of the fact that Mary Ellen Smith 'loves people,' and so seems to know intuitively how to bring harmony out of discord."[15]

To Robertson, what Smith had said was not as important as how she had said it and the authority that she, as a woman, had brought to the occasion. There was no doubt that Smith was a wife and a mother. Indeed, in the first paragraph it was even noted that she was a grandmother. It was also without question that Smith projected through her poise and demeanour a distinctive femininity. But these characteristics did not limit her. Instead, they provided her with credibility in the eyes of the returning veterans and motivation to extend her purview beyond that of hearth and home, although notably remaining within the scope of social welfare and the improvement of living conditions for Canadian men and women.[16]

It is unlikely that Mary Ellen Smith would have been content to simply apply the new lip shade "Military Red" in support of the men overseas during the Second World War. By the 1940s, however, when Canadian women entered the workforce in unprecedented numbers, *Chatelaine* underscored the importance of the beautiful housewife heroine to the war effort. And, in many ways, *Chatelaine*'s wartime images of Canadian women persisted into the postwar years.

Chatelaine magazine, a monthly Canadian periodical that began in 1928 and is still in production, is an excellent vehicle through which to explore popular perceptions about the past because it had a wide national circulation and it had a rich format that exposed readers to an array of articles and advertisements.[17] Through its design, *Chatelaine* consciously reached out to "modern" middle-class Canadian women. Indeed, *Chatelaine*'s producers remarked in 1930 that "The quality of homes reached by *The Chatelaine* is reflected by the high type of its editorial content."[18] The pages of the magazine included the latest fashions. Each month, *Chatelaine* provided readers with: recipes for meals to be prepared quickly from small budgets; national and international news items; and short stories which allowed an escape from reality while still reflecting

Canadian society. Advice on a range of topics, such as how to be a good wife and mother and how to change a flat tire, was published and readers were given the opportunity to write directly to the staff. As the increase in sales and numerous reader responses and debates that appeared suggest, *Chatelaine's* largely female readership poured over the magazine's contents and eagerly anticipated each month's new arrival – it also appears that some husbands and brothers perused the periodical as well.

The Chatelaine[19] first appeared on news-stands in March 1928. It appeared at a time in which Fraser Sutherland suggests in *The Monthly Epic: A History of Canadian Magazines, 1799-1989,* that "The sharp division between myopic specialists and mass homogenizers had become the norm. Class was giving away to crass."[20] *Chatelaine* was unquestionably a mass circulation magazine that targeted white, Anglo-Saxon, middle-class Canadian women for its readership.[21] It was certainly not crass, however.

Mrs. Hilda Pain, a rancher's wife living in Eburne, British Columbia was the winner of the contest to name the new magazine. As she explained, "I pictured in my mind's eye, the cover of the new-women's magazine decorated with the gracious figure of a chatelaine, standing at the head of a flight of steps, inviting with outstretched hands the women of Canada to enter and enjoy the restful charm of her home." According to Pain, in addition to standing for "attributes a woman naturally desires to posses," the chatelaine, with her French origins, could also serve to connect French and English Canadians.[22] These sentiments were echoed in that month's editorial, "The Chatelaine Sets a Lamp in Her Window." Editor Anne Elizabeth Wilson described the magazine's intended audience: "…it is from the Canadian Woman herself that the lamp's hail has called forth the greatest response. To her, we believe it has seemed a beacon burning on the borders of a new country. … The Chatelaine's lamp will be held high to light the way for the women of Canada."[23]

Wilson appeared to be appealing to all Canadian women. Class, race and ethnicity, however, undoubtedly mitigated the call. Despite Mrs. Pain's optimism to bridge French/English tensions, *Chatelaine* was an English magazine for white, middle-class, Canadian women – true to Mrs. Pain's image, the type of woman who could afford to live in such a home.[24] As Fraser Sutherland notes, "*Chatelaine* was resolutely middle-class."[25]

Chatelaine met with instant success and became Maclean Publishing's most profitable and long lasting woman's magazine.[26] By December of its first year, *Chatelaine's* sales had surpassed 57,000.[27] Within two years, 122,000 copies were printed and the magazine was closing the gap on the *Canadian Home Journal's* 132,000 annual circulation.[28] In May 1930, in an advertisement that appeared in the magazine, it was remarked that "The progress made by The Chatelaine since its inception just two years ago, is quite the most remarkable thing of its kind ever witnessed in Canadian journalism."[29] By 1950 *Chatelaine* had an annual circulation of 378,866 and, over the next decade, its circulation almost doubled reaching 745,589 by 1960.[30] Moreover, according to a *Chatelaine* advertisement, "by 1959 one of every three English-speaking women in Canada, or a total of 1,650,000, read each issue of *Chatelaine*."[31] While this last estimate may be slightly exaggerated, it is undeniable that the magazine reached a large audience of Canadian women.

Chatelaine did not present a uniform model of Canadian womanhood throughout its first thirty years of publication. The images of womanhood of the late 1920s and early 1930s were in many ways quite different than those of the 1940s and 1950s. Yet, even in particular periods, no one single model applied. At the same time, however, whether she was reading *Chatelaine* in the early 1930s or in the mid 1950s, all Canadian women were presumed to share a number of attributes. They tended to be white and middle-class and they were, in *Chatelaine's* understanding, unquestionably "modern." Most were wives and mothers;

many worked for wages and/or participated in club work; and *Chatelaine* encouraged its readers to support world peace and to help build a strong national identity. What this meant both for individual women and for Canadian womanhood changed over time.

There is no doubt that the coming of war in 1939 – and indeed the fear of war two or three years earlier – was one of the factors that made a difference in how women, and men, were portrayed in *Chatelaine*, but it did so in complicated ways. In its first ten years, *Chatelaine's* modern woman was capable and competent in both the private and public sphere, as well as feminine. In the late 1930s, *Chatelaine's* modern woman became increasingly connected to the private sphere, and excluded from the public one, as her roles as wife, mother and home-maker became even more central to her character. Femininity too started to be underscored in the magazine and often overshadowed other aspects of Canadian womanhood. Interestingly, the images of modern Canadian womanhood expressed in *Chatelaine* actually changed in 1936/37, at the same time that the magazine was also publishing articles that suggested that another European war was inevitable and that the survival of democracy might be at risk. Indeed, the traditional periodization of the study of gender, war and society might be slightly off; threat perception might be a more valuable starting point.

One of the central concerns regarding the possible effects of war on society is the question of whether war was an agent that "liberated" women from a subordinate role within the nuclear family and confine-ment in the private sphere of the home. Indeed, the emphases on the importance of motherhood and femininity to the development of womanhood during periods of conflict have created a framework through which most academics, consciously and unconsciously, have measured changes in gender norms. Women are less likely to be consid-ered "liberated" if they are associated with motherhood and the home;

conversely, women's association with the public sphere is often used to suggest "progress." Ideas of femininity are also connected with women's liberation in some of the same ways that motherhood has been. For example, Ruth Roach Pierson is clear when she declares that in Canada following the Second World War, "feminism was once again sacrificed to femininity," thereby implying that feminism and femininity are incompatible concepts.[32] In fact, Pierson's definition of femininity leaves no doubt about this connection. "Through dress, deportment, mannerisms, speech, facial expression, cognitive style, and emotive range and mode," Pierson writes, "femininity 'both signifies and maintains' women's difference from, deference toward, and dependence on men."[33] Only recently has Canadian historian Jeffrey A. Keshen questioned the all or nothing nature of femininity versus feminism in this context.[34]

In general terms, there are three main schools of thought as to how the two world wars affected social attitudes about women's places in societies. A number of commentators argue that the wars taught women independence and helped to "liberate" them from the home. Other historians suggest that the wars actually hampered women's fight for equality and that women were pushed or ran back to the home with renewed vigour in 1918 and again in 1945. A third school of thought proposes that the wars were not watershed moments and women's social status was unaltered during, or immediately after, either conflict.

According to many women at the time, particularly those of the Great War, each world war brought with it a brief sense of gender equality – or at least less inequality. Their sentiments were later seized upon by some political and military historians wishing to incorporate women, even if marginally, into the historical account. For example, historian Deborah Thorn illustrates how part of the British museum's commemoration of the First World War, which was orchestrated by the early twentieth century feminist Agnes Conway, was gendered in its representation of events and clearly favoured the portrayal of women in non-traditional roles such as munitions work. According to Thorn, the exhibit underscored changes in women's behaviours between 1914 and 1918 and paid little attention to the continuities of the period. In her opinion, the image of the housewife/mother was underrepresented in the exhibit. This absence caused Thorn to remark that it was obvious that Conway "was entirely devoted to the idea of the war as benefit, rather than loss, for the image of women and their capacities."[35] Many women in the 1920s are believed to have shared Conway's convictions. Author Deidre Beddoe chronicles that "Some [British] feminists … genuinely believed that the war had revolutionized men's minds about their conception of the sort of work of which ordinary everyday women were capable."[36] The implication was that as a result of their participation in the war effort of 1914-1918, women had "liberated" themselves from the confines of home and family and the necessity to be overtly feminine.

Certainly, the most tangible evidence of women's "social climb" was their newly acquired right to vote.[37] When Arthur Marwick states in his 1974 book, *War and Social Change in the Twentieth Century*, that the "success story" of women in the First World War is well known, he is directly referring to women's suffrage. Marwick is careful to explain, however, that British women had gained this right not because of the contributions that they had made between 1914 and 1918, but because of the associated need for the British government to redefine men's suffrage during the war.[38] Yet, in an apparent dismissal of his previous statements, Marwick concludes that, "…once all differences are stated, the process by which women's participation in the war effort brought considerable social, economic and political gains can be traced in a straightforward manner. The first issue to stress … [is] the desire of governments to offer reward for services rendered. …"[39]

In a recent study of Canadian propaganda and censorship during the Great War, Jeffrey A. Keshen also concludes that World War One lessened the subordination of women to men in the postwar period. He argues that between 1914 and 1918 women acquired an "unprecedented feeling of independence" that fuelled their self-confidence. He suggests, however, that with the armistice, many women were less concerned with continuing "such liberating trends" and turned once again to "catching a husband" while their married counterparts "eagerly abdicated the double bind of home-based and outside work for sole custody over the domestic sphere."[40] Family life once again became their number one priority. But Keshen also asserts that "Such alterations, when combined with the new female voting rights, no doubt produced difficulties in many domiciles, especially since more than a few men [had gone] overseas to re-assert masculine dominance over the feminizing aspects of modern society."[41] Apparently, the potential for husband-wife tension in the home and women's newly acquired suffrage, when compared to the actual return of women to the home, was enough for Keshen to conclude that the Great War increased male-female equality. Keshen, however, provides little evidence in support of his arguments except to reference Veronica Strong-Boag's "New Girl of the New Day." But the "New Girl of the New Day" had much in common with her predecessors and was more illustrative of continuities than of discontinuities with the past. "The Great Depression of the 1930s," Veronica Strong-Boag writes, "only confirmed what Canadians in the main already appreciated: changes in human behaviour were hard won, deeply resisted, and not always what they seemed."[42]

Nonetheless, the "watershed theory" continues to hold popular appeal. Author Yvonne Klein notes, with some disappointment, in her anthology of women's wartime autobiographical writings that "...seventy odd years after the Great War, my students tell me confidently every year that the war was a good thing for women: it gave them the vote and jobs."[43] This theory has also been applied to World War Two. Marwick and Keshen are each convinced that World War Two, like the Great War, facilitated progress towards an enhanced status for women.[44] While the post-1945 period offers less concrete evidence with which to measure "women's gains" some historians, like Jeffrey Keshen, cite the postwar push for equal pay between the sexes as evidence of progress.[45] Others, such as Gordon Wright, feel that women's augmented presence in the workforce during the war is enough to conclude that women gained social status in the postwar period.[46]

Some contemporary women of the post-1945 period also felt that their war work would assure them a place in the public sphere following the war. A number of commentators during and immediately after the Second World War suggested that women's contributions to both the labour force and the military between 1939 and 1945 taught Canadian women independence and led to a reconstruction of male-female roles that favoured more liberal attitudes regarding women in the postwar period. Indeed, remarking on the opportunity that women's wartime contributions created for gender reconstruction, Lotta Dempsey, a frequent contributor to *Chatelaine* and *Maclean's* magazines in the 1930s, 1940s and 1950s, wrote to *Maclean's* readers in 1943: "You can tell your great-grand-daughter some day that this is the time and the place it really started: the honest to goodness equality of Canadian women. It began to happen that hour when Canadian girls left desks and kitchens ... stepped into overalls and took their places in the lines of workers at lathes and drills."[47] Norma E. Walmsley, a newcomer to the employment market during the war, likened the war years to a "Pandora's Box," claiming that although many things "returned to the status quo, [after 1945] women proved their ability in many fields ... and now they knew they had choices."[48] Doris Anderson's description of life in her parent's home in the immediate postwar period also illustrates how even subtle changes in women's behaviour brought about because of the war had lasting effects on their lives: "Home life was a more congenial place. ... Everything still revolved around my father, but mama had her own circle of friends in the neighbourhood. ... The knitting group became the focus of my mother's social life. She and her friends talked on the telephone almost every day. After the war ended, they continued meeting at one another's homes for the rest of their lives."[49]

The basic arguments that war was "good" for women, however, often rest on the testimony of a few participants and these conclusions have not been universally accepted. The emergence of second wave feminism in the 1960s, among other things, gave some historians the impetus to revisit the past with a more critical eye. During the next few decades, the new interpretation was that of female "oppression" in 1918 and again in 1945. The world wars were seen as having a "feminizing" effect of the images of women by increasing the importance of women's traditional roles as wives, mothers and homemakers as well as placing renewed interest in their physical appearance. The messages being sent to the women of the 1920s and late 1940s were interpreted by at least some historians, and a limited number of contemporaries, as suggesting that women's full – and often only – potential lay in motherhood. To fulfil this destiny, women needed to be feminine and attractive in order to "catch" a man.

Deidre Beddoe notes that the harsh fact was that British women were "turfed out of the workforce" in 1918.[50] She states unequivocally that women were repeatedly and audibly reminded that their place was in the home.[51] Moreover, according to Beddoe, the image of women as housewives and mothers was the only socially acceptable and desirable image presented to women by the British media in the interwar period.[52] In his study of women's employment in France from 1890 to 1930, historian Francois Thebaud also argues that the Great War exacerbated gender divisions and pushed women into the home. The conflict of 1914-1918 is interpreted as having re-emphasized women's roles as mothers and homemakers. He notes that slogans such as "there is still a housewife inside the woman making shells" and "the *munitionettes* have contrived to keep all their charm" were common in France during World War One.[53] Beddoe and Thebaud's interpretations suggest that "the mother" and "the liberated woman" were incompatible.

Many authors have reached similar conclusions with respect to the Second World War, which they argue also firmly repositioned women into the home. Scholar Denise Riley remarks that during World War Two "rhetorically, [British] women were over-personified as mothers and de-sexed as workers."[54] She suggests that the political and social languages of Britain in the 1940s, including the continuous descriptions of women as "mothers," "girlish employees," or "docile mother workers," contributed to the feminization of women.[55] Riley dismisses what some contemporaries of the 1940s, and later historians, had argued marked progress for women – improved and democratized access to contraceptive and obstetric services, renewed consideration of the lives of orphans, and the introduction of family allowances – as having actually repositioned women in the character of mother and thereby solidified them in a "traditional" role that was anything but "liberating."[56]

Others use the "mass exodus" of women from the paid workforce in 1945 to surmise that the Second World War had a negative impact on the "liberation" of women. United States historian Jo Freeman concludes that following World War Two, opportunities for American women outside of the home became so limited that they had no alternative but to return to their traditional roles of wives and mothers. She suggests that, "Both men and women had heeded their country's call to duty to bring the struggle to a successful conclusion. Yet men were rewarded for their efforts and women punished for theirs." To substantiate her point she explains that, "The returning soldiers were given the GI bill and other veterans benefits. They got their old jobs back and a disproportionate share of the new ones created by the war economy. Women, on the other hand, saw their child-care centres dismantled and their training programs cease. They were fired or demoted in droves and often found it difficult to enter colleges flooded with ex-GIs matriculating on government money." She concludes with the rhetorical questions: "Is it any wonder that they heard the message that their place was in the home? Where else could they go?"[57]

Similarly, Betty Friedan remarks that:

> The one lesson a girl could hardly avoid learning, if she went to college between 1945 and 1960, was *not* to get interested, seriously interested, in anything besides getting married and having children, if she wanted to be normal, happy, adjusted, feminine, have a successful husband, successful children, and a normal, feminine, adjusted, successful sex life. She might have learned some of this lesson at home, and some of it from the other girls in college, but she also learned it, incontrovertibly, from those entrusted with developing her critical, creative intelligence: her college professors.[58]

Many Canadian historians share these sentiments. For example, Sylvia Fraser judges that: "After the war the door was again flung wide for women – out of the work force and into the ranch house."[59] And Ruth Roach Pierson concludes in *They're Still Women After All*, her excellent account of perceptions towards middle-class Canadian women in the paid labour force from 1939 to 1945, that "the war's slight yet disquieting reconstruction of womanhood in the direction of equality with men was scrapped for a full-skirted and re-domesticated post-war model...."[60] Pierson, however, also shows how femininity was a continuous undercurrent in the description of Canadian womanhood during the war years.

A relatively recent interpretation rejects the idea that the world wars were a watershed for gender relationships and instead argues that the wars had little impact on women's positions relative to men's in the postwar periods. Authors Margaret R. Higonnet and Patrice L.-R. Higonnet provide a model of a double helix to help explain gender relationships during war: one strand represents women's roles, the other strand is indicative of men's positions, and the twisting of the strands symbolizes social change. What is important to note is that the relative distance between the "male" and "female" strands is always constant. While acknowledging that many women gained economic independence and assumed familial responsibility during both world wars, the Higonnets stress the impermanence of these wartime transformations.[61] Popular assumptions about appropriate gender roles were not easily reconstructed.

A number of scholars have both consciously and unconsciously supported the Higonnets' model. Susan S. Grayzel discovers that traditional constructs of femininity and masculinity survived the Great War in both Britain and France. Throughout the war and later, in war memorials, women were inextricably connected with motherhood in the same way that men were associated with the role of soldier. Grayzel concludes that "...the gender system was not a casualty of the war."[62] In a separate article, Grayzel again concludes that there was little evidence of female "liberation" between 1914 and 1918 or in the postwar years. She argues that the sexual and moral double standard did not end during or after the war. For example, unmarried pregnant women, or women who were pregnant despite the long absence of their spouse, continued to have a moral stigma attached to their situation.[63]

A selection of essays published in a revisionist account of the First World War titled, *Evidence, History and the Great War: Historians and the Impact of 1914 – 1918*, also supports the theory that the First World War had little effect on gender relationships. The editor, Gail Braybon, suggests that historians who do not recognize this are ignoring the evidence. Indeed, she writes that, "The concept of the war as a watershed has become a cliché, and one which has been accepted unthinkingly by many historians who should know better. The fact that women's history is not their area of expertise does not excuse the sloppy repetition of generalisations, and the re-cycling of material that is merely anecdotal...."[64] She also references a 1920s' commentator who cautioned that books about the war were already "a series of illusions of the past dressed up in the shape of the historians' own predilections."[65]

The rejection of war as a watershed also holds true with respect to recent analyses of the Second World War. Historian Penny Summerfield's study of official policy concerning the situation of British women in the Second World War found that "continuity with pre-war attitudes and practices towards women was considerable in the areas of both domestic work and paid employment."[66] Summerfield argues that the logic of mobilizing women for war would have suggested that the British Government take steps to facilitate childcare, the availability of prepared foods and the structuring of the working hours of men and women to ease the burdens of the "double day." She discovers, however, that the British government took minimal steps in these areas.[67] Women were mobilized during the war, but expectations of marriage, home and dependency remained and were instrumental determinants of government policy.[68] Scholar Sonya Michel also argues that World War Two (re)cemented the importance of the associations of women to family and family to state by placing the American middle-class nuclear family at the centre of a democratic ideal. In this model, women and children were subordinated to their male "protector." This image apparently helped to provide men with a reason to fight.[69]

Placing women at the centre of a democratic ideal that relied on their acceptance of traditional gender roles also allowed men to remain the dominant sex even when women entered "male jobs." Women's work in munitions or in uniform for example, was usually considered temporary and acceptable only so long as men were unavailable to fill the spots. In "The Bren Gun Girl and the Housewife Heroine," Canadian historians Alison Prentice, Paula Bourne, Gail Cuthbert Brandt, Beth Light, Wendy Mitchinson, and Naomi Black argue that "traditional attitudes towards women were ultimately reinforced during the war, in spite of initial challenges."[70] Among other things they cite the official mottos of the various women's services in the army, navy and airforce: "We are the women behind the men behind the guns"; "We serve that men might fly"; and "We serve that men might fight," as evidence of this.[71] M. Susan Bland shares this assessment. In her analysis of images of women portrayed through advertisements in *Maclean's* magazine in the 1940s, she notes that, "While these ads" directed at women war workers between 1942 to 1944 "do not underestimate the contributions and sacrifices made by war workers, we are continuously reminded that these women have feminine qualities."[72] Heather Rymell also finds no change between the images of women in Canadian magazine advertisements from the 1930s and 1940s. She concludes that "A review of these magazines shows the employment of women [from 1939-1945] was merely a temporary expediency, which would end and have no lasting influence. Women would further prove their femininity by gracefully retiring to the home when the emergency ended."[73] Maureen Honey uses the popular United States (U.S.) media to explore the effects of the Second World War on images of American women. She too discovers that the war ultimately failed to alter traditional ideas about women's place in society – although propaganda was seen as an expedient way to shift social norms.[74] Notably, femininity was again largely viewed as incompatible with female "liberation."

The sometimes heated debates about the impact of war on the roles and expectations of women in society rest on readings that try to assess whether women's equality with men was advanced by their participation in the war effort. These scholars often rely on evidence of changes to women's involvement in the public world of paid employment and politics. A few, like Ruth Roach Pierson, have also addressed how public perceptions of women as seen in government propaganda and in the popular media changed in respect to the coming of war in 1939. Relatively little work, however, has been done in Canada that systematically examines if, or how, the Second World War changed popular perceptions of Canadian womanhood. Authors also often begin their detailed analyses with the outbreak of war itself. Few consider the question in a larger chronological context.

Lipstick and High Heels is primarily a study of public perceptions as reflected in *Chatelaine* magazine from 1928 to 1956; it is not a study of government policy or of women's actual involvement in the war effort. The interplay between the popular media, gender identity and war has received relatively scarce attention. Works that look at this topic often do so from a limited perspective and generally fail to consider periods pre- and post-belligerence.[75] One notable exception is Cynthia L. White's history of British magazines. While the effect of the world wars on the magazine industry in Britain is not White's central interest, her book nonetheless deals with the topic masterfully.[76] She concludes that in most British magazines both world wars heralded a return to a feminine ideal.[77] Following World War One, White remarks that "The growing middle-class orientation of the women's press and the new emphasis on home service were accompanied by an intensification of the pressures encouraging a domestic role for women associated with the aftermath of the war." The British presses expressed the belief that, "'Miss Fluffy Femininity carries off the prize.'"[78] In the post-1945 period, White notes that British magazines "used their influence positively to discourage women from trying to combine work and marriage."[79] *Lipstick and High Heels* supports White's conclusions in the Canadian context while additionally providing a thorough analysis of the war years.

Largely, however, researchers who explore gendered images within popular culture do not directly ask whether war affects this relationship. Indeed, much research on the images of women in magazines uses 1945 as a general starting point and seeks to connect an evolving representation of women in magazines with the emergence and spread of second wave (liberal) feminism[80] in the 1960s and 1970s.[81]

One of the first authors to consider the popular press as an historical tool to help understand women's place in society was American Betty Friedan. Many feminists who desired to find a solution to "the problem that has no name" applauded Friedan's 1963 book, *The Feminine Mystique.* The problem, as Friedan interprets it, was that popular culture imposed feminine ideals that were not only unattainable by most, they were also largely unfulfilling for the women who tried to become ideal housewives by focusing their attention on home, family and appearance.[82] The result was that many women lost a sense of identity separate from their roles of wives and mothers – what Friedan terms "the feminine mystique." Friedan suggests that it was time to recognize and deal with the "voice within women that says: 'I want something more than my husband and my children and my home.'"[83]

Of particular interest for *Lipstick and High Heels* is Friedan's chapter on "the Happy Housewife Heroine." In this section, Friedan traces the "evolution" of the image of "the spirited career woman" in 1930s and 1940s mass circulation magazines, to the "housewife-mother" of the 1950s and 1960s.[84] Relying largely on fiction published in popular U.S. women's magazines in the 1930s through to the early 1960s, Friedan suggests that in the pre-1939 period, and to an extent up to 1949,

the image of women in mass circulation magazines – while usually connected with romance – did not deny women an identity of their own
that was distinct from their biological roles as wives and mothers.
As Friedan writes, "…the moral, in 1939, was that if she kept her commitment to herself, she did not lose the man, if he was the right man."[85]
She argues that, up until 1949, for the idealized woman represented in
mass circulation magazines, a career meant more than a job. A career
represented the opportunity for self-fulfilment beyond existing within
and through the identity of others.[86] By 1950, according to Friedan, the
representation in the media of an ideal of modern womanhood had
changed, however. The new modern woman of 1950 was expected
to idealise the home and family.[87] With this shift came a loss of
identity that by the 1960s had created a state of crisis for many American
women.

Friedan suggests two principal reasons as to why these changes may have
occurred in the 1950s: first, female editors were being replaced with male
editors[88]; and second, there was increasing competition for advertisements that may have pushed men to see women principally as consumers
while still situating them within their traditional roles of wives, mothers
and homemakers.[89] Nonetheless, Friedan concluded that the "problem
that has no name" was largely without a catalyst.[90] Interestingly,
the Second World War does not seem to be an important factor for
Friedan's interpretation. As this work shows, *Chatelaine*'s understanding
of women's lives and their changing place in Canadian society in the
1930s, 1940s and 1950s did not always follow this trajectory.

In her reassessment of postwar mass culture, author Joanne Meyerowitz
challenges Friedan's widely accepted "dominant ideology, the conservative promotion of domesticity" in postwar America.[91] Instead, in her
research on American women's magazines, Meyerowitz suggests that
images of women in mass circulation magazines "reveal ambivalence and

contradictions in postwar mass culture, which included a celebration of nondomestic as well as domestic pursuits and a tension between individual achievement and domestic ideals."[92] Meyerowitz also comments that unlike in the early 1960s when Friedan wrote, new theories in cultural studies denied the unquestioning repressive force of mass circulation magazines on women's identity. The new view was to accept that "mass culture is rife with contradictions, ambivalence, and competing voices."[93] This was certainly true of *Chatelaine* between 1928 and 1956.

Friedan was nonetheless a pioneer researcher on the images of women in mass circulation magazines and her legacy is still debated. Newer studies, however, tend to be more aware of the importance of situating their findings into their own context of time and place; they also rely more heavily on quantitative rather than qualitative research methods. For example, Meyerowitz is conscious to include a systematic review of magazines in the 1930s and 1940s before concluding that postwar culture represented a change in the status of women's domesticity. Additionally, she supports her findings with a statistical analysis regarding women's representations in specific roles, for example paid employment.[94] In stark opposition to Friedan, however, Meyerowitz concludes that "postwar magazines differed from earlier magazines in emphasis if not in kind. ...the proportion of articles that focused on motherhood, marriage, and housewifery was actually smaller during the 1950s than during either the 1930s or the 1940s."[95]

How best to assess and analyze images of women (or other subjects) in the popular media is a subject of considerable debate. For Canadian author Valerie Korinek, comparing the number of occurrences of a particular image provides more concrete evidence and a more reliable interpretation than qualitative analyses can afford. She cautions that this later type of selective sampling "leaves the impression that the magazine always presented a single dominant message. ..."[96] However, as a

number of scholars have shown, qualitative research that is done systematically can allow for insights that might otherwise be lost. Heather
Molyneaux in *The Representation of Women in Chatelaine Magazine
Advertisements* chose to conduct her research qualitatively for exactly this
reason.[97] Mary Vipond, in her analyses of the representation of working
women in mass circulation magazines in the 1920s, also follows this
technique,[98] as does Jennifer Scanlon in her examination of the emergence from 1910 to the 1930s of a consumer culture in the *Ladies Home
Journal*.[99] *Lipstick and High Heels* rests on a careful and systematic
analysis of *Chatelaine* to learn about the production and formation of
gendered identities in Canada in the 1930s, 1940s and 1950s.

Much research suggests that the mass media both reflects and shapes
popular assumptions in societies. For example, using statistical analysis to
compare the images of women between 1955 and 1976 in non-fiction
articles from *Ladies Home Journal* with those in *Redbook*, its younger
counterpart, and to American society at large, L. Ann Geise discovers that
"changes found in both magazines ... paralleled a number of important
societal changes."[100] While each magazine tended to emphasize the role
of the housewife/mother, Geise concludes that these were certainly
not the only topics addressed; women were seen to take their careers
seriously and to be interested in topics beyond the scope of the home,
including politics.[101]

Additionally, two recent studies of the representation of women in mass
circulation magazines have augmented their analyses by considering
the readership of the periodicals under examination. In *Girl Talk*, Dawn
H. Currie explores the influence that popular teen magazines have on
the lives of readers through interviews with forty-eight thirteen- to
eighteen-year-old young women living in and around the Vancouver,
British Columbia area. She concludes that readers are both influenced
by and in turn influence the content of the magazine; the identity of

young women is shaped through this interchange.[102] Moreover, like Janice Winship, author of *Inside Women's Magazines*, Currie also argues that the femininity expressed in women's magazines is not necessarily in opposition to feminist beliefs.[103] Valerie J. Korinek, author of *Roughing It in the Suburbs*, perhaps the most influential study of a Canadian woman's magazine, comes to a similar conclusion in her analysis of *Chatelaine* magazine and its readership in the 1950s and 1960s. Korinek argues that the popular women's magazine disseminated feminist beliefs in the 1960s. According to Korinek, this appealed to the magazine's readership. She notes that "it would appear that the vast majority of *Chatelaine* readers agreed with liberal feminist goals by the end of the sixties."[104]

In her study of the relationship between mass media content and social change in Canada, Susannah Jane Foster Wilson provides a model to explain how magazines reflect and shape social change through mediating factors, such as staff and advertiser. Magazines may not necessarily accurately reflect society, but their content is influenced by and helps influence their target audience.[105] Author Naomi Wolf also argues that magazine content is in a way always a representation of readership. In an expansion of Friedan's work, Naomi Wolf claims in *The Beauty Myth*, a study of how the American media manipulates women into feeling unhappy and insecure with themselves, that in the 1970s the "feminine mystique" was replaced with the "beauty myth." This new image rests on the belief that most women are dissatisfied with their physical appearance and continuously want to improve their looks with the use of cosmetics and other products. According to Wolf's logic, the women's movements of the 1960s and 1970s challenged the survival of corporations that relied on targeting housewives as their buyers and the magazines in which they advertised their products. Advertisers needed a new target audience. As Wolf notes, "The beauty myth, in its modern form, arose to take the place of the Feminine Mystique, to save magazines and advertisers from the economic fallout of the women's revolution."[106] Interestingly, Wolf notes that the shift in balance of power from editor to advertiser only occurred in the 1950s. In the second half of the century, Wolf contends, advertisers had the upper hand.[107] In the first part of the twentieth century, however, magazine editors had been instrumental in determining magazine content. This certainly seemed to be the case with *Chatelaine*. As Wolf notes, up to 1950, magazine editors had a responsibility to present both an ideal of womanhood and to reflect current trends of the gendered nature of twentieth century America:

> Though many writers have pointed out that women's magazines reflect historical change, fewer examine how part of their job is to determine historical change as well. Editors do their jobs well by reading the *Zeitgeist*; editors of women's magazines … must be alert to what social roles are demanded of women to serve the interests of those who sponsor their publications. Women's magazines for over a century have been one of the most powerful agents for changing women's roles, and throughout that time … they have consistently glamorized whatever the economy, their advertisers, and, during wartime, the government needed at that moment from women.[108]

Through editorial content and design, magazine staff were able to reflect and shape their readership, a role that was particularly instrumental as mass circulation magazines gained in popularity throughout the 1920s, 1930s, 1940s, and 1950s. As Heather Rymell concludes, "It is commonplace to assert that magazines and other forms of media serve as a mirror of society. They are also responsible, to some degree, for creating the scene they reflect."[109]

This examination of *Chatelaine* between 1928 and 1956 suggests that the war and, in most cases, the threat of war did prompt, and perhaps reflect, a change in popular assumptions about the role of Canadian women at home and in society at large. A careful examination of the pre-war images in *Chatelaine* provides a baseline and shows that certain images gained in importance in the late 1930s. For example, motherhood was increasingly venerated and so too was women's place in the home. Canadian women were also increasingly lauded for their physical attractiveness and not their competence. Many of these images continued after the Second World War.

Lipstick and High Heels provides a glimpse into popular understandings of Canadian women's lives during these three formative decades by looking at all departments featured in the magazine as well as advertisements.[110] The "modern" woman of *Chatelaine*, however, was never necessarily a singular construct. This lens, however, allowed *Chatelaine's* staff the luxury of writing about, and occasionally for, a female middle-class ideal. At the same time, the realities of consumerism mandated that Canadian women relate to the magazine's contents. In this way, *Chatelaine's* modern woman represented, to a degree, simultaneously who Canadian women were and who at least some part of the population thought she could, or should, be.

This book begins by looking at *Chatelaine's* concept of the "modern" woman and the editors who were instrumental in making her image. Looking at *Chatelaine* editorials from 1928 to 1956 suggests that the editors generally reflected maternal feminist views. In addition to home and hearth, middle-class women were expected to be interested in spreading national pride, social welfare and world peace.

Chapters three through six then consider particular themes and issues that made up the changing images of modern Canadian womanhood in

Chatelaine. *Chatelaine* was written for wives, mothers, homemakers, wage earners, nation builders and peace advocates. Given the number of roles that women were expected to play, at a cursory glance some conclusions may appear contradictory. Indeed, paradoxical images could often be published in the same issue, a phenomenon that Joanne Meyerowitz found in her assessment of American periodicals.[111] But, upon reflection, what we end up with is an appreciation of the diversity of the images presented in *Chatelaine* and an idea of how they moulded together to paint a portrait, albeit a dynamic one, of modern Canadian womanhood.

The issues that *Chatelaine* considered to be of concern to women did not really fluctuate in the nearly thirty years under examination, but how *Chatelaine* represented modern Canadian womanhood changed noticeably with the perceived threat to peace in the late 1930s. In concert with an overt threat of war in 1936/37, and war itself in 1939, the images of women in the magazine shifted from being characteristically female to characteristically feminine and women were increasingly connected to the private sphere of hearth and home.

Endnotes

1   Helena Rubinstein, *Chatelaine*, March 1942, 23.

2   Middle-class is used as distinct from working-class and upper-class.

3   *Chatelaine*, November 1942, 71.

4   *Chatelaine*, May 1942, 76.

5   *Chatelaine*, January 1943, 18.

6   *Chatelaine*, November 1942, 81.

7   *Chatelaine*, March 1943, 28.

8   *Chatelaine*, August 1943, 4.

9   Wives who worked for wages were also generally expected to take care of the home.

10   *Chatelaine*, August 1943, 4.

11   *Chatelaine*, March 1943, 29.

12   *Chatelaine*, August 1944, 29.

13   The private sphere refers to the realm of hearth and home whereas the public sphere refers to the domains of politics and business. It should be noted that scholar Gail Cuthbert Brant cautions historians about the over dependency of using the public-private model to explain gender relationships. She argues that the use of this dichotomy often underscores gender differences because it fallaciously assumes that the public and private spheres are independent of each other. Gail Cuthbert Brandt, "Postmodern Patchwork: Some Recent Trends in the Writing of Women's History in Canada," *Canadian Historical Association* 9 (1988), 445-446.

14   Femininity in *Chatelaine* was never clearly defined. It was generally used as a counterbalance to masculinity. It usually referred to how women dressed and their use of makeup and was likely associated with current fashions. Femininity could also be used to help define women in their roles as wives, mothers and homemakers.

15   C.B. Robertson, *Chatelaine*, March 1930, 69.

16   Ibid.

17   The *Canadian Home Journal* (1905-1959) would have been a logical choice as well. Throughout the 1930s, 1940s and 1950s, the sales of *Chatelaine* and the *Canadian Home Journal* paralleled each other reaching between 400,000 – 500,000 in the 1950s. In 1950, *Chatelaine* sold for 15 cents compared to the *Canadian Home Journal*'s 10 cent price tag. Still the *Canadian Home Journal* was losing money and it was sold to Maclean Publishing in 1958, and was merged shortly thereafter with *Chatelaine*. Fraser Sutherland, *The Monthly Epic: A History of Canadian Magazines, 1799-1989* (Markham: Fitzhenry & Whiteside, 1989), 249. It should also be noted, however, that in the early 1950s, while John Clare was editor of *Chatelaine*, the periodical failed to make a profit and circulation was less than that of the *Canadian Home Journal*. Valerie J. Korinek, *Roughing it in the Suburbs: Reading Chatelaine Magazine in the Fifties and Sixties* (Toronto: University of Toronto Press, 2000), 268. Certainly, a study of the *Canadian Home Journal* would also be of value.

18   *Chatelaine*, May 1930, 56.

19   "The" was dropped from the title of the magazine in January 1932. From this point on, the magazine will simply be referred to as *Chatelaine*.

20   Sutherland, *The Monthly Epic*, 37. According to Sutherland this transition occurred around the time of the Great War.

21   Ibid., 159; and Korinek, *Roughing it in the Suburbs*, 33. Interestingly, Gaye Tuchman, Arlene Kaplan Daniels and James Benet suggest that "despite the large variation in women and in women's magazines … all women's magazines ultimately project a similar image of women's feminine characteristics. Supportive of others and concerned with emotional well-being, woman supposedly strives to please. When she fails to cater to the concerns of others, she is politely damned." Gaye Tuchman, Arlene Kaplan Daniels and James Benet (eds.), *Hearth and Home* (New York: Oxford University Press, 1978), 93.

22   Hilda Pain, *Chatelaine*, March 1928, 30.

23   Anne Elizabeth Wilson, *Chatelaine*, March 1928, 16.

24   A French edition of *Chatelaine* began in 1960.

25   Sutherland, *The Monthly Epic*, 159.

26   Maclean Publishing also owned *Canadian Homes and Gardens* and *Mayfair*. Sutherland, *The Monthly Epic*, 158. Until the 1930s, the company was known as the J.B. MacLean Company. The "L" subsequently became lower-cased and the firm then became Maclean-Hunter. From this point on the company will be referred to as "Maclean Publishing." For a more detailed account of Maclean Publishing see Ibid., 129–152.

27   Korinek, *Roughing it in the Suburbs*, 35.

28   Sutherland, *The Monthly Epic*, 160.

29   *Chatelaine*, May 1930, 56.

30   Korinek, *Roughing it in the Suburbs*, 35.

31   Cited in Ibid., 72.

32   Ruth Roach Pierson, *They're Still Women After All: The Second World War and Canadian Womanhood* (Toronto: McClelland and Stewart Limited, 1986), 220.

33   Pierson, *They're Still Women After All*, 20. While femininity is certainly a contrast to masculinity and should be viewed within a gendered paradigm, I suggest that one should be cautious to assume that that which is feminine is automatically subordinate to that which is masculine, or simply not feminine.

34   Jeffrey A. Keshen, *Saints, Sinners, and Soldiers: Canada's Second World War* (Vancouver: UBC Press, 2004), 151. It should be noted that Pat Kirkham and Gerard J. De Groot also argue that ideas of femininity should be understood in their proper context and their presence alone should not take away from the work that women were doing. Pat Kirkham, "Beauty and Duty: Keeping Up the

(Home) Front" in Pat Kirkham and David Thoms (eds.), *War and Culture: Social Changes and Changing Experience in World War Two* (London: Lawrence & Wishart, 1995), 26; and Gerard J. De Groot, "'I Love the Scent of Cordite in Your Hair': Gender Dynamics in Mixed Anti-Aircraft Batteries During the Second World War," *History* 82 (1997), 91.

35   Thorn also suggests that the Women's Collection – which by its very presence is suggestive of a gendered view of warfare – represented change in women's roles because continuities were simply not as interesting to document. Ironically, however, Thorn notes that, "Just as most British feminists before the war emphasized, not undermined, sexual differences so the Museum which one feminist helped create was to underpin assumptions about gender roles in the subsequent history and historiography of women and war." Specifically, the exhibit assumed that gender above all was the dominant division between peo-ple in wartime. Deborah Thorn, "Making Spectaculars: Museums and how we Remember Gender in Wartime," in Gail Braybon (ed.), *Evidence, History and the Great War: Historians and the Impact of 1914–1918* (New York: Berghahn Books, 2003), 62, 64.

36   Deidre Beddoe, *Back to Home and Duty: Women Between the Wars*, 1918 – 1939 (London: Pandora Press, 1989), 13-14.

37   With the removal of gender discrimination, most women gained the right to vote in federal elections in Canada in 1918, in the United States in 1920, and universally in Great Britain in 1928. In Great Britain many women had already achieved this right in the immediate postwar period. French women did not win suffrage until 1944.

38   Marwick also attributes the strength of pre-war Women's Rights Movements as being an instrumental factor in women gaining the vote in some countries, specifically Britain and the United States, before others such as France. Arthur Marwick, *War and Social Change in the Twentieth Century: A Comparative Study of Britain, France, Germany, Russia and the United States* (London: The Macmillan Press, Ltd., 1974), 76-77.

39   Marwick, *War and Social Change in the Twentieth Century*, 76-77.

40   Jeffrey A. Keshen, *Propaganda and Censorship During Canada's Great War* (Edmonton: The University of Alberta Press, 1996), 200.

41   Keshen, *Propaganda and Censorship*, 200.

42   Veronica Strong-Boag, *The New Day Recalled: The Lives of Girls and Women in English Canada, 1919-1939* (Markham: Penguin Books, 1988), 2.

43   Yvonne Klein, *Beyond the Home Front: Women's Autobiographical Writing of the Two World Wars* (New York: New York University Press, 1997), 1.

44   Although Marwick clearly draws the aforementioned conclusion, para-doxically, he supplies more evidence to suggest that the war had little impact on women's social positions and he suggests instead that there was no abandonment of the feminine image during the war. Marwick, *War and Social Change*, 175. For a critique of Marwick's thesis, see Harold L. Smith, "The Effect of War on the Status of Women," in Harold L. Smith (ed.), *War and Social Change: British Society in the Second World War* (Manchester: Manchester University Press, 1986), 208-229. Smith argues that "…the war's most important legacy for [British] women was a strengthening of traditional sex roles rather than the emergence of new roles." Smith, "The Effect of War on the Status of Women," 225.

45   Jeffrey Keshen, "Revisiting Canada's Civilian Women," *Histoire Sociale / Social History* 30 (1997), 266.

46   Gordon Wright, *The Ordeal of Total War* (New York: Harper and Row, Publishers, 1968), 248.

47   Cited in Keshen, "Revisiting Canada's Civilian Women," 254. Some women in the 1940s, however, particularly those who had also experienced the Great War, cautioned the optimism expressed by those who felt that gender equality was just around the corner. In a work published during the Second World War, Mrs. Laughton Matthews, the director of the Women's Royal Naval Service in Great Britain, suggested that some female recruits would be disap-pointed in many of the same ways that women had been in the interwar peri-od. Cited in Susan Gubar, "'This is My Rifle, This is My Gun': World War Two and the Blitz on Women," in Margaret Randolph Higonnet, Jane Jenson, Sonya Michel and Margaret Collins Weitz, (eds.), *Behind the Lines: Gender and the Two World Wars* (New Haven: Yale University Press, 1987), 228-229.

48   Cited in Keshen, "Revisiting Canada's Civilian Women," 242.

49   Doris Anderson, *Rebel Daughter: An Autobiography* (Toronto: Key Porter Books Ltd., 1996), 72.

50   Beddoe, *Back to Home and Duty*, 13.

51   Ibid., 3-4.

52   Ibid., 8.

53   Francois Thebaud, "Work, Gender, and Identity in Peace and War France, 1890 – 1930," in Billie Melman (ed.), *Borderlines: Gender and Identity in War and Peace* (New York: Routledge, Inc. 1998), 409. Moreover, the first secular Mother's Day was celebrated in Lyons in 1918. Notably, Thebaud cites some advances in women's status in France – such as the improved educational oppor-tunities available to middle-class girls – yet, he nonetheless concludes that: "Work and maternity are always in opposition; women cannot be mothers and workers

at the same time. Thus, while the war shifted work structures and the gendered division of workers, at the same time it seems to have had a rather conservative effect on matters of identity." Thebaud, "Work, Gender, and Identity," 415.

54   Denise Riley, "Some Peculiarities of Social Policy Concerning Women in Wartime and Postwar Britain," in Higonnet et al. (eds.), *Behind the Lines: Gender and the Two World Wars*, 260-61.

55   Riley, "Some Peculiarities of Social Policy," 270-271.

56   Ibid., 267.

57   Jo Freeman, *Women: A Feminist Perspective*, 3rd Edition, (Palo Alto: Mayfield Publishing Company, 1984), 554.

58   Betty Friedan, *The Feminine Mystique* (New York: Norton and Company, Inc., 1963), 156.

59   Sylvia Fraser, (ed.), *A Woman's Place: Seventy Years in the lives of Canadian Women* (Toronto: Key Porter Books, 1977), 165.

60   Pierson, *They're Still Women After All*, 220.

61   Margaret R. Higonnet and Patrice L.-R. Higonnet, "The Double Helix," in Higonnet et al. (eds.), *Behind the Lines: Gender and the Two World Wars*, 32.

62   Susan S. Grayzel, *Women's Identities at War: Gender, Motherhood, and Politics in Britain and France During the First World War* (Chapel Hill: the University of North Carolina Press, 1999), 246. See also Jonathan F. Vance, *Death So Noble: Memory, Meaning and the First World War* (Vancouver: University of British Columbia Press, 1997).

63   Susan Grayzel, "Liberating Women? Examining Gender, Morality and Sexuality in First World War Britain and France," in Grayzel (ed.), *Women's Identities at War*, 119-126.

64   Gail Braybon, "Winners or Losers: Women's Symbolic Role in the War Story," in Grayzel (ed.), *Women's Identities at War*, 93.

65   Braybon, "Winners or Losers," 106.

66   Penny Summerfield, *Women Workers in the Second World War: Production and Patriarchy in Conflict* (London: Croom Helm, 1984), 1.

67   Summerfield, *Women Workers in the Second World War*, 3.

68   Ibid, 190.

69   Sonya Michel, "American Women and the Discourse of the Democratic Family in World War Two," in Higonnet et al. (eds.), *Behind the Lines: Gender and the Two World Wars*, 154.

70   Alison Prentice, P. Bourne, G.C. Brandt, B. Light, W. Mitchinson and N. Black, "The Bren Gun Girl and the Housewife Heroine," in R. Douglas Francis and Donald B. Smith, *Readings in Canadian History: Post-Confederation*, 3rd

edition (Toronto: Holt, Rinehart and Winston of Canada, Limited), 447.

71   Prentice et al., "The Bren Gun Girl and the Housewife Heroine," 448.

72   M. Susan Bland, "Henrietta the Homemaker, and 'Rosie the Riveter': Images of Women in Advertising in *Maclean's* Magazine, 1939-1950," *Atlantis*, 8 (1983), 75.

73   Heather Rymell, "Images of Women in the Magazines of the 30s and 40s," *Canadian Woman Studies*, 3 (1981), 99.

74   Maureen Honey, *Creating Rosie the Riveter: Class, Gender, and Propaganda during World War II* (Amherst: University of Massachusetts Press, 1984), 211.

75   While some works do look at the interplay of war and gender in the media, in addition to often failing to adequately represent the pre- and postwar periods, they also tend to examine the subject from a limited perspective. Nonetheless, many provide valuable insights into the field. See for example: M. Susan Bland, "Henrietta the Homemaker, and 'Rosie the Riveter': Images of Women in Advertising in *Maclean's* Magazine, 1939-1950," *Atlantis*, 8 (1983), 61-86; Heather Rymell, "Images of Women in the Magazines of the 30s and 40s," *Canadian Woman Studies* 3 (1981), 96-9; Maureen Honey, *Creating Rosie the Riveter: Class, Gender, and Propaganda during World War II* (Amherst: University of Massachusetts Press, 1984); and Yvonne Mathews-Kline, "How They Saw Us: Images of Women in National Film Board Films of the 1940s and 1950s," *Atlantis* 14 (spring 1979), 20-33.

76   White does not look at the war years in her analysis because she believes they would be "unrepresentative of normal coverage during peace-time." Cynthia L. White, *Women's Magazines, 1693 – 1968* (London: Michael Joseph, Ltd., 1970), 18.

77   White, *Women's Magazines, 1693 – 1968*, 100, 135. White's claims are supported more in the case of the First World War.

78   Ibid., 99.

79   Ibid., 135.

80   "Liberal feminism" refers to equality based feminism whereas "maternal" feminism rests on selected rights for women based on women's supposedly innate predisposition to further the betterment of societies.

81   Some of the research that focuses on the post Second World War period does include a brief pre-war assessment, however, a through examination of the antebellum period is often lacking. Moreover, few researchers ask directly if the war affected gendered images. See for example: Betty Friedan, *The Feminine Mystique* (New York: W.W. Norton & Company, Inc., 1963); Naomi Wolf, *The Beauty Myth: How Images of Beauty Are Used Against Women* (New York:

William Morrow and Company, Inc., 1991); and Korinek, *Roughing it in the Suburbs*. Writing on an earlier period, Jennifer Scanlon, connects the emergence of a consumer culture in *The Ladies' Home Journal* from the 1910s to the 1930s with maternal feminism and the idea of women doing for others. Jennifer Scanlon, *Inarticulate Longings: The Ladies' Home Journal, Gender, and the Promise of Consumer Culture* (New York: Rutledge, 1995). While recognizing that the United States only entered the Great War in 1917, it is nonetheless surprising that the belligerence from 1914 to 1918 receives no direct attention in Scanlon's book. Mary Vipond also wrote on women in mass circulation magazines in an earlier period, the 1920s. Vipond begins with the premise that the Great War "brought disillusionment with reform and idealism ... [and] in the 1920s, the prevailing mood was a desire to return to ... 'normalcy'." Her examination of images in mass circulation magazines, however, is restricted to the 1920s and does not include a pre-war foundation upon which to argue that these images were indeed changed or maintained because of the war. Mary Vipond, "The image of Women in Mass Circulation Magazines in the 1920s," in Susan Mann Trofimenkoff and Alison Prentice, (eds.), *The Neglected Majority; Essays in Canadian Women's History* (Toronto: McClelland and Stewart, 1977), 116-124, quote, 116.

82   Friedan, *The Feminine Mystique*, 16-18.

83   Ibid., 32.

84   Ibid., 54. Much of Friedan's work, however, is concentrated in the post-1945 period.

85   Ibid., 39. White argues that this was not the case in British periodicals during the interwar years. She suggests that the following Victorian anecdote is symbolic of women's representations in British mass circulation magazines from 1919 to 1939: "Heroic girl: 'Where's the young man who applauded so loudly when I rescued that little boy from drowning?' Reply: 'He's over there, proposing to the girl who screamed and fainted.'" White, *Women's Magazines, 1693 – 1968*, 99-100.

86   Friedan, *The Feminine Mystique*, 40.

87   Ibid., 41.

88   Ibid., 54.

89   Friedan asks of this change: "Does this frantic race force the men who make the images to see women only as thing-buyers?" And she observes that, paradoxically, "The fact is, the troubles of the image-makers seem to be increasing in proportion to the increasing mindlessness of their image. During the years in which that image has narrowed women's world down to the home, cut

her role back to housewife, five of the mass circulation magazines geared to women have ceased publication; others are on the brink." Ibid., 65-66.

90   Friedan, *The Feminine Mystique*, 68.

91   Joanne Meyerowitz, "Beyond the Feminine Mystique: A Reassessment of Postwar Mass Culture, 1946 – 1958," in Joanne Meyerowitz (ed.), *Not June Cleaver: Women and Gender in Postwar America, 1945-1960* (Philadelphia: Temple University Press, 1994), 230.

92   Meyerowitz, "Beyond the Feminine Mystique," 238.

93   Ibid., 231.

94   Ibid., 249 and note 59, 260.

95   Ibid., 249.

96   Korinek, *Roughing it in the Suburbs*, 15.

97   Heather Molyneaux, *The Representation of Women in Chatelaine Magazine Advertisements* (M.A. Thesis, The University of New Brunswick, 2002), 1-2.

98   Vipond, "The image of Women in Mass Circulation Magazines in the 1920s."

99   Scanlon, *Inarticulate Longings*.

100   L. Ann Geise, "The Female Role in Middle Class Women's Magazines from 1955 to 1976: A Content Analysis of Nonfiction," *Sex Roles* 5 (1979), 51.

101   Geise, "The Female Role in Middle Class Women's Magazines," 61.

102   Dawn H. Currie, *Girl Talk: Adolescent Magazines and Their Readers* (Toronto: University of Toronto Press, 1999), 8, 282.

103   Ibid., 8; and Janice Winship, *Inside Women's Magazines* (London: Pandora, 1987), xiii-xiv.

104   Korinek, *Roughing it in the Suburbs*, 99.   Korinek was not the first researcher to claim that *Chatelaine* had feminist leanings in the 1960s. See for example, Inez Houlihan, *The Image of Women in Chatelaine Editorials March 1928 to September 1977* (M.A. Thesis, University of Toronto, 1984), 5; and Sutherland, *The Monthly Epic*, 246.

105   Susannah Jane Foster Wilson, *The Relationship Between Mass Media Content and Social Change in Canada: An Examination of the Image of Women in Mass Circulating Canadian Magazines 1930-1970* (Ph.D. Dissertation: University of Toronto, 1977), 38.

106   Wolf, *The Beauty Myth*, 66.

107   Research relating the importance of advertisements in the second half of the twentieth century is plentiful. See for example, Ellen McCracken, *Decoding Women's Magazines from Mademoiselle to Ms* (London: The Macmillan Press Ltd., 1993). McCraken concludes that based on the profits of mass circulation mag-

azines the "master narratives they construct succeed quite well in channeling women's desire to consumerism." She continues, "Readers individual and sometimes shared modes of resistance to representations in magazines have not affected radical changes in the structure of capitalist society nor even in the magazines themselves. The senders and receivers of these cultural texts participate in an immensely unequal power relation; readers have little input into the monthly representations that claim to be about their lives, notwithstanding publishers' acute awareness of the demographics of readers and target audience's probable receptivity to various representations." McCracken, *Decoding Women's Magazines*, 301. McCracken's theory, however, does little to explain changes in the images of women in mass circulation magazines or the diversity in the products being sold. Joan Barrell and Brian Braithwaite provide a more balanced account of the relationships between advertisers, editor and audience in mass circulation magazines, suggesting that each contributes to the final product with somewhat equal weight. Joan Barrell and Brian Braithwaite, *The Business of Women's Magazines*, 2nd edition (London: Kogan Page, 1988).

108   Wolf, *The Beauty Myth*, 64. Currie also discusses the relationship between reader, editor and content. Currie, *Girl Talk*, 308.

109   Rymell, "Images of Women in the Magazines of the 30s and 40s," 96.

110   The entire twelve issues were read for every fourth year beginning in 1928 and ending in 1956. For the remaining twenty-one years, only odd-numbered months were looked at. In total, two-hundred and twenty-two copies of *Chatelaine* were fully examined.

111   Meyerowitz, "Beyond the Feminine Mystique," 231.

Chapter Two

The Staff Behind *Chatelaine*'s Modern Woman

The twentieth century witnessed the development of what those at the time called the "modern" Canadian woman. What this statement meant differed from one generation to another and from one group of women to another. Often one generation of women described themselves as modern to distinguish themselves from their mothers and grandmothers. In other instances, being modern was a hallmark of class aspirations or was understood differently if one was married or single. As Mary Lowrey Ross noted to *Chatelaine* readers in 1929, in many ways,

> The truth of the Modern Girl doesn't exist. She is as legendary a creature as the sea-serpent or the unicorn. She was invented by a journalist with a column to fill every day. Her father is the Press, her mother is the deeply believing public, and she herself will come into being only when all the world turns paper and all the seas turn ink.[1]

Despite this comment, the editors and contributors of *Chatelaine* were seemingly writing for and presenting images of their understanding of the modern Canadian woman.

The images of Canadian womanhood presented in *Chatelaine* thus served to both reflect and shape ideas about middle-class Canadian woman-hood. As will be shown throughout *Lipstick and High Heels*, some of the images of modern Canadian women in *Chatelaine* represented trends occurring in Canadian society; others subtly challenged the norms. At no point, however, were the popular images of women presented in the magazine – as wives, mothers, homemakers, nation builders and peace advocates – too far removed from the realities of middle-class, English, Anglo-Saxon Canadian society that spawned their creation. Indeed, *Chatelaine* served as a microcosm for the general evolution of gendered identities in post World War One Canada.

Chatelaine's female editors from 1928 to 1956 conscientiously organized *Chatelaine* to both reflect and help shape modern middle-class Canadian womanhood through the Great Depression, the war years, a postwar economic boom and into the Cold War. As Naomi Wolf notes in respect to the production of U.S. magazines, in the first half of the twentieth century editors were instrumental in shaping periodicals.[2] To fully appreciate *Chatelaine's* content it is therefore important to appreciate the points of view of the editors and the historical context in which they wrote. Interestingly, the topics addressed in the editorials reflect the predominant images of middle-class Canadian womanhood portrayed in *Chatelaine.* Looking at editorial content separately, however, provides context for the rest of *Lipstick and High Heels.*

For over a year, (March 1928 – August 1929), Anne Elizabeth Wilson edited the young magazine.[3] When she left to marry, the position was filled by Byrne Hope Sanders who, except for an absence while serving as Director of the Consumers' Representative Branch at the Wartime Prices and Trade Board, held the reins of the woman's magazine for nearly twenty years (September 1929 – January 1952). During Sanders' leave, Mary Etta Macpherson acted as the editor (March 1942 – December 1946). When Sanders retired, Lotta Dempsey, a long time contributor, briefly stepped in (February 1952 – September 1952). Subsequently, John Clare took over (October 1952 – August 1957).[4] He was the first male editor of the woman's magazine and his term was marked by a noticeable lack of specific editorial content. This silence occurred even though he was helped by Doris McCubbin, later Anderson, the famous feminist editor of *Chatelaine* in the 1960s and 1970s. During this nearly thirty-year period, the female editors of *Chatelaine*, particularly Sanders, were instrumental in shaping modern assumptions about Canadian womanhood in the magazine.[5]

Anne Elizabeth Wilson's editorials aligned with the ideas of maternal feminism.[6] The maternal feminists of the late nineteenth and early twentieth centuries saw themselves as the moral watchdogs of society. The Great War provided an excellent forum for the growth of the movement. As historian Thomas P. Socknat notes, "In particular, their [Canadian feminists'] disillusionment with the First World War gave rise to a new wave of feminism which was based on a radical critique of society and which, in the following two decades, found its major expression in the campaign for peace and social justice."[7] The Great War also brought a sense of disillusionment with British imperialism and maternal feminists considered it their duty to foster strong nationalist sentiments among Canadians. "One of the lessons of the Great War," notes Socknat, "appeared to be that the British imperial connection had propelled Canada into the European war, and might do so again unless counteraction was taken."[8] Women, with their newly granted right to vote, were considered particularly good candidates to fight for peace and spread national pride. As an extension of the Social Gospel Movement, however, this resurgence of pacifism and developing nationalism in the interwar period remained largely ethnocentric. Indeed, consistent with Anne Elizabeth Wilson's affiliation with maternal feminism was her obscuring of race, ethnicity and class divisions; for her, Canadian womanhood was painted in pale white homogenous middle-class hues.

Two of Wilson's editorials are particularly reflective of the social concerns of maternal feminists. These editorials also suggest an acceptance of many traditional gender roles. "Teaching Men to Legislate for Women: a Remedy for the Loss of Canadian Motherhood" was the title of Wilson's July 1928 editorial. This piece addressed the issue of maternal mortality. It was noted that in terms of political reform, "like most women's business, it lies in the hands of men." Wilson nonetheless appealed to *Chatelaine*'s readership: "If this is 'women's business,' then perhaps, for the first time since the franchise came to us, women may have some national and non-partisan issue on which to concentrate the strength of their influence. May that realization come to women soon – and may it be brought home no later to the men in whose hands the lives of so many women lie."[9] Wilson wanted women to work towards a collective goal, but she did not suggest that this objective should lie beyond their traditional domestic purview.

These sentiments were echoed in the next month's editorial titled "On the Importance of Women Being Women." In August, Wilson observed that "Public office is a small outlet for the floods of influence. Moreover, the very holding of office presupposes politics – and women's destiny in the affairs of nation lies along a broader highway than the partisan path." Wilson continued with her gendered interpretation of women's public destiny: "The soundest and most powerful women in public and private life to-day are doing their work in a woman's way. For the most part they are concerned with the humanitarian side of the world's work. ... they are primarily fine, gentle and intelligent women, doing women's work."[10]

Wilson's interpretation of women's place in society was largely formed in the context of maternal feminism. These examples show how Canadian women were expected to have a strong sense of national pride and to feel a social obligation to improve society. Equality with men was not a direct issue because men and women were presumed to be on different, yet compatible, plains.[11] Without directly challenging the primacy of men in the public sphere, Canadian women pacifists in the 1920s and 1930s were nonetheless developing a sense of "world mindedness."[12]

When Wilson vacated her position to become a wife in August 1929, Byrne Hope Sanders took over. Sanders was born in Port Alfred, South Africa and emigrated at the age of eleven to Canada where she attended St. Mildred's College. At seventeen she worked as a newspaper reporter for the *Woodstock Sentinel Review*, then she spent three years as a copy-writer for the T.E. Eaton Company, followed by three years as editor of *Business Woman*. In 1932, She married Frank Sperry.[13] The new wife, then mother, remained the principal wage earner in the family because "her artist husband's income was erratic."[14] She nonetheless was generally a maternal feminist.

The transition from Wilson to Sanders was smooth and *Chatelaine* entered the depression in the same way that it had exited the 1920s: as a magazine for all Canadian woman, blind to the complexities of this ambition, and espousing the tenets of maternal feminism. As Sanders noted in her first editorial, "Had not your former editor or myself gently drawn to your attention the fact that one had departed hence to practise what she has preached as a chatelaine on her own account, and that the other had arrived to preach what she would practise, there are probably thousands of you who would not realize that a change had taken place."[15] Indeed, throughout the 1930s and into the 1940s Sanders continued to report on the principal issues of the time – the depression, the peace crisis and the Second World War – through the prism of maternal feminism. On occasion, however, her editorials challenged the limits of contemporary feminist thought. But these exceptions remained largely hidden within the plethora of more traditional editorials.

According to Sanders, an important thing that the modern Canadian woman could do during the depression was to keep up the morale of men. In February 1932, Sanders wrote that one of the hardest jobs that women faced was fighting "the fear complex." She continued, "I know so many women who are finding that because they worry and fret over the tomorrow, or because they are facing new poverty now, it is harder to prevent quarrelling. Husbands seem to get so unreasonable, so touchy, so morose. Can't men realize, we think, that women have the hardest end of the job – that of trying to keep things going in the home?" In addition to providing a "happy home" for their distraught husbands, Sanders encouraged women to spend money on consumer goods in order to get out of the depression. She queried, "What could be a stranger anomaly than the sight of women, who, if their country needed them, would give their sons gladly to fight her battles, yet who cling tenaciously to their dollars because they are afraid, or selfish – or both?" In this way she supported the federal government's campaign to increase spending in order to revitalise the economy; at the same time Sanders emphasized women's "obligation" to sacrifice for public good. She also suggested that because the depression underscored social challenges in a less overt way than during times of war, this was actually a harder situation for men and women to face. "Come on, chatelaines!" she pleaded, "We've got as dramatic work to do as any of our pioneer grandmothers did. It takes more courage to face a possible loss of employment for a husband than to face a band of red Indians."[16]

In the early 1930s, one way that *Chatelaine* readers were encouraged to help men to maintain their white masculine identities was by not taking jobs away from them. Sanders lamented in July 1932 that there were "So many girls eking out a bare existence, half fed, eager for friendship and the gaiety of youth," at the same time that there were "so many young men unable to find employment of any kind." She asked, "Should we not pause and consider seriously this rushing of our daughters into any sort of work?" Her solution was for young women to return to the home and to eliminate the "bachelor girl" phase that was increasingly bridging a young woman's parental home with her conjugal residence.[17] Six months later, as a working wife, Sanders wrote her editorial as though her proposed solution had been accepted by Canadian women. In January 1933 she stated, "It is obvious that the free-for-all opportunities of a few years ago for girls everywhere to go into 'business' have gone, probably never to return." She even suggested that "Health authorities everywhere will declare in favor of an earning life spent in the home to the nervous work of office or factory; and it is up to the women of Canada to see what can be done to put domestic service on the same professional plane as other work for girls."[18]

Historian Margaret Hobbs suggests that de-emphasising women's right to paid employment in the 1930s and alternatively arguing that women workers needed their wages helped to confirm a sense of feminism based on innate gender differences, not similarities. For middle- and upper-class women who apparently had no "need" for an income their choice would most certainly have been to stay at home. "If I could stay at home and have my early tea brought to me," an unmarried typist bemoaned during the depression, "[I could then] get up when I liked, and spend all day playing golf or tennis, or motoring and have all the frock I wanted, I should imagine I was in heaven."[19] Even in the late 1930s, the Canadian government continued to assume that women would be cared for economically by husbands or fathers.[20] As Margaret Hobbs and Ruth Roach Pierson note, the federal government's Home Improvement Plan showed a "clear assignment of [middle-class] women to domesticity [and] reflected the strong opposition during the Depression to the gainful employment of the married woman and the prevailing assumption that her right to work should be sacrificed to the needs of the male breadwinner."[21]

Interestingly, while prioritising men's rights to paid employment over women was certainly the predominant position in Sanders' editorials of the early 1930s, exceptions did occur. Notably, in March 1931, Sanders chastised women for not believing more strongly in and supporting women professionals. She commented that she had "heard women in all branches of modern professions, state frankly that women never went out of their way to support or help them." Sanders concluded that, "just as a prophet is not without honour save in his own country, a woman is not without recognition save among her own sex."[22]   As Margaret Hobbs notes of the debate between women's right to paid employment and their "need" to work in the 1930s, "The ascendancy of one rational need not entail the demise of the other." She explains, "Nor is there always a clear separation between those using need arguments and those articulating the legitimacy of women's choices and preferences independent of their needs. The two often overlapped."[23] As will be shown in chapter five, ambivalence about women working for pay was a continuous undercurrent in *Chatelaine*.

The topic of world peace was also a central concern for Sanders. This subject was discussed in editorials as early as May 1930 and again illustrates how Sanders interpreted events loosely within the paradigm of maternal feminism. As chapter six highlights, *Chatelaine* was usually abreast of national and international news items. Of particular concern was the outbreak of another global war. Combined with, and likely accentuated by the depression, this threat was omnipresent in *Chatelaine* throughout the 1930s, yet surfaced with particular vigour towards the end of the decade. In the May 1930 editorial, Sanders encouraged women to educate themselves on issues affecting world peace. Once informed of the situation, Sanders suggested that Canadian women could then "really help to mould the public opinion that is so important in the passing of any great reform or the attainment of any public endeavor."[24] Sanders recognised great potential in Canadian women – women had the vote and they had recently been declared "persons" under the law. Sanders assumed that this power would be harnessed for public good. In the interwar period, as Veronica Strong-Boag notes, "Many female activists believed ... that 'the woman's outlook on life is to save, to care for, to help. Men make wounds and women bind them up."[25] Sanders obviously fit into this category.

In 1934, world peace again took precedence in terms of editorial content. Events in Europe were likely a catalyst for the editorial; however, it was equally clear that four years of depression had shown what Canadian women could do. In January 1934, Sanders explained that "during the past four difficult years women have kept the faith of their great tradition of homemaking. ... homes everywhere are hiding untold stories of heroism and courage." Because of this evident strength, Sanders described what a united womanhood could do: "A united womanhood could stop wars. An intelligent, understanding womanhood must educate the coming generation to be peace-minded. Women must talk peace not only at home, but in the community where their activities can be felt. Women must spread the knowledge of how war propaganda is originated. ..." In essence, women were expected to train the youth of the day to abhor war and to be peace-minded.[26] At least three other editorials that year echoed these sentiments.[27] In the early 1930s, according to *Chatelaine*, world peace provided a legitimate cause for women to enter the public sphere.

In the late 1930s, some of Sanders' editorials did appear to subtly question the limits of maternal feminism while never overtly suggesting that modern women's public roles should extend beyond the welfare of home and community. In 1936, on the topic of women who gave up their "freedom" to care for others, Sanders declared that "there is nothing sadder than a woman who is suddenly left in middle life with no niche in life other than that at some bedside. ..." And yet she also commented that "after all, what a serene confidence in a life well worth the living, is the mark of those who do give the best years of their life for someone else."[28] The message was mixed. On one hand, it was a tragedy for Canadian women to give up their youth to care for family members; on the other hand, it was interpreted as the most fulfilling role that a modern woman could have.

Sanders' March 1939 editorial was more direct. It suggested that women should concentrate their energies on social welfare. "Conscripting the Woman-power is a phrase which is going to be echoed down the years ahead," wrote Sanders. She continued, "I believe women are gradually becoming aware of what they could do in public matters – if they really wanted to. They seem to be slowly realizing the truth behind the cold statistics – that they have the greater voting power at the polls." Sanders was "urging women to make the death toll on the highways their own responsibility"; she was not suggesting that women's responsibilities lay beyond the welfare of the community.[29] By July 1939, however, Sanders applauded the registration of women in the event of war. Under the caption "Women are Thinking" she noted that, "up and down Canada, women are discussing the plan for the registration of women with fast-increasing interest – and many, many points of view. One of the happiest signs of the time is this awakening of consciousness among women."[30]

This joyous occasion was arguably subdued by the onset of war in September 1939. World War Two, at least in terms of *Chatelaine's* editorial content, suggests a strengthening of women's commitment to be the social guardians of society. In March 1940, Sanders remarked that the war was causing a renewed interest in women's clubs, something that had been waning, particularly among young modern women in the 1930s. Unlike their predecessors, however, the young volunteers of the war years appeared to be as concerned with their femininity as they were with contributing to the war effort. For example, in a letter to Sanders cited in the same editorial, a young woman engaged in a mechanics course noted the following obstacle: "The big trouble ... is your nails. How to keep them decent? You can't wear rubber gloves. And the work is ruination to your nails." "But does that stop any of the girls," Sanders asked rhetorically.[31]

The increased employment of women because of the war was likely a major factor for why Sanders recanted her depression era commitment to women giving up their "bachelor girl" days to train for their wifely duties in their parental home. In contrast to the dominant position she took in the early 1930s on women working for pay, in her editorial of March 1941, Sanders applauded a brief period of paid employment for women before marriage. In fact she now felt that it was essential. Sanders noted of *Chatelaine's* modern woman of the 1940s that "Our women are learning, apparently, that the arts and crafts of running a home can be learned by any intelligent woman. But that the important thing is the point of view she brings to it. That point of view, they believe, must be learned somehow in the outside world, before it is brought, with too much concentration, into the home."[32]

Home and family, however, were still considered to be a woman's main interest. In one of Sanders' last wartime editorials in early 1942, she clearly expressed the predominant message that she had been sending Canadian women for over a decade: women were expected to be responsible for the social welfare of the state and the best way to meet this mandate was from the purview of the home and through volunteer work. In January 1942 she remarked: "In Germany, it all depends on Hitler; that's Nazism. Here it all depends on me. That's democracy." She told readers that, "Until you can make Democracy a reality in the minds and hearts of your children, you will fail in your job as Number One Morale Builder. Describe it to them, as shown in the daily news events. Talk about it at the table. Show them why it's worth fighting – and dying for." And she hoped that Canadian women would be "great enough to take from the year ahead the majestic ideal it offers – in keener intelligence, hard, hard work, and absolute self-sacrifice."[33] Indeed, Sanders left *Chatelaine* readers with the message that they were responsible for the moral welfare and future of society. Through their roles as wives, mothers and homemakers, and by placing the concerns of the community above individual aspirations, the women of Canada could save democracy. As Ruth Roah Pierson points out, the Canadian federal government did not need to inspire women's volunteer contribution to the war effort which was "by far and away the largest contribution made by Canadian women." Women persevered as they always had with the care of hearth and home, but because of the need to save the democratic family, "the war effort brought public acclaim to that everyday labour women perform[ed] as housewives and mothers." Women's club work also focused on the war effort and new societies and clubs were created expressly for this task.[34] *Chatelaine* recognized this appeal and helped middle-class Canadian women channel their energy in this pursuit.

Under the editorial direction of Mary Etta Macpherson, wife of Herbert McManus editor of *Mayfair* and then *Saturday Night*,[35] patriotism continued to be a central theme in *Chatelaine*. In her editorial debut with *Chatelaine*, in March 1942, Macpherson explained to readers that Sanders had gone to Ottawa to act as the Director of Consumer Representation on the Wartime Prices and Trade Board. Sanders was going to be "a dollar a year woman." Macpherson highlighted the fact that part of Sanders' qualification for the job was that she was a wife and mother and therefore a consumer. Macpherson remarked, "As Mrs. Frank M. Sperry in private life, and the mother of two young children, [Sanders] has abundant personal experience of the role of homemaker and family shopper." Macpherson appealed to all Canadian women, especially mothers and homemakers, to do their part for the war effort by shopping intelligently.[36] Canadian women responded enthusiastically.

The Wartime Prices and Trade Board divided Canada into fourteen administrative areas, each with a Women's Regional Advisory Committee. Subcommittees reported to their respective regional committees and through this network an estimated one million of Canada's three million adult women were mobilized to keep watch on price and production restrictions.[37]

Another way that *Chatelaine* suggested that women could show their patriotism was by boosting the morale of soldiers, specifically male soldiers. Macpherson devoted the April 1944 editorial to describing what types of letters women should send to the men overseas and what they should put in their packages. She reminded women that "The labored letter written out of a sense of 'duty,' or the long drawn out report of all the little vexatious problems of daily life at home seldom gladdens a man's heart.... Make the letters cheerful and don't backslide on the cigarette orders."[38] This call to be "number one morale booster" was repeated in the next month's editorial. It read in part, "A soldier's duty is to fight, to face death. Our duty makes no such supreme demand on us, but it is nevertheless clear-cut and explicit. We must back up that fighting man with everything we have – the highest sympathy of our hearts, the understanding of our minds, and the practical support of our dollars."[39] Notably, *Chatelaine*'s editorials from 1939 to 1945 were in line with government propaganda on spending and consumption.[40]

While the April and May 1944 editorials were clear in their belief that women should support the men overseas and the government at home, the June 1944 editorial was explicit about the fact that women could do so best from their positions as housewives. Macpherson explained of the housewife, "She had always been a nice person, and a pretty important one to everyone whose life she touches. She is the indispensable heart and spirit and practical head of the home. ...." Macpherson continued, "Sometimes she looks wistfully at the women who make the headlines, the ladies of legislatures and platforms and careers; she remembers that rather dreary vocational title 'housewife,' entered opposite her name in tax papers and census returns." And yet as Macpherson pointed-out, "She was the most surprised person in this Dominion when the Government dumped one of its biggest problems [price control] right into her lap and said, 'Please deal with this – you're the only one who can.'"[41]

Certainly, remnants of maternal feminist thoughts are apparent in these 1944 editorials. The September 1944 was also similar in content and again underscored women's "obligation" to their communities. "Government can give important leadership in legislature, financial grants, etc.," Macpherson wrote, "but they can never achieve the practical day-by-day neighborliness which must inspire community undertakings." And she made the point that this responsibility was a woman's duty. She continued, "That will remain a job for citizens, and especially for the voluntary women workers. ..."[42]

Ironically, however, only a year earlier, after taking her first ride on a bus driven by a woman, Macpherson had applauded women's wartime emancipation. She told readers, "If you think hard, you may be able to remember 1939, pre-war. The term 'womanpower' had yet to be coined. There wasn't a woman in Canada, we venture, who knew how to manipulate a welding tool; not one who had ever entered a shipyard as a worker. ..." Macpherson's point of view was clearly middle-class. She encouraged college girls to write a thesis entitled "What War Has Done to Improve the Status of Canadian Women," noting that "If one could stand far enough back to keep the historian's detached point of view, yet still bring the march of events into the exciting sharp focus they deserve, what a prize-winner that would be!"[43] But this type of editorial, which was at least suggestive of liberal feminist thought, was truly an anomaly for Macpherson. More typical were her comments in 1942 when she described a female industrial worker as follows: "Here is a picture of a woman working. We don't know her name, we can't recognize her features because of that curious contraption she wears, but the smooth high forehead, the well brushed dark hair, lead us to suspect she is young and attractive."[44] As chapter five shows, *Chatelaine*'s modern working woman of the war years was undeniably feminine.

Chatelaine acknowledged that during the wartime emergency women would have to fill jobs previously restricted to them because of their gender, but the magazine also reminded readers that they were still women – even the bus driver had been described as petite and feminine. To help emphasize this point, the May 1943 issue of *Chatelaine* was dedicated to brides. Several were interviewed and the editorial commented that "the brides – all of them in their twenties, [are] all eager to tell us that marriage is incontrovertibly the greatest thing in the world."[45]

The tone of Macpherson's postwar editorials returned women emphatically to their roles of wives, mothers and homemakers, and, importantly, social guardians. This should not be surprising given postwar social norms. As Douglas Owram points out, "Though family has always been central to social institutions, during the fifteen years or so after the Second World War the values of marriage and family were exalted to new levels."[46] Some of the social welfare programmes being put forth by the state also encouraged women to assume their traditional roles as wives, mothers and homemakers. Historian Annalee Golz illustrates how the debates surrounding the 1944 Family Allowance Act and the Canadian Citizenship Act of 1946 placed the state at the centre of the family. Particularly with respect to the Family Allowance Act which, whenever possible, a cheque would be made out to the mothers in support of their offspring, Golz shows how the government thereby transformed motherhood into a vocation that could be on par with other forms of paid employment.[47] Reflecting the emergence of the social welfare state in the post Second World War period, in *Chatelaine* the roles of wives, mothers and homemakers took on new significance as women were encouraged to lobby for more social welfare programmes. For example, the January 1946 editorial suggested that health should be women's new collective goal. "The state of our health – family, municipal, provincial, national – could and should be on the agenda of every women's organization," Macpherson declared. She continued, "The place of voluntary groups in educating public opinion, urging measures for the general good and counting the practical results, has never been so admittedly important as it is today."[48]

Macpherson had acted as the editor of *Chatelaine* during a period of unprecedented opportunity for women to redefine their gender identity. Canada's total war effort, on the home front at least, demanded a re-negotiation of many traditional norms. For example, women's employment increased by over 10 per cent between 1939 and in 1944 and they held jobs previously restricted to men.[49] Yet, Macpherson's editorials largely emphasized the importance of marriage and motherhood to the development of middle-class Canadian womanhood.

When Sanders returned to *Chatelaine* in 1947, many of her editorials also positioned modern women of the postwar period in the roles of wives and mothers. However, some also challenged the limits of maternal feminism and pushed for more equality between the sexes. To claim as Valerie Korinek has done that Sanders was simply a maternal feminist who was "convinced that the power of the household should have an impact on the nation and that wives and mothers were a force to be reckoned with,"[50] is to miss many of the complex nuances that surfaced in Sanders' editorials from 1947 to 1952. As Inez Houlihan suggests, this was a period of transition for *Chatelaine*'s editorials. Houlihan argues that from August 1945 to February 1960 *Chatelaine*'s "editorial focus shifted from a confidence in women's traditional roles toward a questioning of women's status in Canada."[51] In a way, however, both Korinek and Houlihan are correct in their interpretations of Sanders' postwar editorials. Many did preach of the power of the household; others, however, challenged the limitation of women within the home.

Sanders underscored the importance of women to the home in her November 1947 editorial titled, "Husband's Jobs and Working Wives." Sanders commented that many women who deplored the idea of working wives did so for two central reasons: "...married men should have all the jobs available as they support families. Married women work for selfish reasons – nice clothes, luxuries." Sanders, however, was more broad in her view that many wives worked because of economic need. She also disengaged "career women" and "cleaning women" from the discussion on the basis that no man would envy these workers. But she concluded that even if wives worked, they were the ones who also had to take care of the home. She commented that "it's a mighty hard life for any woman." And noted that "Very few would undertake it unless they had excellent reasons."[52] Yet, when the topic of working wives outside the home resurfaced in *Chatelaine*'s July 1950 editorial, Sanders viewed it as a modern necessity. She wrote that "For good or ill, mankind is pressing forward to some unknown goal. Somewhere in that progress, surely, lies the principle of the right to earn money – provided one can and provided one wants to."[53] Her comment suggests a strong middle-class bias and a genderless right to paid employment.

In *Chatelaine*'s September 1947 editorial, it is clear that Sanders was once again stressing women's affinity towards peace because of their roles as mothers. She pondered why women had up until that point been unable to eliminate wars in the twentieth century and she reminded women of their "natural" calling. "Women have always been the natural protectors of the human race," Sanders wrote. She continued, "Somehow we've got to find a way to learn the hopelessness of being fiercely protective of our own sons and daughters, yet refusing to use our strengths as women to try and save them from the destruction of war."[54] Her October 1948 editorial had a similar tone although it concentrated more on how women could improve their communities rather than eliminate war. Sanders wrote of Canadian women, "Painfully, laboriously, we are learning that the welfare of each family in our community is our personal concern. We are discovering that efficiency in administration and scientific techniques in approach are the strongest support a warm heart and a generous impulse can have." The "wrongs" in the community that Sanders believed women could "right" included "broken homes, sick children, ailing old people, youngsters in need of guidance and recreation."[55]

By 1950, however, Sanders questioned women's dedication to home and community. She suggested that women's fundamental problem was that they cared too much. In one editorial she commented that "For in caring too much, they try too hard. This tends to build an awkwardness when men and women work together for a community cause. ... It tends to build a resentment in the minds of men, who automatically feel that the woman is trying to 'show them up.' It makes them feel uncomfortable." Her recommendation to women was that they learn "to be easy and relaxed in their approach to any problem."[56]

Perhaps Sanders' suggestion for women to be more "man-like" stemmed in part from the growing dissatisfaction that she chronicled among Canadian wives. In April 1948 she lamented that, "Progress has given our girls a chance for education in the professions; in the arts; in business. Women make brilliant students in all these phases of work. But at marriage the majority must put this promise of personal expression away, and turn their talents to housework." She suggested that the modern wife was missing the opportunity for "self-expression" outside of the "treadmill of housework, childcare, [and] community service." Her recommendation was for the women of Canada to "somehow find time in their busy lives for the things they want to do as individuals."[57] In just over a year, however, Sanders blamed the women for their discontent. In September 1949 she observed, "Look around and check the people you know. Isn't it the woman who has brought an almost humorless devotion to the task of raising a family, or working for the community, who is first to complain of ingratitude? 'And I've given them the best years of my life!'" To which Sanders commented, "Oh – why give them, if you don't have fun doing it?"[58]

Reflecting the changing state of the Canadian nation in the post World War Two period, another theme that surfaced in Sanders' postwar editorials was that of ethnic diversity. After the Second World War, as historian Valerie Knowles notes, "The Canadian government's demonstrated sympathy for European refugees and displaced persons was another factor that augured well for the development of a less restrictive immigration policy."[59] Amid the fears of the Cold War, however, racism and ethnic biases were hard to quell. At times, *Chatelaine* tried to embrace Canada's budding diversity. "Race Hatred and You" was the title of the March 1947 editorial. Sanders cautioned her readers that they were "in countless thoughtless ways … building intolerance, misunderstandings and ill will." And she observed that "…one of the tests of true democracy is a tolerance of minorities. We Canadians are a nation of minorities.…" In this way she was ever so slightly moving beyond the white, middle-class blinders of maternal feminism. However, she did suggest a solution based on traditional gender roles. To her female readership she wrote, "The nations of the world can never be truly united until they understand and trust one another. They can only do that working through the communities of the world. That means your hometown, and you."[60] While she spoke of Canada being a nation of minorities, Sanders was clearly appealing to white, Anglo-Saxon, middle-class women to show tolerance of others. Indeed, Sanders comments in her

July 1948 editorial in which she wrote about a reception for foreign guests that she had attended in Virginia were clearly race conscious. At the function she met a young Iranian woman who had come to North America to learn about ways to prevent infant mortality so that she could return home and educate her Iranian sisters. Sanders asked the young woman, "Tell me honestly ... you have been in this country for several years. You have learned a great deal from us. But, apart from our knowledge of the proper way to care for mothers and their babies – do you feel our civilization has much to offer the women of your country?" The Iranian replied: "Oh, no! ... There really isn't much else that I would like to take back to my countrywomen. You see, we have a wonderful home life. I think it's because every girl is trained from the time she's a baby to believe this one thing. 'One God, one man, one home.'" Sanders celebrated the virtues of "one God, one man, [and] one home"[61] and encouraged Canadian women to live by this motto, yet her comments also suggest that she was quite aware of racial and ethnic differences between North Americans and Iranians and, as a white Anglo-Saxon, Sanders inadvertently expressed sentiments of racial superiority.

Sanders' return to *Chatelaine* after World War Two was reflective of a schizophrenic period for Canadian women in which many tried to (re)define a place for themselves in postwar society. Within this five-year period Sanders' editorials were characterised by paradoxical shifts in attitude. At times she strongly supported the values associated with maternal feminism, yet some of her editorials also suggested a yearning for something different.[62] In her farewell editorial of January 1952, however, she was clear. She bid "good-by and good luck" to readers and left them with the following words: "It's been exhilarating to watch your growing pride in your work as homemakers and in an understanding of the vital roles we play in the nation's life as wives and mothers."[63]

When Sanders retired from *Chatelaine* to join her brother in conducting Gallup Poll research, Lotta Dempsey took her place. Dempsey had begun as a newspaper reporter in Edmonton and then moved to Toronto in 1935 where she freelanced for a variety of presses. By 1950 she had written over 316 articles, many under pseudonyms.[64] She was also married and a mother. During the war she took on the additional task as a "staffer" with the Wartime Prices and Trade Board. In her autobiography she describes the war years as "a hectic, challenging period."[65] Despite Dempsey's long association with *Chatelaine*, Valerie Korinek labels Dempsey as a "feisty outsider," and suggests that "The difference in Dempsey's tone from that of Sanders was readily apparent." She concludes that Dempsey was more encouraging to her readers than her predecessor had been and that she recognized the influential role that she, as the editor of one of Canada's foremost women's magazines, played in the lives of many Canadian women.[66]

Dempsey made a concerted effort to address current issues that affected modern Canadian women beyond the confines of hearth and home. In April 1952, for example, because of her shock and disappointment over Canada's first female Member of Parliament Agnes Macphail not being re-elected, Dempsey devoted her entire editorial to the famous Canadian woman. Dempsey was clear about her personal feelings on the patronage system. She felt that Macphail had been reduced to "a state of proud poverty."[67] She concluded that "If all these quite plausible things [specifically, taking a non-partisan approach to the situation] happened, Agnes Macphail might feel called upon to graciously decline (if she hadn't already accepted it) the one post, as I write this, which has been offered to her in tribute to three decades of national service – That of matron of a mental institution."[68]

In May 1952, Dempsey again addressed an issue that she felt affected many Canadian women: the feeling of having no time to complete everything that needed to be done. At a time when the "super woman" myth was beginning to emerge, Dempsey was able to remark on some of the challenges that faced modern middle-class women who tried to balance paid employment and a family without automatically suggesting that women return to their traditional roles of housewives. This editorial was certainly of a less personal nature than April's had been, but it also shows Dempsey's desire and enthusiasm to influence her readership. In a morose way, Dempsey reminded women, and men for that matter, to focus on important matters in their lives – but she left it up to her readers to decide what these priorities were. She told the story of a woman who, discovering that she had a terminal illness, penned a farewell letter to her husband. It read simply, "So short, So sweet."[69]

The same could be said of Dempsey's term as editor of *Chatelaine*. In August 1952, after only eight months on the job, Dempsey vacated her position to become a columnist with the *Globe and Mail*.[70]

Dempsey's replacement, John Clare, was *Chatelaine*'s first male editor. His term was characterised by a noticeable lack of editorial content and a decline in subscription rates.[71] In lieu of editorials, Clare provided a feature called "*Chatelaine* Centre" in which he published anecdotes about "contributors, producers and readers of the periodical."[72] Valerie Korinek remarks, "Unlike the other editors, he did not understand his audience of female readers. This is not to say that a male editor could not interpret the '*Chatelaine* ethos' to the readers; rather, the criticism that an uninterested male editor, with no desire to learn about or interact with the readers, could not create editorial material that had much resonance with them."[73] According to members of his staff he "hated his time at *Chatelaine*" and could not wait to return to his previous post as managing editor of *Maclean's*.[74] This lack of editorial content came at a difficult time for Canadian women as they tried to find their place in postwar Canada amid the growth of a consumer culture and suburbia.

While Clare was editor, Dorris McCubbin, later Anderson, was able to exercise considerable influence in terms of the magazine's direction and content. Initially she was in charge of "editorial promotion" and her job was to get the magazine mentioned on radio and television. Later she managed the service department and she became managing editor under Clare. She also wrote many articles for *Chatelaine*.[75] Anderson has since become famous for her term as *Chatelaine*'s "feminist" editor from 1957 to 1977.[76] In her autobiography she recalls, "Even as a lowly editorial assistant, I had been itching to make changes to *Chatelaine*. Now [1957] with the go-ahead from management, we redesigned everything. ... I'm sure they would never have approved my plans – had they known about them in advance."[77] In the early 1950s, however, although despair became a common sentiment attached to the suburban housewife, there was little evidence of equality-based feminism in the magazine.

Certainly, a review of *Chatelaine* and its editors in the 1930s, 1940s and 1950s, provides insight into the dynamic and complicated gendered relationships that existed within Canadian society. Not only did *Chatelaine* editors write for the modern Canadian woman, in subtle, and occasionally not so subtle, ways they also tried to shape modern conceptions of womanhood. The female editors of *Chatelaine* influenced and were influenced by their readership and the world in which they lived. The depression, the war, a postwar economic boom and the Cold War all affected editorial content and the other images presented in the magazine. The perceived threat to democracy that grew in the late 1930s and continued into the Cold War was of particular concern for the editors. The more severely democracy was perceived to be threatened, the more the images of modern Canadian womanhood in *Chatelaine* were associated with the private sphere of hearth and home. According to the editors of *Chatelaine*, by the late 1930s, women could best fight for peace and the survival of democracy as wives, mothers and home-makers and this persisted well into the 1950s. As the next chapter shows, this placed an added stress on the need for women to "catch" a man.

Endnotes

1   Mary Lowrey Ross, *Chatelaine*, May 1929, 5.

2   Naomi Wolf, *The Beauty Myth: How Images of Beauty Are Used Against Women* (New York: William Morrow and Company, Inc., 1991), 64.

3   There is little published material about Anne Elizabeth Wilson's personal life.

4   Inez Houlihan does a good job of tracing the editorial staff of *Chatelaine*. Additionally, Houlihan provides a chart that details the number of editorials in a given time period. For example, from 1928 to 1945, 59% of the issues are recorded to have had editorials, from 1945 to 1960 the number is 54%. Inez Houlihan, *The Image of Women in Chatelaine Editorials March 1928 to September 1977* (M.A. Thesis, University of Toronto, 1984), 2-8.

5   Fraser Sutherland, *The Monthly Epic: A History of Canadian Magazines, 1799-1989* (Markham: Fitzhenry & Whiteside, 1989), 246.

6   Houlihan also makes reference to this fact. Houlihan, *The Image of Women in Chatelaine Editorials*, 18-23.

7   Thomas P. Socknat, "For Peace and Freedom: Canadian Feminists and the Interwar Peace Campaign," in Janice Williamson and Deborah Gorham (eds.), *Up and Doing: Canadian Women and Peace* (Toronto: The Women's Press, 1989), 67.

8   Thomas P. Socknat, *Witness Against War: Pacifism in Canada, 1900-1945* (Toronto: University of Toronto Press, 1987), 92.

9   Anne Elizabeth Wilson, *Chatelaine*, July 1928, 16.

10   Ibid., August 1928, 16.

11   Wendy Mitchinson, "The WCTU: 'For God, Home and Native Land': A Study in Nineteenth-Century Feminism," in Linda Kealey (ed.), *A Not Unreasonable Claim: Women and Reform in Canada, 1800s-1920s* (Toronto: The Women's Educational Press, 1979), 161.

12   Veronica Strong-Boag, "Peace-Making Women: Canada 1919-1939," in Ruth Roach Pierson (ed.), *Women and Peace: Theoretical, Historical and Practical Perspectives* (London: Croom Helm, 1987), 170, 174.

13   Sutherland, *The Monthly Epic*, 160. In 1953, Sanders and Margaret Aitken co-authored *Hey Ma! I did it. Hey Ma!* told the triumphant story of Aitken's election to parliament. Reading the book reveals both Sanders' progressive nature in regard to women's rights and the fact that she saw things in the only way that she could have, through the gendered lenses of 1940s and 1950s Canada. For example, when deciding on which riding to run for, they decided on York-Humber because as Aitken put it "well, just because I liked York-Humber." Apparently actual figures were too difficult to calculate because there were "so many 8's and 9's." It is doubtful whether their male counterparts would have used the same logic (or, at least, whether they would ever have admitted to it). Margaret Aitken and Byrne Hope Sanders, *Hey Ma! I did it* (Toronto: Clarke, Irwin & Company Limited, 1953), 14, 12.

14   Valerie Korinek, *Roughing it in the Suburbs: Reading Chatelaine Magazine in the 1950s and 1960s* (Toronto: University of Toronto Press, 2000), 44.

15   Byrne Hope Sanders, *Chatelaine*, September 1929, 16.

16   Ibid., February 1932, 4.

17   Ibid., July 1932, 2.

18   Ibid., January 1933, 2.

19   Cited in Margaret Hobbs, "Equality and Difference: Feminism and the Defence of Women Workers during the Great Depression," in Wendy Mitchinson, Paula Bourne, Alison Prentice, Gail Cuthbert Brandt, Beth Light and Naomi Black, *Canadian Women: A Reader* (Toronto: Harcourt Brace & Company, 1996), 213.

20   Ruth Roach Pierson, "Gender and the Unemployment Insurance Debates in Canada, 1934 – 1940," in A.D. Gilbert, C.M. Wallace and R.M. Bray, *Reappraisals in Canadian History: Post Confederation* (Scarborough: Prentice Hall Canada Inc., 1992), 356.

21   Margaret Hobbs and Ruth Roach Pierson, "'A kitchen that wastes no steps…' Gender, Class and the Home Improvement Plan, 1936-40," *Histoire Sociale/Social History*, 21 (1988), 36.

22   Byrne Hope Sanders, *Chatelaine*, March 1931, 84.

23   Hobbs, "Equality and Difference," 214.

24   Byrne Hope Sanders, *Chatelaine*, May 1930, 16.

25   Strong-Boag, "Peace-Making Women," 170.

26   Byrne Hope Sanders, *Chatelaine*, January 1934, 1.

27   See for example: Mrs. James Ince, guest editorial, *Chatelaine*, March 1934, 2; Hon. Irene Parlby, guest editorial, *Chatelaine*, May 1934, 2; and Byrne Hope

Sanders, *Chatelaine*, November 1934, 2. The topic did not disappear after 1934. See for example, Byrne Hope Sanders, *Chatelaine*, May 1935, 2.

28   Byrne Hope Sanders, *Chatelaine*, November 1936, 2.

29   Ibid., March 1939, 2.

30   Ibid., July 1939, 48.

31   Ibid., March 1940, 84.

32   Byrne Hope Sanders, *Chatelaine*, March 1941, 1.

33   Ibid., January 1942, 50.

34   Pierson, *"They're Still Women After All,"* 35, 33, 37.

35   Sutherland, *The Monthly Epic*, 249. There is little published material about Mary Etta Macpherson's personal life.

36   Mary Etta Macpherson, *Chatelaine*, March 1942, 76.

37   Pierson, *"They're Still Women After All,"* 39-40. Perhaps because of the traditional association of women to the private sphere, Canada's "dollar a year woman" has received noticeably less historical attention than the men who volunteered for Canada's war effort.   Sanders, however, was named a Companion of the British Empire for her war work. Sutherland, *The Monthly Epic*, 244.

38   Mary Etta Macpherson, *Chatelaine*, April 1944, 90.

39   Ibid., May 1944, 96.

40   For a discussion on how wartime advertisements, including government propaganda, targeted women in their roles as wives, mothers and homemakers see Pierson, *"They're Still Women After All,"* 41-48.

41   Mary Etta Macpherson, *Chatelaine*, June 1944, 76.

42   Ibid., September 1944, 90.

43   Ibid., September 1943, 76.

44   Ibid., September 1942, 64.

45   Mary Etta Macpherson, *Chatelaine*, May 1943, 1.

46   Owram, *Born at the Right Time*, 12.

47   Annalee Golz, "The Canadian Family and the State in the Postwar Period," *Left History* 1,2 (1993), 16.

48   Mary Etta Macpherson, *Chatelaine*, January 1946, 56.

49   Jeffrey Keshen, *Saints, Sinners and Soldiers*, 149-150.

50   Korinek, *Roughing it in the Suburbs*, 261.

51   Houlihan, *The Image of Women in Chatelaine Editorials*, 69.

52   Byrne Hope Sanders, *Chatelaine*, November 1947, 2.

53   Ibid., July 1950, 3.

54   Ibid., September 1947, 3.

55   Ibid., October 1948, 3.

56   Byrne Hope Sanders, *Chatelaine*, November 1950, 3.

57   Ibid., April 1948, 2.

58   Ibid., September 1949, 2.

59   Valerie Knowles, *Strangers at Our Gates: Canadian Immigration and Immigration Policy, 1540-1997* (Toronto: Dundurn Press, 1997), 125,131.

60   Ibid., March 1947, 112.

61   Byrne Hope Sanders, *Chatelaine*, July 1948, 1.

62   While not directly discussing *Chatelaine*, Naomi Wolf argues that "Though many writers have pointed out that women's magazines reflect historical change, fewer examine how part of their job is to determine historical change as well." Naomi Wolf, *The Beauty Myth: How Images of Beauty Are Used Against Women* (New York: William Morrow and Company, Inc., 1991), 64.

63   Byrne Hope Sanders, *Chatelaine*, January 1952, 3.

64   Sutherland, *The Monthly Epic*, 244.

65   Dempsey, *No Life for a Lady*, 64.

66   Korinek, *Roughing it in the Suburbs*, 264-265.

67   Ibid., 265.

68   Lotta Dempsey, *Chatelaine*, April 1952, 3.

69   Ibid., May 1952, 1.

70   Sutherland, *The Monthly Epic*, 245.

71   Korinek, *Roughing it in the Suburbs*, 267-268.

72   Ibid., 259.

73   Ibid., 260.

74   Ibid., 45.

75   Sutherland, *The Monthly Epic*, 246.

76   For more on *Chatelaine* in the 1950s and 1960s, particularly on Doris Anderson's tenure as editor, see Korinek, *Roughing it in the Suburbs* and Doris Anderson, *Rebel Daughter: An Autobiography* (Toronto: Key Porter Books, 1996). Interestingly, Anderson has gained popularity as a feminist editor, however, Wilson, Sanders, Macpherson and Dempsey were also feminists – just of a different sort.

77   Anderson, *Rebel Daughter: An Autobiography*, 148-149.

Chapter Three

Learning to Live with a Man and Love It: Romance in *Chatelaine*

Marriage, apparently, is still considered the ideal state, and people continue to fall in love. Why, then, can't they live more happily together?

... "women" seek relief from the annoyances of everyday existence more often than men. When a man asks for divorce, it is generally for some cogent reason – infidelity on the part of his wife, neglect of his children, or because he has fallen in love with another woman. But the wife wants "relief" from the ennul [sic] of little things ... Said a recent divorcee to me: "John will make a splendid husband for some other woman. There was no fault I could lay my finger on. He just had a way of rasping my nerves past endurance. That's all!"

Madge MacBeth
Chatelaine, November 1928[1]

In November 1928, *Chatelaine* published a story about Carrina, a fictitious grandmother. Carrina, the quintessential Victorian, had committed herself as a young woman to a marriage of convenience that merged the wealth of two prominent families. In its wake she abandoned her true love, the handsome yet poor, Peter Shane. Carrina later justified her choice by the advantages it gave to her daughter. "Had she not done the very best for her child?" she asked. "It was the child that mattered," she continued. "The finest of silk, the softest of cambric for that tender little body, such care! Oh surely this was the greatest love that life could offer, surely this was worth her sacrifice – this mother-love." The child, Mina, grew up selfish and spoiled. At a young age she married a man who was "fat and comfortably well off." Mina, however, was soon widowed with an infant girl of her own, Arletta. Mina quickly absolved herself of her parental responsibility and left Arletta to be raised by her grandmother, Carrina. Meanwhile, Mina enjoyed her newfound freedom and endless wealth. When Arletta entered her twenties she, like her grandmother, had to decide whether to marry for love or money. She asked her grandmother for advice. Without hesitation, Carrina encouraged her granddaughter to follow her heart.[2]

Whether motivated by love or money, between 1928 and 1956, marriage was of paramount importance to the modern woman of *Chatelaine*. To many, husbands were a prize. Their value did not lie predominately in their physical attributes – although physical attractiveness was certainly recognized. A more important criteria for judging a suitor's potential was the lifestyle that he could provide. Simultaneously, however, for a growing number of *Chatelaine*'s women, marriage was no longer seen as life's panacea. As a January 1929 article stated: "The modern woman … steps out to make her own place in the sun, dependent on no man."[3]

From 1928 to 1956, *Chatelaine* published in its editorials and also in short stories, opinion pieces and advice columns, a range of middle-class views concerning courtship and marriage. *Chatelaine*'s shifting views on marriage can be loosely categorized into three phases. In the early years, marriage was viewed as a welcomed luxury, but not as a necessity for modern Canadian womanhood. For example, first time romances between elderly couples were described, men and women lived together outside of the bonds of matrimony, and working women supported themselves without the need for a husband. In its first few years,

Chatelaine's "modern woman" generally married for love. And she stayed married for the same reason. The depression challenged these notions but it did not dislodge them. The women of the early 1930s who married for economic gain usually wed to improve their situations and not out of dire necessity. For the unhappy wife, divorce appeared to be a socially acceptable option. By the time of the Second World War, however, a different picture of courtship was being presented. *Chatelaine's* modern bride was young and marriage was increasingly seen as an integral step in the life of every modern woman. Moreover, the dynamics of the male-female "chase" were being redefined. Initially, power rested with the woman who, at her leisure, selected a husband for emotional and/or economic reasons. By the mid 1930s, with an increased pressure on young women to wed, *Chatelaine's* modern woman relied heavily on her femininity to "trap" a man and a woman's appearance became increasingly important in this pursuit. Moreover, once married, it was up to the bride to ensure the durability of the conjugal relationship. In the postwar years, the role of wife, now a critical stage in a woman's lifecycle, also subordinated her to husband. Certainly, there were challenges to the images of wifely obedience published in the magazine but, paradoxically, in the end they too reinforced "traditional" gender roles that often connected men with the public sphere and women to the private. Additionally, in this last phase, men moved to a relative position of power within the evolving courtship ritual.

A common motivation for women to wed that appeared in *Chatelaine* throughout its first three decades was a desire to improve their social and/or economic status. Under these circumstances, at least until the mid 1930s, marriage was considered a woman's best choice, but it was not her only option. In many instances young women wanted to marry to escape the confines of home life. For example, in November 1929, there was a short story about a young woman, Norma, who agreed to elope to escape from her strict, upper-class father. The man, Vincent, who she agreed to wed, projected the illusion of being well-off by borrowing from and manipulating friends. On the night of the elopement, to help "free" Norma from her father's house, Vincent procured the help of his male friend Beverly, to whom he was two thousand dollars in debt. The plan went terribly wrong. Vincent ended up being caught by Norma's father while Norma and Beverly narrowly escaped. After hearing of the "repressed" conditions in which Norma was forced to live, Beverly could not face returning her to her home. Norma admitted that the only reason why she had wanted to marry Vincent was to escape from her father's purview. She had not been in love with him. Realizing this situation, Beverly, who had just met Norma, professed his love to her. Interestingly, Norma never confessed to being in love with Beverly. Yet, the two were immediately married. Beverly was actually all that Vincent had pretended to be, wealthy, well educated and socially upwardly mobile.[4]

Beverly was unquestionably the hero of this rather far fetched story, but it was Norma who had controlled the situation. Norma knew that she wanted a husband. When it did not work out with Vincent, then Beverly became the preferred candidate. Throughout the late 1920s and into the 1930s, it was common for the men of *Chatelaine* to be portrayed as "saviours," particularly through the role of the provider. As this story suggests, however, the women of *Chatelaine* were often aware of the benefits that husbands could provide and these advantages could sometimes supersede the individual qualities that a particular man would bring to the role.

Certainly, once the depression began to manifest itself in Canadian society in the early 1930s, marriage was again seen by many Canadian women as the easiest way to improve their standard of living. Like Norma, many women were apparently willing to overlook true love for the perceived economic security that a husband could provide. As a contributor to *Chatelaine* wrote in 1931: "When it comes to leaping off the deep end, beauty has it over brains … Give me a cute nose and I won't need to know how to spell. Correct spelling will bring me $25 a week, perhaps, but a cute nose will give me a meal ticket to punch for the rest of my life. … An ounce of complexion is worth a pound of grey matter."[5] However, not all women agreed with the above statement. A couple of years later a woman remarked in *Chatelaine*: "We are living in 1933 … Marriage is no longer the chief end of woman. There are many careers open to her and she had learned the joy of independence."[6]

Despite their difference of opinion, both contributors interpreted the role of wife as a "job" for women and a means of providing for their economic security. This became a common theme in *Chatelaine* and reflected at least some middle-class interpretations of marriage. Indeed, many historians have suggested that the representations of middle-class women in the popular media were predominantly as wives. The concept of a family structure built on gender division whereby the woman supported the earning capacity of her husband by taking care of the home and children and acting as a hostess and social companion when occasion demanded lasted well into the twentieth century and is reflective of a middle-class bias.[7] *Chatelaine* both embraced and rejected this image, but at no point did the magazine distance itself too far from this popular discourse.

Many contributors to *Chatelaine* in its first decade expressed the opinion that women should only accept the "position" of wife if their motive was love.[8] Indeed, the contributor from 1933 who was adamant regarding employment options for women continued, "If some man comes along and wins her love, she will consider the matter very carefully. Is it worth giving up her job and her glorious freedom for a husband, home and children? If she decides that it is and she goes to the marriage altar, it is because Love, the greatest force in the world has led her there."[9]

While the value of a potential suitor could depend on two measurable variables – how much money he could provide and how desired he was by other women – according to *Chatelaine* love usually worked its way into the recipe as well. "Secret Banner," a March 1934 love story had all three ingredients. Lorna and Scotty were married right after college graduation. Scotty had been the star of the football team during his school years and their lives had been full of excitement and popularity. When school ended, fame vanished. Scotty took a job at a sporting goods store and the couple lived comfortably, but with no appearance of upward mobility. Lorna was unhappy. She considered leaving Scotty. She recalled a friend of hers who had been in a similar situation and who had broken her engagement a year after graduation. Lorna remarked enviously of her friend, "[She'd] waited a year – she'd given herself a chance to find out how Tom would appear. She'd been able to get away then because she hadn't lived with him – hadn't gotten herself all tangled up with emotions."[10] When Scotty heard that Lorna's friend was now engaged to a wealthy tennis star he remarked sarcastically, "Well, she'd better hurry up and marry him before he isn't a hero anymore."[11] It was obvious that Lorna and Scotty were aware of the gulf that was growing between them. After Scotty was taken to the hospital for a foot injury, however, Lorna admitted: "I shall always love him. I don't want to, but I can't help it."[12] The marriage was saved. Lorna accepted Scotty's position and, more importantly, she realized his "social decline" had probably not been easy on him either. Lorna reflected: "He [Scotty] had been the idol of the whole school, the city, but now there was another Flying Scotchman on the hill and Scotty was selling sporting goods in a downtown store, patronized by persons who, two years ago, would have bragged about meeting him. You never once heard him complain."[13] Even though Lorna had flirted with the idea of divorce, like many of *Chatelaine*'s modern women she realised that love was the key ingredient to marriage.

There was, however, no guarantee that every young woman would fall in love and marry. According to *Chatelaine*, this became more of a problem for middle-class parents of daughters during the depression and was associated with the decrease in job opportunities for women. "Can She Manage Alone?" that appeared in April 1932, addressed this topic. The article claimed that, "Most mothers have held the view that marriages were made in heaven; it would be nice if the girls found the right men, but it was none of the parents' business." The article pointed out, however, that "it begins to look as though careers for women are not so assured, and marriage may again become their most certain means of livelihood." While the article began by suggesting that parents were nonchalant about their daughters getting married, it was also quick to point out that a son-in-law was indeed what every girl's parents wanted. "Nearly all parents want their daughters to marry because they think it means the greatest happiness for them," the author stressed. She continued, "Any normal parent will cheerfully see a girl give up a dazzling career for a mere man."[14] Indeed, the message was mixed. However, the association of the wife as the husband's employee was direct. And the mere presence of the article suggests that the modern woman of 1932 refused to be forced into wedlock.

Indeed, in the early 1930s *Chatelaine* appears to have over represented the choice among young women to remain single compared to the number of single women living in Canadian society. In her study on the relationship between mass media content and social change in Canada, Susannah Jane Foster Wilson averaged out marriage rates for the forty-year period beginning in 1930 and found that in fiction in *Chatelaine*, 55 per cent of heroines were single and 36 per cent were married by the end of the story. Comparatively, 28.1 per cent of the Canadian female population above fifteen years of age were single during the same time period and 62.0 per cent were married.[15] Although this data does not take race, ethnicity or class into account, it is probable that articles in *Chatelaine* over represented the possibilities for single middle-class women. For example, in a 1929 article that alluded to the fading appeal of marriage among young Canadian women, *Chatelaine* reported that a vote among a dozen modern women at a tea party held in honour of a bride-to-be was equally split between those who wanted to marry and those who did not.[16] Yet, the reality was that most young women would be married by the age of twenty-five.[17] *Chatelaine* however stressed choice over destiny in its description of young womanhood.

In the early 1930s, the modern woman of *Chatelaine* knew that she had choices. "Dinner Dance" which was published in July 1931 told the story of Elinor, a young working woman whose only connection with wealth was through her paternal aunt. Her aunt invited her for a weekend in the country where she re-encountered an old boyfriend, Hal. Initially, Hal did not recognize Elinor among the swarm of young women vying for his attention. At a formal dinner dance Elinor was determined to confront Hal. Watching other diners she observed of the new modern young women: "They depended on nothing, not beauty, nor clothes, nor any quality that dazzles. … She saw other girls snatch-ing the men they wanted and galloping off with no self-consciousness whatsoever." She concluded that, "These girls did not care, they took what they wanted with gay impudence. … There was not one of them who would have cried in a pillow for any man that walked."[18] Elinor was eventually empowered by the assertiveness of the young women around her and manipulated a moment for herself and Hal to be alone. They kissed. At that instant Hal remembered the long lost love of his youth. The ending was left open, but it was clear that it was the mod-ern woman who could be in charge of the romance and she was not des-perate to have a ring on her finger. There was no suggestion that Elinor was looking to live happily-ever-after with Hal. She knew she had options. Notably, this conclusion challenges Veronica Strong-Boag's statement that, "Despite disquiet on every side about the state of marital relationships, women were directed relentlessly to the pursuit of husbands."[19] This 1931 short story suggests that there is more to the popular courtship story of the 1930s.

The men of *Chatelaine* during this era also appeared to be at least somewhat aware that women on occasion manipulated them. A man spoke out on the subject in "I Wish I Were a Woman" that appeared in April 1932. The author remarked, "Funny, isn't it, how the brains and resources of the men of the world are concentrated on developing and improving the well-being and comforts of women."[20] The author envied the beauty products available to women and the "ease" of their lives, filled with visits to the park and gossiping with friends. He noted that "men are the Pollyannas of the world, who, because women expect it of them, uncomplainingly swelter in heavy suits on the hottest day, and brave the rigors of the coldest weather in Derby hats."[21] While there was a satirical quality to the article, there was also a genuine tone to the longing.

Not everyone agreed, however, that women were the advantaged sex in marriage. In May 1932, the author of "The Vainer Sex," Beverley Owen, remarked that women "are quietly aware that vanity is by no means exclusively of the feminine gender. Married women soon discover, on the contrary, that it is the chief ingredient of the masculine morale. If a man hasn't room to strut he's no good."[22] Owen, a mother of three, remarked that, "Taking care of my own husband's egotism and nourishing his self-sufficiency to the level where it produces dividends is a bigger job than looking after my babies. If a man's vanity suffers or he develops an inferiority complex, down come the earnings."[23]

Certainly, a common theme in *Chatelaine* was to discuss which sex gave more in marriage. In many respects, particularly in its first decade,

Chatelaine provided readers with a forum in which to debate "modern" views concerning romantic relationships. On several occasions these discussions turned into arguments, generally between men and women, concerning the roles of wives and husbands. The specific topic of who had more privileges – wives or husbands – was played out in one form or another over the course of several years. Interestingly, the disputes often hinged on the ability, or lack thereof, of women to support themselves economically and the associated stereotype of the husband/provider.

"Do wives give more than husbands?" queried the title of the May 1930 article, by F.E. Bailey, a frequent contributor to *Chatelaine* who had already earned a reputation for eliciting many and varied reader responses. "In my opinion," Bailey wrote, "when Mrs. Smith marries, she drives a bargain that would turn an Aberdeen merchant green with envy."[24] Bailey observed that women on the brink of a divorce often complained that they had given the best years of their lives to their ungrateful, soon to be ex-husbands. He further noted that the age of the woman on her wedding day and the length of the marriage seemed to be of little relevance when a scorned wife wailed of the loss of her "best years." This ambiguity allowed Bailey to conclude that wives did not have much reason to claim that they had sacrificed the best years of their lives to their marriages. In his view they had simply "bartered them for home, protection, a chance of motherhood, and … 'the name, and lines to show'."[25] Husbands on the other hand, according to Bailey, had truly given their best years to the marriage and they had also given their entire fortunes.

In July 1930, *Chatelaine* published responses from women on both sides of the debate concerning which sex benefited most in marriage. One woman who agreed with Bailey was frank in her assessment of what her life would probably have been like as a single woman. She wrote: "With my education and ability I know I could not have bought a house nor a car nor have saved so much toward an old age fund." She continued, "None of my unmarried contemporaries has a home of her own nor a car to use as she likes, with none of the dirty work of keeping it up – the men do that – nor [do they have] a perpetual escort." She further chastised the women who were offended by the May article when she stated: "If these scornful ladies ... had ever done a man's work hanging on beyond one's endurance, and sticking to it even beyond breaking point, they would know why men die younger than women, and why they should spend their lives doing everything to make their men happy." The letter was penned "A Successful Wife."[26]

On the other hand, several readers argued that both husbands and wives contributed equally in modern marriages. One respondent wrote, "Few indeed of our average wives in rural or urban districts are 'kept' by their husbands, are merely a bill of expense; on the contrary they give value for value received." She related her views to the development of the nation. She argued that husbands and wives were far too busy with "helping to make Canada a great country" to concern themselves with the nonsense that filled Bailey's article.[27] Another woman simply dismissed Bailey's opinions as being unrepresentative of the majority of Canadian marriages.[28]

When "a diplomatic husband" wrote the January 1932 article, "Why I Let My Wife Spoil Me" he loosely categorized his wife as his employee; and yet the tongue-in-cheek nature of his article hinted at more gender equality than inequality in his marriage. While obviously exaggerating, he described how he intentionally left the bathroom dirty so that his wife could pick up after him; how he never helped with the dishes; and how he would bring home work that could have been done by his secretary, for his wife to do in the evening. Why? "Because she likes it," wrote the diplomatic husband. He continued, "As all women, she likes to feel that she's a martyr to a cause. I'm the 'cause' and she is never so happy as when she thinks I am imposing on her good nature and generosity."[29] But while he admitted to allowing his wife to spoil him, the author readily acknowledged that he also spoiled her and that the two of them were deeply in love.

Undoubtedly, *Chatelaine's* modern middle-class bride of the early 1930s did apparently enter into a roughly equal partnership with her husband – for good or for bad – and she was not expected to stay married at all costs. According to *Chatelaine* she continued to have choices, even after her wedding day. This fact again speaks to the English middle-class urban character of *Chatelaine's* modern woman. Divorce, a process that still favoured men in the 1920s and 1930s, also lay predominately within the purview of the middle-classes and was largely an urban phenomenon.[30] According to historian James G. Snell, in the first half of the twentieth century those who argued for a more liberal divorce law and those who maintained the rigidity of the existing process "both ... rested on the vital position of the family as the cornerstone of society. Both had in mind the same sort of family, one that reflected and upheld the powerful middle-class norms of the period." Snell continues, "The family was seen as the primary unit in society controlling, guiding, and supporting people. In short, advocates of both positions accepted the essential elements of the dominant familial ideal; state instruments, including the courts and the law, ought to be used in the most effective manner to support that ideal."[31] Divorce law thus remained restrictive and required proof of adultery and/or abandonment.

In its first decade, *Chatelaine* tended to support the need for reform to the current divorce law while not undermining the sanctity of marriage. In a July 1935 article that suggested revising the divorce law, the Reverend G. Stanley Russell cautioned readers against making a hasty choice when choosing a mate. He wrote, "Sometimes a pretty face, or a common interest, or general boredom enthusiastically shared, brings two people to the altar – and then to the courts...."[32] While happily married and eternally committed to his wife, the Reverend acknowledged that not every couple was so well suited. By legally requiring that adultery be committed to allow for divorce, the Reverend suggested that, "the whole atmosphere of marriage is degraded and a cattle market mind is imported which is disgusting and abominable."[33] He argued that social and spiritual unions were more important. Consequently, dysfunction within these domains should also be cause for divorce. He cited the example of a school friend who was "forced" to commit adultery before getting a divorce from a woman who equally wanted to separate from him. As Russell summed up: "There are couples wrongly assorted, married in haste or in glamor, who will hate each other until they are no longer tied together, when they may possibly become quite good friends."[34] He also asserted the need for mutual feelings in the decision to keep a marriage together or the choice to dissolve it. If he were revising the law, he wrote: "I would also remove every possible relic of the idea that the man has any 'property' in the woman, or that she is not absolutely an equal partner in the making of all decisions and arrangements concerning their common life."[35]

In June 1936, *Chatelaine* published responses by several Canadian men and women who had been interviewed on the topic of divorce. One of the questions asked was: "Does the growing independence of women contribute to divorce?" Miss Vera L. Parson, Ontario's only woman divorce lawyer in 1936, and Mr. Silcox, then general secretary of the Social Service Council of Canada, answered "yes" to the above question. Their reasoning was that "many [women] who are now economically independent refuse to 'sit back and take' any sort of shameful treatment."[36] A divorce court judge explained that divorces were becoming more common, "because many advanced thinkers believe a bitterly unhappy marriage is worse than a broken one." Marriage was also intricately connected with the development of the state; as the Judge wrote, "an unsound marriage does not promote the good of the state."[37] The convictions of Mrs. R.I. Eagleson, an Irish-Canadian wife, appeared to be in the minority and outdated with respect to *Chatelaine's* modern woman. Eagleson stated that, "If you want a lasting marriage you must marry for life."[38] The article did point out that the length of the marriage that ended in divorce was decreasing. Using Statistics Canada as a source, the article reported that, "in 1935, the average marriage (divorced) lasted six years; in 1934, twelve and a half years, and in 1932, eighteen years." But, based on these findings, it was concluded that, "it isn't the youngsters who take a dive in and quit when they meet the first breaker."[39] *Chatelaine's* modern wife of the early 1930s had choices and she was not always young when she exercised them.

Chatelaine encouraged couples to adapt marriage to their particular needs, even if these requirements challenged traditional norms. In December 1936, an article about marriage preparation provided advice for those about to embark on this potentially life-long journey. The author told the story of a college friend, Peter, who was in love with a beautiful young woman. Peter wanted to give up his promising career as a journalist to marry. His girlfriend, however, would not allow him to make that sacrifice. She said to him: "You have been living your own life up till now the way a man in your line should live it. That's why I like you – why I fell in love with you in the first place. And if you try to fit yourself into every little groove of my life, giving up all these other things which make you so attractive I wouldn't like you at all." The couple did marry and Peter kept his career. The author attributed their continued happiness to the fact that, "they found out early in their acquaintance how to remain two people while becoming one."[40]

The predominant view expressed in *Chatelaine* from its inception in 1928 until the mid-1930s was that marriage was, or should be, an equal partnership between a man and a woman. It was difficult, especially during the depression, to shake the paradigm of marriage as a career choice for women, but *Chatelaine* continued to underscore romance in male-female unions. More importantly, the magazine made it clear that marriage was a choice for women; it was not a social or economic necessity. *Chatelaine* also supported the idea that a woman should maintain her own identity. It made clear to women the fact that they still had choices after their wedding day. Divorce was not encouraged by the magazine, but there was also no social stigma attached to it.

By the late 1930s, as fear of another world war was gaining momentum within Canadian society, *Chatelaine's* man increasingly rose to a position of power in the romance arena. Additionally, an inextricable connection between marriage and womanhood began to appear in the magazine. Now women were expected to do everything in their power to "catch" a husband and then to keep him happy, healthy and above all else hers.

According to *Chatelaine*, by the late 1930s, romantic success depended on both the man and the woman assuming traditional gender roles. In 1936, "You're the Boss" told the story of Miss Alberts, a thoroughly modern woman and a successful entrepreneur who worked diligently at her business while romance passed her by. One day, Mr. Hughes, an old acquaintance of Miss Alberts' who she happened to have danced with years before, came by in search of a job. Although Miss Alberts had no vacancies, she created a position for the seemingly desperate man. Miss Alberts, however, appeared interested in having more than just an employee. She enjoyed his masculine company although she remarked that, "her pleasant pride in him was spoiled by a treacherous regret that he could not be as important and dominant as he looked."[41] Regardless, she justified her decision to hire him and noted "as she snuggled up to her shining important desk half an hour later, she had bought something. Bought a man in about the way, some centuries earlier, a high-born lady might have bid off the debtors auction block some luckless friend."[42]

Mr. Hughes proved to be an excellent addition to the company as well as a frequent and enjoyable dinner companion for Miss Alberts. The first time Miss Alberts asked Mr. Hughes out to "dine and dance," she made it clear that she intended to pick up the tab. Mr. Hughes protested. Miss Alberts retorted: "You're the most pre-war person. You know very well I can't ask you and then have you pay. Or even dutch it. It isn't manners."[43] Miss Alberts got her way. But later, when Mr. Hughes kissed her, she wondered if it was because he liked her or because she was the boss. She could not keep her insecurities to herself and the relationship appeared to be doomed. Before much could happen, however, Miss Alberts went bankrupt. Having foreseen the situation, and through a series of good fortunes, Mr. Hughes had secured himself a partnership in a competing firm. With new financial independence and a corporate identity he was finally able to become a complete man in Miss Alberts' eyes. And, with his newly found financial security and masculinity, Mr. Hughes observed to Miss Alberts that "there was an opening in the Bellair-Hughes Company for a bright pretty little woman …" And he proposed, "Do you think you could manage home and a career at the same time?" In response, Miss Alberts "made herself look fragile and clinging in the way even the strongest and most capable of women can, when they wish to, in plain violation of the laws of optics." She replied, "It's up to you, dear, you're the boss."[44] Indeed, *Chatelaine's* modern man was slowly becoming the boss in the realm of romance and, as a consequence, *Chatelaine's* modern woman became a supporting actor in the developing drama.

While romantic advice was always a staple of the magazine, by the late 1930s *Chatelaine* directly encouraged women to make personal sacrifices to "catch" a man. The title of Lorna Slocombe's September 1938 article asked *Chatelaine* readers "Are You a Good Date?" Slocombe observed that "there are plenty of girls who are homely, unobtrusively virtuous, pedestrians perforce – and still popular. If your dates are infrequent and unsuccessful, there must be a reason."[45] She pointed out common errors that many women made when on a date. These included paying attention to others and not talking enough about their companion. Another major roadblock for securing a future date was being boring. A possible solution to this problem was to dress appropriately. Slocombe wrote: "Your appearance is one way you can keep things interesting. Don't invariably wear powder blue, just because it's your best color. Dazzle your beau some night, by bursting forth in cherry red … Change your coiffure frequently, and ask his opinion on each change. …"[46] Most importantly she advised women to act like they had had a wonderful time. "Even if the movie is the dullest epic that ever came out of Hollywood, find something nice to say about it," Slocombe recommended.[47]

This trend of *Chatelaine*'s modern woman acting submissively feminine continued with the onset of the Second World War as the magazine increasingly published material about young single women on the hunt for prospective husbands. This is not surprising given that the Second World War did accelerate marriage rates in Canada. War in 1939, as Veronica Strong-Boag suggests, heralded an end to the new woman of the new day. Women put aside their collective issues as they "were increasingly preoccupied with the very terms of survival."[48] To an even greater degree than in the late 1930s, marriage was an expected part of young adulthood and women were encouraged to wed. As Jeffrey A. Keshen points out, "as soon as war broke out, the marriage rate in Canada almost doubled."[49] Many couples may still have chosen to wed for financial reasons; for example, the federal government's dependant's allowance programme, which was passed in August 1939, provided additional income for the spouses (generally wives) of military personnel. Undoubtedly, however, many also married for the emotional comfort and strength that they hoped wedlock would provide for them.[50]

The war ushered in a fear of moral degradation and marriage acted as a sign of respectability, particularly for women. Rates of venereal disease, prostitution, illegitimacy and divorce all rose during the war.[51] Generally, young, single women were blamed for the falling moral standards. For example, in response to early Canadian Women's Army Corps (CWAC) recruiting propaganda that targeted young, single, English-Canadian women, a "whispering campaign" emerged in late 1942 that accused CWAC personnel of being sexually loose. To counterbalance the rumours, the government replaced the images of independent and adventurous young women characteristic of early CWAC propaganda with those of feminine, patriotic girls.[52] CWAC officers tried to deny the accusations of sexual promiscuity among their recruits; however, pregnancies and venereal disease were hard to mask. The CWAC officer corps, all university graduates, instead blamed "mass recruiting" and the influx of "undesirable types" for the less than perfect moral standards among recruits.[53]

The middle-classes, however, were not exempt from social scrutiny when it came to accusations of moral impropriety. In "Under the President's Gaze: Sexuality and Morality at a Canadian University During the Second World War," Catherine Gidney shows how "The university and the broader Canadian community expected students, who were privileged not to be at the war front, to be serious and upright members of the community in both their social activities and their military training." Deviation from these norms was not accepted. The university not only provided students with an academic education; it also took the prerogative to instill moral righteousness among its middle-class citizens. "The university helped construct, reinforce, and regulate the ideal of heterosexuality," Gidney writes, "seeing family as the outcome of proper relations between men and women. Its purpose was to recreate a particular type of citizen: industrious, Christian, heterosexual, capable of leadership – none of these elements could be missing from the whole, well-adjusted person."[54]

Marriage – for both men and women – helped to stabilize fears of moral dissipation that many felt could erupt in times of war. John Modell and Duane Steffey argue that "World War II actually enhanced nuptiality in the United States." They reasoned that both government policy and public sentiment represented a yearning on the part of Americans to protect the family as an institution.[55] Within the Canadian context, historian Doug Owram remarks of the fifteen years following the Second World War that, "Marriage and family was the young adult's route to respectability. …Those who did not marry were the subject of suspicion, for they were, in a sense, deviant in terms of cultural norms."[56]

Certainly, from the late 1930s on, *Chatelaine* projected the assumption that for many middle-class Canadian women, marriage was and should be their primary pursuit. In August 1942, *Chatelaine* reported that after arriving in Ottawa to work for the war effort, and discovering that there were seven women to every man in the city, one young woman remarked "Gee, I'll never get married here – the competition is terrific, and I can't even get a date. I think I will go back to Calgary!"[57]

According to *Chatelaine*, even women in uniform returning from overseas service above all wanted to be wives, something that readers who feared that the war had irrevocably altered gender roles must have found reassuring. A December 1944 article that profiled women war veterans began, "their favorite postwar plan is matrimony. …" It reported that "more than 90% of the girls in uniform rate as their first job preference:

matrimony." The article continued, "And they want to make it an all-out full-time business, with plenty of dividends of the pram and diaper variety. Competition for postwar jobs in the business and professional man's world would not come from them, if they had their choice."[58]   Indeed, a January 1949 article reminded Canadian women that they were lucky. "It's not our push-button kitchens or private bank accounts the women of Europe and the Near East envy" they were told. "It's what we've always taken for granted – the right to have a man of our own. ... With some 370, 000 surplus men in Canada, marriage is an expected part of your lives!"[59]

Chatelaine's modern man of the war years could sometimes be ignorant of the appeal that he held among his female counterparts. For example, Kay, the young, beautiful heroine of January 1944's "Waiting Can be Too Long" was in love with Eric. Eric, however, was almost always away on war work. Although Kay's family was rumoured to have lost their wealth, Kay let several eligible bachelors slip away as she waited for Eric. The town's people thought her foolish and speculated that Eric, like his uncle, would be a bachelor forever. Finally, Kay decided to confront Eric. Eric was shocked by the revelation of Kay's emotions for him. He explained that he felt that she would not want to marry him because he was always away. When Kay declared that a ten-day leave pass was ample time to get married and have a honeymoon, Eric agreed. He had been in love with her since the day he had met her four years previously, but he had been too shy to tell her.[60] While Kay did finally take the initiative in revealing her emotions to Eric, she only did so after years of patiently waiting.

A similar theme was played out in "Pigeon Love," a story that appeared in March 1945. A teenage girl, Janie, was growing tired of her same-age boyfriend, Skiz. She felt that he was too juvenile for her. Instead, she set her heart on her neighbour's nephew Phil, a handsome twenty-two year old war hero. On his visit to his aunt's, Phil noticed Janie right away and the two spent some time together at the beach. Phil revealed that he had been in love before the war, but his sweetheart had left him. He recalled to Janie, "I was engaged when I was in training – or I thought I was. But before I went across I found out there's nothing in that old gag about absence making the heart grow fonder, anyway not on a woman's part." He surmised that, "It's always the fellow who's nearest the jar who gets the cookies."[61] Phil did not know, however, that his ex-fiancée Peggy was still in love with him. Aware that Phil was visiting his aunt, Peggy had arranged to travel to the same town to stay with family friends. While there she toured around with the friend's son, who was also coincidentally Janie's "boyfriend," Skitz. One evening the two mix-matched couples met up at the soda shop. It was obvious that Peggy and Phil were still in love, (and it was also clear that Janie and Skiz were quite fond of each other). It was revealed that Phil had thought that Peggy had left him because he never received any letters from her when he was overseas. Meanwhile, Peggy, who had diligently and lovingly replied to every one of Phil's letters, was stunned when the mail stopped arriving. She concluded that he had left her. In the end, the romance was rekindled.

During the war, *Chatelaine* also suggested that some men, particularly those in uniform, might be quite eager to marry. Romance, and specifically marriage, was of particular importance during the war because it symbolized a democratic ideal for which men could fight. Historian Joshua S. Goldstein notes of the phenomenon: "The moral support of family and friends, and most importantly a connection with (often idealized) wives and girlfriends, helps keep soldiers going." He continues, "A soldier who has just received a 'Dear John' letter (from a girlfriend who has dumped him in his absence) is considered a danger to himself and his group."[62] Sonya Michel elaborates on the importance of women's roles in marital relationships: "In this system of meaning, the family was regarded as a key link in the nation's defenses and women were deemed essential to the family's survival and stability." She continues, "This discourse not only reinforced traditional views of women's role but also invested the family with major political significance, thus making it more difficult for women to challenge the social division of labour without appearing to be virtually treasonous."[63]

Marriage was the keystone of this democratic ideal and even if initially timid like Eric and Phil, *Chatelaine*'s man in uniform was not usually shy about "acquiring" a wife. For example, in "Note to the Future" Libby, a beautiful young woman, had just lost her fiancé to the war. Then, at a tea party, she met a charming and handsome man who proposed immediately. Libby was shocked, yet interested. The stranger, Bill persisted in intensely courting her. Within twenty-four hours the two were married and it was revealed that Bill, who had been wearing civilian clothes at the tea, was really a Navy Captain. Libby was quick to move into base housing before her husband's ship sailed.[64]

The eagerness of some soldiers, sailors and airmen to marry could have negative consequences for some women. A July 1943 short story, "A Kind of Armor" again suggested that *Chatelaine*'s military man was looking for a wife. If romance with a particular woman did not work out, then the soldier should waste no time in looking elsewhere, just like Norma from the November 1929 story had wasted no time in finding a husband. In this wartime article, Tippy is supposed to learn the rules of romance from her wise roommate, Mab. Mab had been madly in love with a young man for several years. They had planned to wed before 1939, yet instead of rushing into it once war was declared, Mab favoured waiting. She reasoned that her fiancé, if he were truly in love with her, would return at the end of the war and they could continue as before. Despite his repeated proposals, she did not want to tie him down. Mab continuously warned Tippy against hasty marriages and young women who got stuck raising babies by themselves after ten-day leaves. Then one night Tippy returned home from a date to find Mab in tears. Her fiancé had married someone before being shipped overseas. Mab explained, "he's leaving for somewhere tomorrow. Tippy, he wanted to marry me. He wanted something to cling to – something to come back to, and I – I just wasn't big enough to risk it." She continued, "Plain love isn't enough for some men. Plain waiting, I mean. There's a kind of man who needs to know there's something they're honor-bound to come back to. It gives the whole thing meaning." And Mab described how she felt all military men were: "There's a little of the old-fashioned knight, I guess, in almost every soldier. And marriage, at a time like this – when there are so many foolish girls running loose, well – it's a little like a kind of armor."[65] According to *Chatelaine*, under wartime conditions men generally controlled romances in the same flippant way that had characterized *Chatelaine*'s modern woman of the early 1930s, and women were increasingly seen to have a duty to marry as part of the war effort.

As *Chatelaine* increasingly underscored the fact that men were taking charge of romance, the magazine, even before war erupted in 1939, tried to help women understand how they could keep their man to themselves. Generally, the woman was in danger of losing her man unless she conformed to traditional middle-class gender norms. She generally did. For example, as early as September 1935 *Chatelaine* ran a serial called "Child Wife." The story was about a husband and wife, Jim and Sandra Hewlett. Sandra was not a particularly dutiful wife. She refused to have children and was often out when Jim returned from work. With his architectural designs slipping and his home life far from ideal, Jim was susceptible to the advances of one of his "office-girls," Miss Murphy. After almost loosing Jim – who returned to Sandra of his own free will – Sandra resigned herself to be the "happy housewife." In conclusion the author noted of Jim, "He would say – years from this night – 'Without you I could not have been what I am today.' He would be able to bring home men to dinner any night, knowing that a good dinner waited. That was it; it must be that way…"[66] Jim's obvious flirtation with separation ended up being the catalyst that drove Sandra to conform to the role a dutiful middle-class wife.

To help women understand their husbands, in July 1937 *Chatelaine* advertised the soon to be released book, *Live With a Man and Love It*, by Anne B. Fisher, an internationally known physician and psychiatrist. Selections from Fisher's book appeared in later issues of the magazine. The advertisement appealed to married women and to anyone who ever hoped to be one. Topics included: "Hints to Girls Who Haven't Caught Their Man; How to Compromise Without a Fight; How to Avoid Being a Nagger; and What to do About the Other Woman."[67] Apparently *Chatelaine's* modern woman needed help with her romantic life. The magazine began to focus more attention on equipping women to catch a man and teaching them how to keep them. Gone were the days where *Chatelaine* underscored women's choice to remain single or to end an unfulfilling marriage.

On several occasions specific guidelines were provided to help women succeed at being good wives.[68] In the article, "How to be a Good Wife," which was published in February 1940, the author suggested that women could be the head of the house if they waited on their husbands. He remarked: "Once there was a wife who said 'before I would wait on my husband I would leave the house and never come back again!' She missed so much in life, poor, silly, little thing. She never was her husbands' boss."[69] While this article did suggest that men could be manipulated, the subtext also implies that men manipulated women by allowing them to feel that they were in charge if they performed certain "wifely" duties. In the end, men got what they wanted: a wife and housekeeper. This article also reminded women that men were not looking for clever wives: "Remember, too, that, many a husband has wished for a dumb wife, but never a man yet has wanted a deaf wife. So be a good listener."[70] Certainly, stereotypical attitudes about women's roles as housewives were being elaborated in the article.

Some women embraced these categories and, not unlike during the depression, they continued during the war years to look at marriage as a career. "Marriage is my career," announced a woman in her forties in a January 1941 article. As an adolescent, this woman had decided that she wanted to be a wife and mother. She immediately started an informal apprenticeship with her mother. Over twenty years later she attributed her success as a wife to the fact that she approached the role as she would have a business career.[71] According to *Chatelaine*, in the 1930s some women took the role of wife as a job; however, by the 1940s many chose it as a vocation.

In March 1941, *Chatelaine* published several reader responses to the January article. The magazine had offered a five-dollar prize for the best response and five secondary prizes of one dollar.[72] While not all respondents agreed that women should approach marriage as they would a career, they all assumed that all women would prefer to be wives rather than businesswomen. "Thank goodness the modern girl can now look on herself as a 'person'!" wrote a woman from Ontario who disagreed with the article under question. She was underscoring the point that modern women had career choices. However, she also added that a woman was "generally wise enough to prepare for a self-supporting career until a suitable husband turns up. ..."[73] A wife from Ontario, who agreed with the view that marriage was a career, recalled that when she worked downtown as a single woman she would hear the other stenographers discussing marriage. She remarked that, "the general consensus seemed to be that it would be grand to be married because then you wouldn't have to go to work!" But after several years of being a wife, she knew how disillusioned they had all been.[74] Housework was real work.

Despite challenges to "wifely obedience" many women continued to view marriage as the alternative to paid employment. A woman from Alberta noted that, "the large majority of 'career' girls are merely earning their own, and often a dependent's [sic] living, to the best of their ability. … With no more than average attractiveness, they have had to give their work all their vitality, with none left over for husband-getting."[75] Whether or not it was viewed as a "career," *Chatelaine* now projected the view that all middle-class women ultimately wanted to be wives and that most of them willingly gave up other jobs to devote themselves to this new vocation.

During the Second World War, and in the period immediately preceding the war, another way that *Chatelaine* suggested that women could "keep" their husbands was through their ability to perform wifely chores such as cooking, cleaning and taking care of the children. Intelligence and ability in other domains were not considered assets in this arena. A March 1939 article put in bluntly: "Men don't want clever wives."[76] The article explained how many men ran away from intelligent women. They "shy at a clever woman as a colt shies at a gate, and [if you see it] you'll witness in action what is so beautifully termed the instinct of self-preservation."[77] The author suggested that this scene was common at social gatherings. Men did not want clever women as wives, according to the article, because they would be less likely to perform, without complaint, the daily tasks of homemaking. Moreover, the author also suggested that the "dumb" housewife would, as part of her wifely duties, overlook adultery on her husband's part. He described an episode when a husband returned home from an alleged night out with the boys and remarked to his wife – chosen from the pool of non-clever women – that it was nice to have a break from women and to socialize with his male friends. While the wife agreed, it was simultaneously noted: "She notices the film of feminine powder on the right shoulder of his [her husband's] dinner jacket, where some girl has put her hand while dancing, or her hand while flirting. Perhaps it is an old mark, perhaps not. [She] keeps his clothes in pretty good shape. She ought to know." The wife was "too wise to say anything about it. And it is at moments like these, ironically enough, that [the husband] thanks heaven he did not marry a clever woman!"[78] The message was clear. If you wanted to be a wife, and it was assumed by the late 1930s and throughout the war years that all of *Chatelaine*'s female readers did want to be wives, then you had to play the role of the happy housewife regardless of what was thrown at you.

In the 1940s, when intelligent women were praised in *Chatelaine* for non-feminine attributes, it was often done in a way that underscored the growing necessity for women to please their men. In an article that appeared in May 1944, *Chatelaine* provided ideas for women eager to live out the fairytale wedding. While most of the advice dealt with keeping up feminine appearances – topics included, for example, how to be your own beautician, keeping trim, and how to keep your hands from looking worn – the article also stated: "Don't let either your mind or your looks go into a slump." It continued, "A happy marriage depends on a lot ... You've got to be mentally alert – keep up with the times and in step with the man in your life. Otherwise he may grow very weary of treating you as a precious little nitwit and laughing at your childish prattle. It's safer and a lot more fun if you can occasionally tell him a thing or two about world events and take a sprightly interest in his problems ..."[79] The main message was not that women should be interested in world events for their own sake, rather they should be knowledgeable so that they could retain their husbands' interest.

For their part, men were expected to take pride in their wife's home-making abilities. *Chatelaine* supported this image by providing women with guidance on how to behave in potentially stressful situations in order to appear the perfect homemaker in front of their husbands. For example, in May 1940, the magazine told women how to act when their husbands unexpectedly brought guests home for dinner. "Don't, for heaven's sake, dissolve in tears or have hysterics. Hold everything. You know very well he wants to show you off and prove what a grand little cook he married. Just show them!"[80] Wives were told not to quarrel with their husbands for placing them in a difficult position, but simply to rise to the occasion. This was, after all, their duty.

This advice was particularly true for the wives of soldiers, sailors and air-men. During the Second World War, these women were given special attention and respect in *Chatelaine*. They were encouraged to be proud and supportive of their husbands. They were also reminded that while their husbands were overseas, their true calling as wives would have to be temporarily put on hold. A soldier's wife reminded other wives of service men that, "You are living in a vacuum, but you keep on living because some day, some day, life will begin again."[81]

Chatelaine suggested that it was nonetheless important for wives with hus-bands overseas to keep up their homemaking skills. *Chatelaine* noted that near a Saskatchewan air force base, "Girls from all over Canada ... are hud-dled in one-room shacks, learning to bake bread, to churn up some but-ter by shaking cream in a jar, and to grow vegetables ... they are the young wives, many of them brides, of airmen. ..." Like their foremothers, they were excelling in traditional gender roles. Indeed, the author asked, "Who said modern girls couldn't stand the rigors of pioneer life?"[82]

For the wives who found that the war years challenged their marriages, *Chatelaine* reminded readers that marriage was "for better [or] for worse."[83] Dorothy Dix, a regular contributor to *Chatelaine*, told readers in May 1944, "If you want to make a go of your marriage, wake up. Be done with your day-dreaming." Dix encouraged women to "quit think-ing of your husbands as a little tin god, or cinema great lover. See him as he is, just a common or garden variety of the genus homo, with plen-ty of faults and peculiarities that get on your nerves, but, for all of that, a fine honest chap who is a good provider."[84] Women were encouraged not to be "matrimonial quitters" regardless of the obstacles that they might face – gone were the days of "free choice" available to the women of the early 1930s. The pages of *Chatelaine* no longer entertained the idea of divorce, although in Canada, divorce rates increased dramatically in the post World War Two period.[85] For the middle-classes, divorce now had a social stigma attached to it and, in popular culture, "divorcees were subject to condemnation."[86]

From the mid 1930s and throughout the war years some instrumental changes occurred in the way that romantic relationships were presented in *Chatelaine*. Men began to take charge as women became more and more reliant on their femininity to secure a partner. Notably, marriage was increasingly being seen as a woman's main vocation and an essential component of her womanhood. These changes proved long lasting.

"Object matrimony" carried into the postwar period and was even the title of an August 1948 article. The article told women how to dress and behave while on summer vacation in order to maximize their chances of meeting Mr. Right. In particular it was geared towards, the "average-looking gal-on-a-budget, a little on the shy side. ..." And specified, "if you've been watching time slipping by for the past few years and feel a bit droopy-mouthed, then now is the hour to size up the situation."[87] Advice included what colour fabrics to choose, what style would most flatter your body type and what men you should target. Like the early 1930s, however, women were reminded that they had choices. "Don't be in too great a hurry to grab at the first available guy who tells you you're his dreamboat type. Take time to look around," wrote the authors. They also cautioned women not to "waste tears on that tall, dark and handsome man, who's always surrounded by wide-eyed innocents … he's probably awfully wrapped up in his own charm, and his conversation may be a nice assortment of cliches." Instead, they asked women, "what about that quiet lad with the nice smile – the one behind the horn-rimmed specs? He may not be the centre of attraction, but he'll make you feel that you are."[88] Unlike their pre-war counterparts, however, the new modern woman of *Chatelaine* was not given the choice to remain a "bachelor girl."

The following poem, "Those Were the Days," likely captured many of the sentiments of *Chatelaine*'s single readers who were finding it difficult to meet the social pressure of wedlock, particularly considering the new dynamics of male-female relationships. It read:

When ladies used fans,
If your skin was a sight
You shaded your face
From the candlelight

Thick legs were a secret
(A glimpse was forbidden)
Your hair was half false,
And your figure was hidden.

Looking helpless was easy
Your bundles were carried.
No wonder so many more
Women married.[89]

Certainly, many women were beginning to realize that catching a husband was no simple task. The envy of Canadian women by their European counterparts regarding their right to a man of their own likely appeared to many *Chatelaine* readers as slightly misplaced.

Chatelaine nonetheless published several short stories in which the woman finally caught her man – she just needed to trap the right one, even if he initially did not appear to be to her liking. For example, a short story published in January 1948 told of a young woman, Sophie, and her attempts to win the interest of her handsome neighbour. The neighbour, however, was not interested because he had a lot of female company. Sophie was distressed by her neighbour's rejection and wondered what was wrong with her. Her friend, Hank, assured her that she had done nothing wrong other than to pursue the wrong man. Hank was secretly in love with Sophie. Finally, through overt efforts on Hank's part, Sophie realized that Hank was in love with her and she saw him for the man that he was, and more than simply her reliable old friend.[90]

Indeed, on occasion, particularly in the post-1950 period, *Chatelaine* reminded its female audience that a man of their own was life's ultimate prize and that one should not miss out on this opportunity by being too selective. In an article that was reflective of Betty Friedan's *The Feminine Mystique,* "No Man's Good Enough for Janie" that appeared in July 1956, was dedicated to all women, "but especially for the proud, lovely girls with polished clothes and perfect hair who sit behind an office desk and watch their life slip by."[91] The article told the story of a young woman, Janie, who took a job as secretary. Janie started with the intention of working for a couple of years before home and family would take over. However, as the years passed and Janie's career advanced, she was less inclined to "settle" for a husband. She had money, a fancy car and freedom. But, as her friends married and had children, the message to Janie became clear; she was wasting her life and allowing happiness to pass her by. She now gratefully accepted dinner invitations to which an "extra" man would also be invited.

Chatelaine was up to the challenge of helping its readers find a mate and the magazine did recognize that the postwar world presented unique challenges in this pursuit. "How does one get a man?" asked the title of a March 1951 article. "How we get to be 30 and still single doesn't really matter," the article continued.[92] The author and protagonist of the piece, Margaret Crofton, wrote of herself: "I can cook, hang curtains and fire a furnace. I'm not too old to start raising a couple of children. But I doubt if I ever will. Because, say what you will about women's emancipation, a woman still needs more than her own skills to meet a man she'd be happy to marry." Crofton assured readers that she was not holding out "for the dream man of romantic love theory."[93] But, despite her willingness to "settle," Crofton could not find a solution to her, and what she assumed to be many other women's, problem: how does one meet a man – even an average one? She did, however, challenge the idea that "older" single women should relocate personally and/or professionally in order to increase their chances of meeting a man. She was holding out for a more pragmatic solution.[94] And hoping that she would find one in the pages of *Chatelaine*.

Had Crofton read the December 1950 issue of *Chatelaine* she may have been able to gain insight to her problem. "Ever since Eve fooled Adam, women have outwitted men," began a December 1950 column about understanding women. "'They drive us nuts,' says the average male," the article continued. The problem according to the author was that men were by and large predictable while women remained, at least to the average male's understanding, largely an enigma. The author was adept, however, at summing up potential romantic motivations of women. "In affairs of the heart," he wrote, "of course, women are particularly susceptible to being set against one [an]other. Women did not go about the business of dividing up the available males on an unbiased and objective basis. There is no calm deliberation about the matter. There is no tendency, for instance, to say: 'I like this one but Dorothy wants him, too, and as she deserves him more than I do she can have him and I'll take this other one.'" Indeed, the author assured readers, and particularly the male audience, that "No such judicial procedure prevails, among women in search of mates. In fact, the very fact that Dorothy did want the particular male would make the other females desire him just that much more." He assured men, however, that "The male, on such occasions, can very often get the female he wants merely by waiting for the females to exhaust one another." In conclusion, the author advised that "The male should diligently strive to amass knowledge of the female sex merely … for his own survival."[95] This need for information included the arena of romantic interactions and all other male-female scenarios. While *Chatelaine*'s modern man of the postwar period may have been striving to become less ignorant of women, he often remained in a position of power.

Perhaps *Chatelaine* was unable to satisfy the needs of all its readers who were hoping to soon be wives, but the magazine nonetheless assumed that most of its readers were married or would be soon, and it offered much advice to wives on how to go about marriage maintenance. Wives were often accused of causing marital strife; their husbands for the large part remained hapless victims. For example, a September 1947 article describing the new Alcoholics Anonymous support group, asked, "Do women drive men to drink?" The answer was a resounding yes! "I nagged my husband into alcoholism," admitted several wives.[96]

According to *Chatelaine*, a main reason why women were seen as the belligerent partners in matrimonial discord was because they often "nagged" their husbands. In November 1949, *Chatelaine* asked wives if they wanted to make over their husbands. Seventy-five per cent of the two thousand women of all age groups and experiences living across Canada who had been anonymously polled answered yes. Interestingly, in *Chatelaine's* first ever polling of husbands, sixty-one per cent of the men were aware that their wives were trying to re-make them. But only half of this group resented it. And of all husbands who answered the questionnaire eighty-three per cent felt that their wives truly appreciated them.[97]

Despite a number of articles and stories that suggested that *Chatelaine's* modern post-World War Two woman was instrumental in the development of her husband's character, *Chatelaine* also published articles that cautioned women about men's largely stagnant personalities. In July 1953 an article warned women that, "The scientists know the guy better than you do." It continued, "Odds are you'll marry him anyway – but a look at his figure will tell you what kind of husband to expect."[98] According to the article muscular men would insist on making all marital decisions, would be mediocre lovers and should be steered away from alcohol because they were likely to be belligerent under the influence. If the man you loved was thin and nervous you could expect to have a socially awkward husband, who at the same time would be "a wonderful lover with a high sex drive." And of men who were fat and easy-going, women could expect a loving and loyal companion. They were warned, however, that while this type of man "idealizes his family and especially mother love, his sexual drive is low." Women were told to "adjust to this fact; to mention it would be a cruel blow to his masculine pride. Appreciate his unending devotion and loyalty, but don't expect a Romeo."[99] The men of *Chatelaine* were thus unveiled according to body type and women were warned that fundamental male characteristics could not be changed. This article also nicely captures the growing acceptance among the middle-classes of the importance of sexual fulfilment for husbands and wives in modern marriages. This sexual evolution, however, remained gendered and "sexual purity" out of wedlock remained the norm, especially for young women. As Doug Owram notes in Canada, "the 1950s was, sexually, a society at war with itself. Amid the cult of domesticity, there was a persistent and significant trend towards the loosening of old strictures on sex." Owram cites the release of the Kinsey report in the United States and the publication of the new American men's magazine Playboy as examples of this transformation.[100]

Other articles in *Chatelaine* published during the postwar period, like the above example, also alluded to the impermeability of the male character.[101] In these instances *Chatelaine's* modern man, through his rigidity, gained some leverage over his female counterpart. Women were often encouraged to be subordinate to their husbands in order to ensure their marriages lasted. For instance, in January 1955, women were educated on how to live with an alcoholic husband. Supposedly many men drank because of their wives and women were told to fix flaws in their wifely behaviour in order to minimize this.[102] Moreover, in August 1956, a family psychologist, Dr. Marion Hilliard,[103] wrote in an article questioning why some men cheated on their wives that "the burden of creating a happy marriage falls mainly on the wife." She continued, "A man's life is much more difficult than a woman's, full of the groaning strain of responsibility and the lonely and often fruitless search for pride in himself." Hilliard noted that "A cheerful and contented woman at home, even one who must often pretend gaiety, gives a man enough confidence to believe he can lick the universe." Indeed, she stated: "I'm certain that the woman who enriches her husband with her admiration and her ready response gets her reward on earth, from her husband."[104] *Chatelaine's* modern man seems to have risen to a position of ultimate power in the post-1945 marital relationship.

An article, "Seven Threats to Marriage," published in April 1949, explicitly stated that to maintain a happy marriage a wife had to be subordinate to her husband. The article presented seven "rules" to follow in order to maintain a traditional marriage. Rule three reminded women to meet their husbands half way *or farther* on all issues.[105] Rule six, however, was the one that most stressed traditional roles for women: "Don't try to handle two jobs. Working in an office after marriage takes too much out of you and ruins your health. *Housekeeping is a full time job.*"[106]

However, as many of *Chatelaine's* articles suggested, not all wives were happy with the roles that they were expected to play. A new aspect of *Chatelaine's* modern wife began to appear in the postwar period. Despair became a regular sentiment associated with the housewife. In November 1948, *Chatelaine* suggested that many wives fought with their husbands because they "feel afflicted, or martyred, or imprisoned in an unbearable situation."[107] The situation that the author was referring to was a traditional marriage in which the woman was a housewife. She asked of the belligerent housewife, "isn't it true that we put our own disappointments and dissatisfactions into our quarrels, and that we could do much to cure home quarrelling if we could make peace with these disappointments and dissatisfactions?" Alternatively she queried, "Or do we make these differences the grand occasion for an all-out offensive to inform our spouse that we resent his ways of thinking and doing?"[108] The sense of frustration among many housewives was clear. However, the solution provided appeared superficial. These women were encouraged to share their feelings with their husbands before allowing them to develop into large-scale fights. *Chatelaine* did not provide them with any other advice for curbing their frustrations.

In general, *Chatelaine's* "frustrated housewife" eventually came to appreciate her blessings, but her pervasive presence in the magazine speaks to

a deeper subtext. While these images of modern wives ultimately reinforced traditional gender roles for women, the unhappiness that they
projected also challenged these norms – a theme that Betty Friedan picks
up on in *The Feminine Mystique*.

The April 1948 editorial addressed the topic of "unhappy wives."
"Progress has given our girls a chance for education in the professions …
But at marriage the majority must put this promise of personal
expression away, and turn their talents into housework," lamented the
editor, Byrne Hope Sanders.[109] Her solution, however, was not that
women should free themselves from the shackles of home and family.
Sanders suggested that women should incorporate time for themselves
into their schedules – schedules that were already full of family
obligations.

Fiction in *Chatelaine* also commonly highlighted unhappiness among
housewives. For the most part, however, by the end of the stories the
wife had discovered new joys in her role as a wife, which, incidentally,
often subordinated her to her husband. For example, a 1947 short story
described Marty, the wife of a philanderer, as having "followed all the
regular rules about how not to lose a husband, until she made the
important discovery that there was an even greater danger of losing
herself."[110] After roughly twenty years of marriage it became apparent
to Marty that her husband was in love with another woman. Marty lost
weight, bought new clothes, developed her skills as a bridge player, a
game that her husband enjoyed far more than she did, and did everything
she could think of to win her husband back. On the verge of collapse,
Marty was about to give up. It was at this point that her husband
re-entered the picture. He had been run ragged by his young girlfriend
and, exhausted, admitted his adultery to his wife. Marty forgave him and
the marriage was saved. It was clear that Marty had no power of her
own. Divorce did not appear to be an option.

A similar story appeared in the March 1949 issue of *Chatelaine*. In this story the wife, already dissatisfied with the way in which her husband provided for her economically, instigated divorce proceedings when she suspected him of cheating. On the morning of the divorce he arrived in a new car and professed his love for her. She was quick to accept his apology and the marriage was saved. No further explanation was required.[111] The reader, however, is left wondering whether the woman reclaimed her husband because of love for him or the new car. The appearance of belonging to the middle- or upper-classes was very important for the post-World War Two modern woman of *Chatelaine* who emerged with the rise of the new consumer culture of the 1940s and 1950s.

In May 1948, a short story about newlyweds, Lisa and Steve, sent the message that women were happiest with their husbands regardless of what they had to put up with. Lisa had worked in advertising before she married Steve, a promising architect. Once married Lisa immediately, and willingly, gave up her career to be a full-time housewife. She did not, however, give up her independence. Lisa soon became friendly with her neighbours. One of the husbands was prone to drinking and social-izing with women, so Lisa encouraged his wife to leave him. Steve for-bade Lisa to appear at the divorce trial. He told her that she had already done enough to wreck that marriage. He explained to Lisa that she was much stronger than her friend. He reminded her that "It's easy to talk proud ... when you're you – and happy and sure of yourself. But remember, Annette [the neighbour] is not in your league. She's never worked, she's highly emotional and I doubt that she's ever made an important decision for herself in her life."[112] But Lisa would not listen. When she returned from the trial, Steve was gone. Lisa was beside her-self with grief but was convinced that a man who would desert her over an issue like that was not worth having as a husband. "No man," said Lisa, "can order my comings and goings! No longer is it necessary, or even customary, for a wife to submit to her husband's will. Modern marriage is a 50-50 proposition ...."[113] As the days passed, however, her resolve faded. She missed Steve and wanted him back and thoroughly regretted having meddled in her friend's affairs. One night Steve arrived home. Lisa was delighted to see him. As it turned out, Steve had only been away on a business trip and all the worry had been caused by a missing telegram that would have explained his absence. Yet, because of the misunderstanding, Lisa had learnt the true meaning of being a modern wife. It was noted that on Steve's return, Lisa "acknowledged him as her lord and master," and that "at the same time she felt herself growing in stature."[114] Even educated, competent, middle-class women were expected to be more fulfilled as the subservient half of a heterosexual couple.

In *Chatelaine*, this type of redefinition of the modern wife was not limited to fiction. In September 1951, the magazine published the anonymous story of a 40-year-old woman's failed suicide attempt. The woman explained that she was chronicling her story because she felt that there were many Canadian women in her position who might benefit from her experience. The woman had a successful husband and four children in their late-teens/early-twenties. They lived in a big house in a wealthy suburb, but she continuously felt like a failure when she visited friends with bigger homes or more successful husbands. This sentiment intensified and was compounded by the loneliness that she felt as her children grew. One Sunday night, during a family dinner, the unhappy wife left the table and overdosed on sleeping pills. Her daughter found her and she survived the ordeal. After months of psychiatric treatment and electric shock therapy the woman reported feeling better than ever. "Today I am a new person," she wrote. She continued, "I eat, talk, sing and laugh again. I enjoy my family and my housework."[115] From total despair the anonymous author managed to find new vitality in her roles as a wife, mother and homemaker.

She wanted other women to be able to find satisfaction in these roles without having to experience her pain.

In many ways, *Chatelaine's* depiction of postwar women and families reflected the new social reality of women's lives in the suburbs. The suburbs, as some historians have noted, provided the ideal setting for the separating of the feminine and the masculine, the private and the public, and are again suggestive of a strong middle-class bias in the popular expression of gender roles.[116] For example, in "Home Dreams: Women and the Suburban Experiment in Canada, 1945-1960," Veronica Strong-Boag argues that "The threat of the Cold War and the Korean War encouraged citizens to prize the private consumption and accumulation of products in the nuclear family household as proof of capitalism's success." She continues, "suburban housewives at home in ever-larger houses epitomized the promise that prosperity would guarantee both individual happiness and the final triumph over communism."[117] The domestic woman of the suburbs – existing as an aberration or normality – helped to uphold both her own femininity and her husband's masculinity.[118] Indeed, the suburbs provided a physical barrier between a masculine "public sphere" and a feminine "private sphere." And, as Doug Owram argues, they became a haven for the middle-classes.[119] Yet, as Betty Friedan remarks and many of *Chatelaine's* article suggest, some women could find the experience isolating and unfulfilling.[120]

Chatelaine's modern wife of the postwar years was very similar to her wartime counterpart. However, in the post-1945 period, *Chatelaine* was much more likely to acknowledge the frustration that many women felt as wives, particularly as housewives. Most of the time, *Chatelaine* suggested that women ultimately found happiness through this role, but despair certainly contributed to the definition of *Chatelaine's* modern wife after 1945.

Looking at the changes and continuities in *Chatelaine*'s portrayal of the modern wife and husband from 1928 to 1956 helps to illuminate a possible effect of World War Two on the images of women in the magazine and the broader aspect of gender relationships. What we see is that for several years *Chatelaine* acknowledged that many women may have wanted to get married, but the magazine underscored the point that women did not "need" a husband. During World War Two – a time when fewer men were around and women were more self-reliant – marriage was beginning to be seen in *Chatelaine* as a necessary part of Canadian womanhood. It was also explained as part of the war effort and used to measure the moral integrity of the nation. As M. Susan Bland notes, women working for wages from 1939 to 1945 were viewed as temporary and they were encouraged to be overtly feminine.[121] Home and family were still projected to be their ultimate destiny. This emphasis carried through into the postwar period. New, however, was a sense of despair that became attached to the image of the modern wife after 1945. Within these thirty years we also witness the rise of male power in the arena of romance, often at the expense and subordination of women.

Interestingly, the dynamics of male-female relationships within *Chatelaine* did not change with the war, but actually shifted in conjunction with the fear of war that began to be pervasive in late 1936/1937. Canadians knew all too well how war could challenge the very fabric of society. It is as though, perhaps unconsciously, editors, particularly Sanders, and readers of *Chatelaine* were determined that that most basic of social relationships – the relationship between men and women and the middle-class Canadian family – could not be a casualty of international warfare. Indeed, reinforcing maternal feminist understandings of "proper" gender roles which were so pervasive at the beginning of the twentieth century was one way to ensure social stability and to reinforce the moral and social fabric of Canadian society. In *Chatelaine*, fear of war seems to have been enough to strengthen these bonds. As the next chapter will show, the war also affected how *Chatelaine* portrayed home-making and motherhood.

Endnotes

1   Madge Macbeth, *Chatelaine*, November 1928, 4.

2   C. Thompson, *Chatelaine*, November 1928, 5, 61, 62.

3   Nancy Leigh, *Chatelaine*, January 1929, 34.

4   R. K., *Chatelaine*, November 1929, 6, 56-58.

5   Cited in Veronica Strong-Boag, *The New Day Recalled: The Lives of Girls and Women in English Canada, 1919-1939* (Markham: Penguin Books, 1988), 19.

6   Constance Nicholson Lea, *Chatelaine*, September 1933, 26. The association of women and work – paid employment and volunteer positions – will be discussed in chapter five. It should be noted that in 1931 47.4% of women aged 20 to 24 years were in the labour force. Strong-Boag notes that the widening of the range of white-collar jobs in the 1920s increased employment opportunities for women and saw the rise of the number of middle-class women in the workforce. "In the 1920s and 1930s," writes Strong-Boag, "it was more likely than ever that women would spend some part of their lives in the paid work force." Strong-Boag, *The New Day Recalled*, 42-43, quote, 70.

7   Many works that deal with the roles of middle-class women in the family in the mid-twentieth century place women at the heart of the family and dependant on the earnings of their husbands. See for example, James G. Snell, *In the Shadow of the Law: Divorce in Canada, 1900-1939* (Toronto: University of Toronto Press, 1991), 21-47. Snell writes, "The doctrine of separate spheres – the public world of paid labour and government of men and the private domestic world of women – had been articulated in the nineteenth century and incorporated into the overlapping imagery of women and family. ... [women's] special skill in nurturing and comforting complemented male aggression and competition in the public sphere. This sense of female-male partnership, of a symbiotic relationship between the sexes, was basic to the dominant view of the family. ... The two spheres were held to be mutually exclusive." Snell, *In the Shadow of the Law*, 23-24. Snell continues to describe that the wife was subordinated to her husband by law and how this reflected a strong middle-class bias in the construction of the ideal of the conjugal family. For a discussion on

women's roles – and the popular ideal of women's place – in marriage during the interwar years see Strong-Boag, *The New Day Recalled*, and Andree Levesque, *Making and Breaking The Rules: Women in Quebec 1919-1939* (Toronto: McClelland and Stewart, 1994). Some historians have also used the gender-bias application of government policies concerning women's economic welfare to suggest that the Canadian government largely assumed that women would be cared for economically by their husbands. Among other things, this represents a class-bias in the assumptions of family welfare by the government. See for example: Ruth Roach Pierson, "Gender and the Unemployment Insurance Debates in Canada, 1934-1940," in A.D. Gilbert, C.M. Wallace, and R.M. Bray, *Reappraisals in Canadian History Post Confederation* (Scarborough: Prentice Hall Canada, Inc., 1992), 336-367; and Ann Porter, "Women and Income Security in the Postwar Period: The Case of Unemployment Insurance, 1945-1962," in Wendy Mitchinson, Alison Prentice, Paula Bourne, Gail Cuthbert Brandt, Beth Light, and Naomi Black, *Canadian Women: A Reader* (Toronto: Harcourt Brace & Company, Canada, 1996), 322-351.

8   Snell argues that a shift towards romantic marriages was occurring in Canadian society in the post-World War One period and that the change was directly related to women's suffrage. He writes, "This belief in the near equality of rights between the sexes was fundamental to suffrage reforms in the first decades of the twentieth century. Also important in the conjugal family was the place of romantic love in marriage. ..." He cautions, however, that this ideal favoured a middle-class interpretation of marriage. Snell, *In the Shadow of the Law*, 22, 31.

9   Nicholson Lea, *Chatelaine*, September 1933, 26.

10   Madelyn E. Ralph, *Chatelaine*, March 1934, 11.

11   Ibid.

12   Ibid., 70.

13   Ibid.

14   Isabel Turnbull Dingman, *Chatelaine*, April 1932, 12.

15   Susannah Jane Foster Wilson, *The Relationship Between Mass Media Content and Social Change in Canada: An Examination of the Image of Women in Mass Circulation Magazines, 1930-1970* (Ph.D. Dissertation, University of Toronto, 1977), 106.

16   Mary Lowrey Ross, *Chatelaine*, May 1929, 5.

17   In 1931 the average age for women at their first marriage was 25.1 years. Snell, *In the Shadow of the Law*, 133. Strong-Boag notes that in 1931, 65.3% of women of British decent between the ages of 20 and 24 were single. For those

between the ages of 25 and 34 the number was 27.3% and those aged 45-54, 11.6% This data clearly indicates that most women of British decent would one day be wives. Strong-Boag, *The New Day Recalled*, 83.

18   Evelyn Murray Campbell, *Chatelaine*, July 1931, 5.

19   Strong-Boag, *The New Day Recalled*, 95. A possible explanation for this difference is that Strong-Boag looks at the interwar years as a collective whole. Although some distinctions are drawn between the 1920s and 1930s, few changes are noted within the decades.

20   R. F. Faryon, *Chatelaine*, April 1932, 19.

21   Ibid.

22   Beverley Owen, *Chatelaine*, May 1932, 15.

23   Ibid.

24   F. E. Bailey, *Chatelaine*, May 1930, 9.

25   Ibid.

26   *Chatelaine*, June 1930, 34.

27   Ibid.

28   Ibid.

29   *Chatelaine*, January 1932, 12.

30   Strong-Boag suggests that divorce was "an expensive process that favoured the well-to-do." Strong-Boag, *The New Day Recalled,* 99. Snell is less direct in his assessment of the connection between class and divorce. He states that "The impact of class on divorce participation was neither straightforward nor simple." Yet, he also argues that as a representation of their overall population, the middle-classes were more likely to petition for divorce than working class members and especially farmers. Snell suggests that the high cost of divorce – parliamentary or judicial – affected these numbers. Snell, *In the Shadow of the Law*, 217-220. Notably, the number of divorces was significantly lower in Quebec than in Ontario from 1900 to 1939. For example, in 1930 Quebec had 41 compared to Ontario's 204, in 1940 the numbers were 62 and 916 respectively. Ibid., 10-11, 14-15.

31   Ibid., 73-74.

32   G. Stanley Russell, *Chatelaine*, July 1935, 55.

33   Ibid., 10.

34   Ibid.

35   Ibid., 11. The divorce law was not dramatically changed in the 1930s and remained both gender and class biased and it helped to reflect the ideal of the conjugal family. It was also based on nineteenth century ideas of patriarchal marriages in which the woman became her husband's property at wedlock. For

more on divorce law and practice in Canada and an interesting account of how gender and class shaped these perceptions see Snell, *In the Shadow of Law.* Notably, in 1925 the law was slightly amended so that wives could petition their husbands on the same grounds that men could sue for divorce: adultery. Alison Prentice, Paula Bourne, Gail Cuthbert Brandt, Beth Light, Wendy Mitchinson and Naomi Black, *Canadian Women: A History* (Toronto: Harcourt Brace Jovanovich, 1996), 292.

36   *Chatelaine*, June 1936, 15. Historian Elaine Tyler May supports this conclusion in her work on marriage and divorce in early twentieth century America. Elaine Tyler May, *Great Expectations: Marriage and Divorce in Post-Victorian America* (Chicago: the University of Chicago Press, 1980), 126-134.

37   Ibid.

38   Ibid.

39   Ibid.

40   R. S. Hoskins, as told to Jack Mosher, *Chatelaine*, December 1936, 16, 46.

41   Francis Bunce, *Chatelaine*, September 1936, 8-9.

42   Ibid., 9.

43   Ibid., 27

44   Ibid., 32.

45   Lorna Slocombe, *Chatelaine*, September 1938, 18.

46   Ibid., 25.

47   Ibid.

48   Strong-Boag, *The New Day Recalled*, 208.

49   Jeffrey A. Keshen, *Saints, Sinners, and Soldiers: Canada's Second World War* (Vancouver: UBC Press, 2004), 121.

50   Keshen, *Saints, Sinners, and Soldiers*, 122.

51   Ibid., 121-144.

52   Jennifer M. Sentek, *"Women at War": Recruiting Images of the CWAC 1942-1945* (M.A. Thesis: Royal Military College of Canada, June 1997), 1-18.

53   Pierson, *"They're Still Women After All,"* 177-178.

54   Catherine Gidney, "Under the President's Gaze: Sexuality and Morality at a Canadian University During the Second World War," in Cynthia R. Comacchio and Elizabeth Jane Errington (eds.), *People, Places and Times, Readings in Canadian History, Volume 2: Post-Confederation* (Toronto: Thomson Nelson, 2006), 234, 240.

55   John Modell and Duane Steffey, "Waging War and Marriage: Military Service and Family Formation, 1940-1950," *Journal of Family History* 13 (1988), 195-218.

56   Owram, *Born at the Right Time*, 12.

57   *Chatelaine*, August 1942, 11.

58   Lotta Dempsey, *Chatelaine*, December 1944, 30, 60.

59   Maria Huldshinsky, *Chatelaine*, September 1949, 17.

60   Elsie Taye, *Chatelaine*, January 1944, 5.

61   Fanny Killsworth, *Chatelaine*, March 1945, 28.

62   Joshua S. Goldstein, *War and Gender: How Gender Shapes the War System and Vice Versa* (Cambridge: Cambridge University Press, 2001), 304.

63   Sonya Michel "American Women and the Discourse of Democratic Family in World War II," in Margaret Randolph Higonnet, Jane Jenson, Sonya Michel and Margaret Collins Weitz, *Behind the Lines: Gender and the Two World Wars* (New Haven: Yale University Press, 1987), 154.

64   Mabel Brown Farwell, *Chatelaine*, January 1942, 5.

65   Mary Frances Morgan, *Chatelaine*, January 1943, 10.

66   Katharine Haviland-Taylor *Chatelaine*, September 1935, 42.

67   *Chatelaine*, July 1937, 63.

68   See for example: Anne Ellis, "Hurray! I've Lost My Job!" *Chatelaine*, November 1942, 2-3, back cover. Ellis told how loosing her paid employment allowed her to concentrate all her energies on being a full-time wife. She explained how more women should devout themselves fully to the home and how they could best go about this business; M.L. Young, "Marriage Is My Career," *Chatelaine*, January 1941, 11, 33. Young explained how best to be a stay at home wife; and Anonymous, "Soldier's Wife," *Chatelaine*, January 1942, 16, told women how to be supportive wives of the men overseas.

69   *Chatelaine*, February 1940, 2.

70   Ibid., 37.

71   M.L. Young, *Chatelaine*, January 1941, 11.

72   It was rare for *Chatelaine* to offer prize money for responses to articles.

73   *Chatelaine*, March 1941, 3.

74   Ibid.

75   Ibid., back cover.

76   James Wedgwood, *Chatelaine*, March 1939, 13.

77   Ibid.

78   Ibid., 39.

79   *Chatelaine*, May 1944, 30.

80   Kathleen Kraft, *Chatelaine*, May 1940, 61.

81   *Chatelaine*, January 1942, 16.

82   Emily M. Gould, *Chatelaine*, November 1942, 51.

83   This view provides a contrast to the November 1938 article called, "Until Divorce Do Us Part." While the 1938 article did not encouraged divorce, it suggested that many Canadians considered marriage temporary. Taylor Bynum, *Chatelaine*, November 1938, 10.

84   Dorothy Dix, *Chatelaine*, May 1944, 9.

85   For information on divorce rates during the Second World War see Keshen, *Saints, Sinners and Soldiers,* 123-124. Keshen notes that divorce rates rose steadily during the war. This trend continued into the post-1945 period. See Owram, *Born at the Right Time,* 28-29.

86   Owram, *Born at the Right Time*, 253.

87   Evelyn Kelly and Adele White, *Chatelaine*, August 1948, 12-13.

88   Ibid., 13.

89   June Grant, *Chatelaine*, February 1948, 51.

90   Elizabeth Inskip Wye, *Chatelaine*, January 1948, 28.

91   Margaret Cravin, *Chatelaine*, July 1956, 14.

92   Margaret Crofton, *Chatelaine*, March 1951, 9. As Owram notes, "In the postwar years the 'ideal' age for marriage advocated by the manuals was twenty to twenty-five for a woman and three or four years older for a man. Yet the insecurities mounted with each year, especially for women. By age twenty-three, the experts said, it was time to worry. ..." This expert advice corresponded with the actual ages of men and women at first marriage. Owram writes, "At the beginning of the war, half of the women were married by the age of 23.2 years. The men they married had held out until the positively stately age of 26.4. A decade later the ages had dropped to 22 and 24.8, respectively, and by 1956 to 21.6 and 24.5." Owram, *Born at the Right Time*, 14, 18.

93   Ibid.

94   Ibid., 92.

95   Frank Tumpase, *Chatelaine*, November 1950, 39.

96   Peter Hanes, *Chatelaine*, September 1947, 15.

97   *Chatelaine*, November 1949, 31.

98   Virginia Morris, *Chatelaine*, July 1953, 24.

99   Ibid.

100   Owram, *Born at the Right Time*, 259, 261.

101   See for example: Jaqueline Roy, "Give Him a Man's Breakfast," *Chatelaine*, May 1947, 90-91, where not only were all husbands considered to be the same, they were expected to be consistent in the dietary needs they required their wives to provide for them; Dorothea Malm, "You Marry a Man's Whole Family," *Chatelaine*, September 1948, 33, 38, 40, 42, 45-46. This short story suggested that

neither the husband or his family were going to change, so the wife should adapt to the situation; and Gerald Walsh, "I'm a Bachelor – and love it," *Chatelaine*, October 1951, 6-7, 100. Walsh was set in his ways and had no intention of changing his habits.

102   Dorothy Sangster, *Chatelaine*, January 1955, 9.

103   Valerie Korinek comments that Marion Hilliard was a vocal lesbian whose columns were often edited to exclude overt associations with homosexuality. Valerie Korinek, "'Don't Let Your Girlfriends Ruin Your Marriage': Lesbian Imagery in *Chatelaine* Magazine, 1950-1969," in Cynthia R. Comacchio and Elizabeth Jane Errington, *People, Places, and Times: Readings in Canadian History, Volume 2: Post Confederation* (Toronto: Thompson Nelson, 2006), 250.

104   Marion Hilliard, *Chatelaine*, August 1956, 9.

105   *Chatelaine*, April 1949, 32.

106   Ibid., 61.

107   Stella Newman, *Chatelaine*, November 1948, 11.

108   Ibid., 18.

109   Byrne Hope Sanders, *Chatelaine*, April 1948, 2.

110   Eleanor Arnett Nash, *Chatelaine*, November 1947, 27.

111   Daphne Alloway McVicker, *Chatelaine*, March 1949, 17, 34-40.

112   Rowan Farrar, *Chatelaine*, May 1948, 23.

113   Ibid., 36.

114   Ibid., 42.

115   Anonymous, *Chatelaine*, September 1951, 4.

116   Veronica Strong-Boag argues that while the American suburbs may have been a haven for the middle-classes, in the Canadian context there was no such homogeny. Veronica Strong-Boag, "Home Dreams: Women and the Suburban Experiment in Canada, 1945-60," in Chad Gaffield (ed.), *Constructing Modern Canada: Readings in Post-Confederation History* (Toronto: Copp Clark Longman Ltd., 1994), 478. Alternatively, the suburbs represented as Doug Owram notes, a shift in the focus of the middle-class from a family of extended kinship to the nuclear form. They were created at the turn of the twentieth century to provide middle-class families with an escape from the "noise and pollution and overcrowding that industrialization brought to their cities." He continues "Aimed at saving the working class from itself, the garden cities that were actually built appealed to that bedrock of suburbia – the middle class." The postwar economic boom may have made the dream of suburbia a reality for more Canadians but, combined with modernization and consumerism, it did not obscure class divisions. Doug Owram, *Born at the Right Time*, 57, 59. See also

Margaret Hobbs and Ruth Roach Pierson, "A Kitchen that wastes no steps …" Gender, Class and the Home Improvement Plan, 1936-40," *Histoire Sociale / Social History* 21 (1988), 9-37.

117   Strong-Boag, "Home Dreams," 479. For a discussion on how the Cold War helped to shape American ideas about masculinity and femininity see K.A. Cuordileone, *Manhood and American Political Culture in the Cold War* (New York: Routledge, 2005).

118   Strong-Boag, "Home Dreams," 484.

119   Owram, *Born at the Right Time*, 57-59.

120   Betty Friedan, *The Feminine Mystique* (New York: W.W. Norton & Company, Inc., 1963), 54.

121   M. Susan Bland, "Henrietta the Homemaker, and 'Rosie the Riveter': Images of Women in Advertising in *Maclean's* Magazine, 1939-1950" *Atlantis*, 8 (1983), 61-86.

Chapter Four

Hearth and Home: The Cornerstones of Modern Womanhood and the Complements of the Father/Provider

Why should I envy her? My neighbor's poor!
No babies romp about the quaint blue door.
Homage men pay her – homage to her gold!
Why should I envy her? I've wealth untold!

Helen Shackleton

Chatelaine, September 1931[1]

In July 1950, *Chatelaine* published a short story about Cora and Charles Bishop and their young daughter Julie. Cora was the stereotypical suburban housewife/mother. She drove her husband to the train station in the morning and had supper waiting for him on his return in the evening. Dutifully, she took care of the house and their little girl, but increasingly she challenged the confines of hearth and home. One evening Cora declared to her husband "I don't want to become a Mom," to which he retorted, "You've already become one." But what Cora was lamenting was not motherhood in the literal sense. She was questioning the limits of this role and she was yearning to contribute to society through waged work. Charles did not approve of his wife's ambition. When Cora supported her desire for paid employment by stating that she wanted "to be a producer," Charles suggested that she "produce another child." Nonetheless, Cora persisted in seeking employment and arranged for her mother to help care for her home and child. Cora's mom was happy to encourage her daughter's business career and had always thought that her daughter's college education had been some-what wasted in the home.

On their first shared commute to town Mr. Bishop was downright rude to his wife and even hissed at her to "shut up" when his boss, a fellow commuter, engaged her in morning pleasantries. Mr. Bishop was embar-rassed by his wife's "need" to work. Indeed, when his boss found out that Cora was working at a local gift shop he assumed it was because Charles had been denied a raise. Charles was immediately granted an increase in pay. His anxieties over his wife's employment grew. After a week of stressing over the fact that his wife worked for wages Charles observed his daughter's behaviour closely, hoping to find a reason for his wife to return full time to the home. Yet Charles discovered, "to his disappointment she [his daughter] was apparently neither frustrated nor developing neurotic tendencies." He also noted that "His wife was keeping up her health and energy. She had got a weekly pay cheque and presented it to him, and he had turned it down. His mother-in-law was running the house." And while Mr. Bishop still disapproved of his wife working, he had to admit that he had little reason to argue. To his delight, however, that evening Cora announced that she had quit. She was going to have another baby. Despite the "obvious" delay that this would impose upon her business career, Cora remarked, "Of course I have to have the children while I'm young."[2]

The story of the Bishops underscores many of the complexities of *Chatelaine's* modern wife, mother and homemaker. It also unveils some common assumptions that were expressed in the magazine about expected gender roles for modern parents: the care of the home and children were the responsibility of the woman; the husband supplied the economic means to accomplish these tasks. There was, however, room for negotiation. These gender roles and the subtle ways in which they shifted in *Chatelaine* from 1928 to 1956, also speak to the middle-class, white, Anglo-Saxon character that filled the pages of the magazine and popular understandings of middle-class Canadian women and men.

Chatelaine always considered that most women wanted to be mothers. But, at first, it did not assume that all women would be good mothers. Nor did the magazine assume that women would devote all their energies to their offspring. Mothers were still able to contribute outside of the home, although their efforts were generally channelled towards leisure pursuits and the welfare of the community. With the coming of war in 1939, the importance of motherhood increased in *Chatelaine* and became directly associated with national survival. The magazine now suggested that all women had natural talents in this endeavour. Motherhood remained centre stage for women in the postwar years and, like Cora, many wives were restricted to the home once the stork arrived. Some, again like Cora, questioned their choices. Interestingly, as mothers gained in social status with the coming of war in 1939, the importance of fathers appears to have diminished.

Before middle-class wives became mothers, they were first housekeepers. Homemaking and all that it entailed was continuously considered the purview of women, irrespective of other obligations or commitments. Housekeeping was never an envied task, but its presence was pervasive in *Chatelaine*. *Chatelaine* offered little leeway from 1928 to 1956 on the subject of women and housework. Women were not expected to like it, but the magazine did assume that it was the wife's responsibility to take care of the home. A clean, organized home was a sure sign of a happy, healthy family. This association was ever present and helped to solidify gender categories for husbands and wives. The Second World War had little effect on this relationship.

Even at a young age little girls in *Chatelaine* were steered towards house-work in their choice of play.[3] As a March 1929 article noted of children playing, "The little girl playing at making cakes is the housewife of the future and the little boy playing soldier will be the warrior of later life."[4] By the 1950s, *Chatelaine* encouraged formal training for girls. "Are our children being trained for Homemaking?" asked a June 1952 article. The article concluded that schools were not spending enough time training girls in the art of homemaking. It was felt that some responsibility for training the future generation of housewives was up to their mothers, but compulsory school courses were also recommended. Interestingly, it was suggested that boys would also benefit from this type of education. However, it was noted that the main advantage to having boys in the class-room was that their presence created an enthusiastic environment that fostered learning among the girls. In conclusion it was noted that, "we [Canadians] should always keep homemaking in mind when planning education for women – even when planning professional education."[5]

After spending a lifetime perfecting homemaking skills – informally as her mother's apprentice and then at school – once married, wives were usually the ones who were responsible for the upkeep of the home. As Veronica Strong-Boag notes, in the 1920s and 1930s, "Very few Canadians questioned that, whatever duties women might have in the world at large, as income earners, voters, volunteers, activists, and so forth, they were secondary to their efforts as housewives and mothers."[6] This assumption could sometimes even be made before marriage. For example, in November 1931 *Chatelaine* published a short story that told about the lives of four adult sisters who lived together following their parents' death. One of the sisters, Elizabeth, was not as bright as the other three. The three other sisters went to work while Elizabeth stayed home to take care of the house. The working sisters would take turns vacationing with their "less fortunate" sister. One summer Elizabeth escaped and vacationed on her own. She met a man and fell in love. Having heard Elizabeth's complaints about keeping house for her sisters, he encouraged her not to return home. Elizabeth asked, "But what should I do? I haven't any money apart from being their housekeeper." Her Prince Charming replied, "If you like, you can come and be mine." Protesting at the social implications of such an arrangement, Elizabeth declined, although she admitted that she would very much have liked to accept his offer. The gentleman quickly continued, "But, my dear girl, we'd be married first…"[7] The connection between marriage and housework was direct. And, in true literary style, Elizabeth's future husband just happened to be one of her sisters' employers. This twist of fate also served to implicitly raise Elizabeth, in her role as housewife, to a higher social status than that of her working sisters. As the previous chapter has illustrated, however, *Chatelaine* did not inextricably connect marriage with Canadian womanhood in the 1930s. Nonetheless, the magazine did, as this article suggests, generally applaud those who chose this position.

With such a direct connection forged between marriage and housework, some women considered their skills as homemakers as a means of keeping their husbands. "Happiness in marriage is not a free gift from Heaven," said a May 1931 contributor. She continued "Like everything else it must be worked for, fought for, bought at a price that has to be paid." Part of the cost of keeping her marriage together was spoiling her husband. The author noted that "at least two women have told my husband that he is wasting himself on me." She also acknowledged, "Goodness knows I am no beauty, and am always being chased down to the hairdresser to get another Marcel wave. I am too solid to enter the sylph class, and am beginning to slide unobtrusively off the scales before the indicator has quite stopped swinging." To make up for her physical deficiencies the woman tried to be the best wife she could. Yet, she pondered, "There is no apparent reason why he should be so unswervingly loyal to me when the world is so full of lovely women and excellent housekeepers."[8] Her solution, and what seemed to have worked for her for over a decade, was to be at his constant beck and call and to be not just a housekeeper, but a personal servant to her husband. Whether the woman liked her work is questionable, but she did relish the reward – marriage.

Generally, articles about women and homemaking in *Chatelaine* assumed that these women were also mothers. Geraldine McGeer Appleby described her life as a homemaker for *Chatelaine* readers in July 1933. She wrote, "my life was that of any housewife whose concern is largely for her husband and her children, and whose life is very close to the boundaries of her own encircling fence." Appleby alluded to having been frustrated by this confinement, but by the time she wrote the article she was a grandmother and had had time to reflect on her life. Ultimately, she was happy that she had dutifully fulfilled her responsibilities as mother and homemaker. She continued, "I am an average wife and mother whose life has known both happiness and sorrow. It means more to me now that my years may be counted more in the past than in the future that my home life has been complete and my family united whether in mirth or sadness." Appleby was provoked to write the article after spending two years in Russia and realizing that Russian women did not keep house. As a housekeeper there she was a curiosity. "Housekeeping as we know it no longer exists there," she wrote. The reason, "Workmen's restaurants and clubhouses have taken the place of the family table and the hearth. ..."[9] Arguably Appleby did not miss the actual housework, but she somehow connected this duty with the pleasures derived from a nuclear family and subtly accepted the gendered division of labour that this ideal entailed.[10]

Chatelaine certainly considered the job of homemaker to be very important. In 1933 the magazine began a regular section called "Homemaking," later changed to "Home Management," in order to provide advice to Canadian women on the best ways to perform household tasks, including instructions on how to shop for the family's groceries and how to keep houses clean and attractive. In March 1938, the editor of "Home Management," Helen G. Campbell, reminded women of their responsibilities as homemakers. Campbell declared, "Cleanliness is still next to godliness in the order of housewifely virtues and should be consistently practised rather than occasionally indulged in."[11] This association, as Veronica Strong-Boag's notes, was strengthened after the Second World War by technological advances.[12]

According to *Chatelaine*, homemakers were also supposed to provide delicious and nutritious meals for their families and as a June 1940 advertisement for Kellogg's Corn Flakes suggested, homemakers were usually the authority in the kitchen. The advertisement asked readers when deciding on a choice of breakfast cereal, "Expert or Housewife – whose vote would you take?" While the advertisement suggested that the expert and the housewife were definitely different people – the expert in this example was represented by a middle-aged man – it conceded that in this instance the housewife was correct.[13]

Not all women, however, shared Campbell's enthusiasm for housecleaning or Appleby's joy of homemaking. In *Chatelaine* it was common for many women to lament their household duties. Women often considered these tasks endless and largely thankless jobs. The following poem, published in April 1948, encapsulates these sentiments. Titled, "Housecleaning," it read in part:

> . . .Then comes out the pail and soap,
>   the mop--
> Till the whole job's done I will not
>   stop.
> But I pause to read or even worse.
> Scribble down something like this
>   verse.

So when that last cobweb is swept

away

I fear I will be old withered and

grey. . . .

. . . When the housecleaning is done,

will I have any friends?[14]

Such attitudes persisted well into the 1950s. As Valerie Korinek notes in her study of images of women in *Chatelaine* magazine during the 1950s and 1960s, "although it was possible to put different spins on meal preparation or decorating, housecleaning by its very nature was tiresome both to read about and to do."[15]

Particularly in the postwar period *Chatelaine* gave voice to middle-class Canadian women who challenged their household responsibilities. In May 1948, the article "Women in Revolt" was published. The subtitle read, "Let's get rid of horse-and buggy Housekeeping." Two of the three contributors wanted reform for homemakers while the third rejected the idea that this role was unfulfilling. The first author declared that she had "broke[n] out of solitary confinement." She asked who would apply for the following position: "Help Wanted Female. Reliable, cheerful woman to cook, sew, dust, scrub, wax floors, market, wash and iron, mend, look after lively four-year-old child. Must have knowledge of dietetics and home nursing. Hours – 7 a.m. to 8:30 p.m. Time off – none. Pay – room, board, small allowance for clothes and personal necessities." When the woman realized that she had been doing that for years she put her son in nursery school and took a job outside of the home. Of course, she only worked for wages part-time because housework did remain her responsibility. She concluded, "… it's strenuous running two shows at one time, and there are more emergencies to be coped with. But I know now that the freer the spirit (where I'm concerned anyway) the stronger the self-imposed ties of devotion and service."[16] The second contributor was in agreement that housework should not take a woman's whole day. Modern appliances were the key for this woman. The potential results as she saw it were that women "might have to sacrifice some of those timeless eulogies on the part of preachers and politicians about the all-sacrificing, all submerging M-O-T-H-E-R. But with women getting out more in the world there'd be less nonsense talked and more action of a constructive sort practised anyway."[17] Apparently housework was dulling Canadian women's minds. The third woman who wrote in admitted that housework was all consuming and that taking care of home and family was a hard job. But she said, "Today, thank heaven, women don't have to marry for a meal ticket. They do it because they love their men and want, more than anything else, to share their lives and raise their children."[18]

From a young age girls were trained in the art of homemaking. For many it became their principal vocation. The Second World War and the demand for female labour that it created had little impact on the assumption that the modern Canadian woman took care of the home. For those who worked outside of the home, the "double day" was always a harsh reality. Few women looked forward to the long hours and slim rewards associated with housework and *Chatelaine* acknowledged their discontent. One of the main reasons why they continued with the daily toil was for the benefit of their children.

Motherhood, according to *Chatelaine*, was a woman's chief aspiration. From 1928 to 1956, *Chatelaine* projected that once married most couples would soon start families of their own. Procreation was commonly considered the main goal of marriage – even if you had married for love. Raising children was thought to be an ultimate joy in its own right and it was often seen as the glue that bound families for life.

An April 1947 article about a woman who stated that she did not want to have any children elicited immediate response. The anonymous wife offered many reasons for her decision; in the end she stated "what it all boils down to is that I think a married woman's prime responsibility is to her husband. . . .I'd rather concentrate on giving what advantages and comforts I can to Jack [her husband] than ask him to keep on giving up things all his life on the assumption that his child will get a full and complete existence."[19] Most women would probably have agreed that their primary responsibility was to their husbands, but the article nonetheless met with much criticism. Husbands might be first among the list of women's priorities but raising a family was supposed to be her true purpose. In response to the article, a mother of four wrote:"... I do not believe that your writer is happy, although she may think she is. ..."[20] A mother of nine suggested that children were not only a crucial component of a woman's life but that they also served to fulfill men as well. She suggested that "... more middle aged men turn nasty and look for other companions, and seek divorce when they have been denied the responsibilities of fatherhood."[21] Many women were aghast that one of their own did not want children, and one could almost hear the sigh of relief when the editors wrote in June: "One moment please! The editors [Byrne Hope Sanders and *Chatelaine*'s editorial staff] are happy to announce, for all readers' peace of mind, that the anonymous writer in question has just telephoned to say Hurray, she is going to have one!"[22]

While the general expectation that most modern women wanted to be mothers was continuously present in *Chatelaine*, what this role meant to Canadian womanhood changed in the thirty year period under examination and reflects some of the changes in the ways that maternal feminists saw the Canadian landscape. Marianna Valverde is clear in her recent assessment of race, reproduction and sexuality in first wave feminism that "the vast majority of English speaking first-wave feminists were not only ethnocentric but often racist."[23] These maternal feminists lobbied for political rights for women on the basis of their role "in bio-logical and social reproduction."[24] Women not only needed to produce the next generation of Canadians, they needed to mother the entire country and make sure that boys and girls grew up with proper moral standards. They were the "mothers of the race." In the early twentieth century, white, Anglo-Saxon, middle-class women were considered to be particularly suited to this task. Alarming, however, was the declining birth rate among this group of women, something that some white writers referred to as the "specter of race suicide," and the rise in birth rates among other ethnic groups, sometimes referred to as "racial uplift."[25] These ideologies raised the status of motherhood to not only a cultural ideal, but also a racial duty.[26]

In Canada, at the turn of the twentieth century the social purity move-ment sought to regulate some of these discrepancies through pro-grammes which included proper sex education and the establishment of a healthy Protestant understanding of sex among all Canadians, some-thing that most educated, middle-class, Protestant Canadians assumed to mean sexual self-denial.[27] By the 1930s, sterilization and less obtrusive forms of birth control were being practiced on the urban poor. As Alison Prentice, Paula Bourne, Gail Cuthbert Brandt, Beth Light, Wendy Mitchinson and Naomi Black note, "A birth control clinic founded in British Columbia in 1932 also counted among its objectives the need for 'good breeding' and recommended the sterilization of the 'unfit'."[28]

These movements prioritized class and race over gender in the realm of a woman's reproductive rights and choices. As Valverde notes of moral reformers at the turn of the twentieth century: "The collectivity thus organized had very specific class, gender, and racial/ethnic characteris-tics, generally supporting the domination of Anglo-Saxon middle-class males over all others but allowing women of the right class and ethnici-ty a substantial role, as long as they participated in the construction of women in general as beings who, despite their heroic and largely unaided deeds in maternity, were dependent on male protection."[29]   Their cause was furthered by the development of the social sciences and the relationships forged between social activism, religion and the new science. By the 1930s, parental advice could be obtained from any one of a number of "professional experts."   Particularly for the middle-classes, the emergence of the social sciences revolutionized modern parenting. Women were no longer considered innately good at this task and as Strong-Boag notes, "Eager tutors in medicine, education and social work contrasted their superior professionalism with maternal amateurism."[30]

The portrayal of *Chatelaine*'s modern parents in the interwar years suggests that the magazine was both encouraging middle-class couples to reproduce and to follow expert advice on how to raise the next generation of Canadians. Those who refused parenthood were socially condemned; those who embraced it could be assured that they had contributed to the development of Canadian nationalism – albeit a specific type of nationalism that idealized white, middle-class, Anglo-Saxon Protestants. It is evident that in its discussion of motherhood in the 1930s *Chatelaine* was talking to a specific group of Canadian women, those who had the good fortune to be born white and middle-class.[31]

Initially, the intrinsic value of motherhood appears to have been questioned in *Chatelaine*. So too was women's "natural" ability for this role. In its first decade, *Chatelaine*'s modern woman did not automatically gain in social status when she had children and became a mother. For instance, in May 1933 the magazine published a debate between Isabel Sampson who considered Mother's Day to be, "An emotional and commercial orgy, offensive to good taste," and Agnes Thomas who thought it "One of the most beautiful gestures of modern life."[32] Sampson objected "to the basic idea that all mothers are a combination of saint and martyr with a well defined halo." She suggested instead that they are "women who have chosen homemaking as a profession instead of some other, and like women in other professions, some make a success of it and some don't." As Sampson stated: "I am a mother because I wanted to be. If I had been unwilling to bear children I could not have married. But, having made my choice, and brought into the world children who did not ask to be born, I feel under an obligation to be as good a mother to them as possible." Sampson considered motherhood a job and she had no sympathy for those who complained about the work. Indeed, in the 1930s, the popularly held view in Canadian society as Veronica Strong-Boag records was that "being a mother was 'the highest of all professions' and 'that no power of imagination on the part of women who have no children can succeed in placing them in the same position as the mothers.'"[33]

Part of what disgusted Sampson about Mother's Day was the commercialism associated with the May holiday. As an alternative, she suggested that Mother's Day should be a "means of recognizing motherhood as a profession, with stress on the need of preparing for it as for other careers, of keeping up with the times, and of cooperating with all agencies for civic or nation wide improvements."[34] It was obvious that for Sampson marriage was foremost for procreation. Given the illegality of birth control devices and the distribution of family planning information in the 1920s, and the scant availability of these resources in the 1930s, it is probable that many still considered marriage a tool for procreation.[35]

The economic depression of the 1930s, however, challenged these positions, particularly for the working-class.[36] Sampson's middle-class views on this issue are thus apparent in her strong association of marriage and offspring in the 1930s. Indeed, white Anglo-Saxon middle-class women who challenged these norms were often accused of "race suicide."[37] It was equally apparent that for Sampson, motherhood by itself did not raise women's social status; she expected Canadian women to work hard at being "good" mothers; and only "good" mothers were worthy of social praise.

Agnes Thomas viewed the importance of motherhood quite differently. Certainly, she too considered motherhood one of life's hardest jobs. Thomas noted that "being a mother is no easy task. She starts out by risking her life to bring children into the world, and proceeds to spend her best years caring for them. She has no personal liberty, day or night; works longer hours with smaller material returns than women in any other calling...." She also acknowledged that women had to work diligently in order to be successful in this pursuit. Unlike Sampson, however, Thomas felt that regardless of the growing commercialism associated with Mother's Day, the holiday provided women with well deserved praise that was often lacking in their day to day lives. "I know that in Utopia there would be a constant love between parents and children lasting the entire year. But we are not in Utopia yet," wrote Thomas. She continued, "until we arrive there, I think Mother's Day should be supported by everyone who loves the good, the true and the beautiful."[38] Like Sampson, Thomas did not think that rearing children automatically raised women's social status and she was also not under the impression that all mothers were equally good at their jobs.

The supposedly innate ability for women to be good mothers was again challenged in the February 1936 article titled, "Debunking the Mother Myth." "Let us get away from all this sentiment about motherhood. Some mothers are good, some are bad, some are intelligent, and some are ignorant," began the author, Evelyn Seeley. She continued, "Having a child, with all due respect for the physical process, doesn't rate all this reverence tradition gives. If you are a good mother, you deserve praise; if you are a poor mother, you should be blamed. You stand on your merits, as in any other job." Seeley did not support what she thought was "a sizeable group of women who, because they have managed to have offspring, merely rest on their laurels and expect to be supported, revered and loved for that natural accomplishment alone." She suggested instead that "maternal halos are in the discard. You have to be a first-class mother who works hard, to make good today." Seeley's remarks represented some of the modern assumptions about mother-hood that emerged with the development of the social sciences, but they also simply reiterated paradoxes about modern and traditional values concerning motherhood that had existed since the Victorian era.[39] To further her point, Seeley told the story of a woman who had lost her five-year-old son in an accident and who addressed a doctor about having another child to fill the void and to save her marriage. The doctor told the woman that she had no right to have a child for those reasons. "It belongs to the ancient myth," said the doctor, "this idea that every woman is entitled to have a child, and, along with that idea, that naturally she will be a good mother. Certain women most surely should not have children."[40] The message was direct and it was clear that the doctor was revered for his "expertise" in childcare and motherhood. Additionally, the advice hints at some concerns that existed over who was considered of "good breeding stock" for the future of Canada. As Veronica Strong-Boag notes, "Wittingly or not, children's behaviour and development were apt to be judged by the standards of middle-class childcare professionals."[41] So too were the behaviours of their parents. Yet, as Strong-Boag concludes, "Not all would or could match a portrait of normality which was overwhelmingly white, Anglo-American and Protestant in character."[42]

Paradoxically, however, while women were expected to work hard to become good mothers, in its first decade of publication, *Chatelaine* did not expect them to devote all of their energy to this. Some women could not be full-time mothers because their circumstances did not allow them the "luxury" of full-time domesticity. In September 1931, for example, *Chatelaine* told the story of the recently widowed Grace and her infant son Timmie. Grace was in dire economic circumstances following the death of her husband in a motor vehicle accident and she needed to earn a living. In her search for a job she met other young women. One friend, Evvie, reminded Grace that she had a lot to be grateful for. Evvie remarked, "if I'd had a year of a man I loved, and had his baby and mine, a baby all my own. I'd – I'd just walk the skies and trample the stars like so many snowflakes." At her own expense, Evvie arranged for Grace to have an interview at an accounting firm. Grace manoeuvred her way into a position by telling the boss, "I'm really like a married man, and you know firms always prefer to employ married rather than single men. I shall make a success of my work because it is necessary for me to do so for the sake of my son." This quote affirms *Chatelaine's* commitment to gendered spheres. Grace quickly became pre-occupied with her tasks. As she recalled, "The next couple of months were hard for me, for the readjustment to business was difficult, my salary was low, and I was anxious about Timmie, alone all day except when my landlady came up to my rooms at stated intervals to feed him or clean him up." She did not often think of Evvie. Then one day her boss recommended that she take a vacation at a local boarding house. To her astonishment Evvie worked there as a mother's helper. Evvie had given up her only chance at employment in the city for Grace, yet, in the end, had found true happiness in the family atmosphere of the inn.[43] The moral of the story is somewhat confusing. On one hand, Grace is to be envied for her success in the business world, yet she must pay the price of leaving Timmie alone. Conversely, Evvie, who once was pitied for her childless state, is now in the midst of family life. Children do appear to have been of paramount importance to modern Canadian womanhood, but *Chatelaine's* modern woman of the early 1930s was not necessarily restricted in her role as mother – although gender divisions of labour were the norm in modern families. Additionally, motherhood could be fulfilled in the literal sense through giving birth or, in the more general sense, of mothering the nation's young as Evvie did.

Other mothers maintained social commitments for their own personal fulfillment and to retain the interests of their husbands. Often children were an integral part of their lives, but again they were not their sole focus – nor did the magazine encourage them to be. For instance, the caption of a November 1934 short story read, "After six weeks in exile with a sick child, she found her husband the property of another woman…" Gertrude, the protagonist of the story, and obviously a woman of some financial means, was jubilant at her release from caring for her sick brood. She declared on her return to her bridge club, "Well, here's the exile returning! And it's swell to be back. Let me tell you that nursing three through the whooping cough is the world's worst joke. …" She continued, "Really, girls, you don't know how grand it is to be going places again. You see, ordinarily I could have left the children now and then with a nurse but they were at their worst at nights and the baby wouldn't go back to sleep if I wasn't right there. We were quite anxious about him for a while, so I just stood by." Gertrude had encouraged her husband Neale to keep up social appearances while she kept an arduous schedule at home: "except for a short walk every day to keep herself in some measure fit, her time had been spent in the strenuous nursing of the children." And she explained, "She had saved Neale all she could. She knew he had plenty of business cares. She had urged him, though, to go to the parties as they came along. He needed some recreation and at night all she craved was a chance to fling herself down to sleep until the first small patient roused her." Neale did keep up his social calendar and, as Gertrude's entire bridge club was aware, he had met a young woman in the process. Gertrude discovered her husband's infidelity and successfully won him back by re-entering the social scene and proving herself more mature and sophisticated than her competition.[44] Gertrude's children were definitely important to her, but under normal circumstances they did not limit her activities and certainly retaining the affection of her husband was at least equally as important. Women were expected to be self-sacrificing and selfless in their roles as mothers, but as this article suggests, for middle-class women this did not mean that they were required to give up all their leisure activities.

Interestingly, in its first decade, *Chatelaine's* modern fathers could sometimes appear even more exuberant over children than mothers. *Chatelaine's* modern father of the 1930s was usually passionate and involved in his children's lives even if they were not his biological offspring. For example, the central character of "Baby Doctor," a short story published in March 1930, was a handsome young doctor who was devoted to providing the best care to his patients. On one occasion a destitute unwed woman about to give birth was admitted to a private hospital despite strict regulations forbidding it. The woman died in childbirth and her son, now an orphan, remained in critical condition in the hospital. The board of directors of the hospital demanded his removal but the young doctor insisted that he remain. One night the infant took a turn for the worse and was on the brink of death. He was in desperate need of a blood transfusion. While completing this risky procedure the doctor had an epiphany. He realized that he loved the young ward and he was in love with his beautiful and competent nurse.[45] Inspired by the bonds of fatherhood, the once socially inept doctor was able to create an instant family.

Children often acted as a catalyst for romantic relationships and it was common in *Chatelaine* in the 1930s for men to be interested in single mothers, either widows or divorcees. In most instances the key to success with the woman lay in how good a father she perceived he would be. In March 1933, *Chatelaine* ran a short story about Frances Harmon, the widowed mother of twelve-year old Jack. Frances was by far the prettiest mother in town and she was constantly being pursued by the local doctor, Fred Easton. But she continuously refused his proposals. As the author explained, "Her sole reason … was that she as a child had had a stepmother; and she had registered a vow that her son should never have a stepfather. Better no father at all than a stepfather.…"[46] Regardless, Dr. Easton remained devoted to both Frances and her son. When Jack was caught jumping on a freight train and dragged home by the police, Dr. Easton was there to comfort Frances and diffuse the situation. Eventually, Frances realized how much Fred loved both of them. The final paragraph reveals the new family life of the Harmon-Eastons – a happy couple with a son who adores his baby half-brother.[47]

"Twice Blessed," published in September 1934, again illustrates how important a suitor's fatherhood potential was for single mothers. This story was about how Mrs. Willson chose between two potential boyfriends with the help of her teenage twin sons. The twins were "devilish" and played unmerciful pranks on the two prospects. In the end, although the unlikely candidate simply could not keep up with the twins physically, he did pass the test of patience. (His competitor had been much less good-natured when he saw his car in the lake.) But, more importantly, he acknowledged that the twins should be paramount in Mrs. Willson's life – although Mrs. Wilson obviously craved more. On the verge of pulling out of the competition he stated, "I see that there are various loyalties in love. And in your own loyalties – if your children hate me, there's no use in my telling you how deeply I care for you – "[48] With his devotion to all of them unquestioned, he won Mrs. Willson's heart and all four agreed that for the sake of each other they could and would get along.

These three examples also illustrate how important in the 1930s the idea of the nuclear family, a husband, wife and children, was to both men and women, at least according to *Chatelaine*. This phenomenon is at odds with what other scholars have found. Historian Cynthia Comacchio notes the absence of fatherhood in the historical assessment of parenting during the interwar years. Comacchio builds on the premise put forth by American historian Robert Griswold that "fathers became 'outsiders' during the interwar years because this emergent 'therapeutic culture' was predicated on the exclusive partnership of mothers and expert."[49] For the most part, fathers were ignored by professionals of the time who offered "superior" advice to women on how to be good mothers in *Chatelaine*. But, as Comacchio's article reveals, they were not pushed to the margins in all accounts of parenting and there is a need to discover, beyond the rhetoric of professional advice, the roles of fathers in the interwar period. Indeed, for the middle-class men represented in *Chatelaine*, fatherhood was more than a "postscript." As the following examples continue to show, according to *Chatelaine*, fathers could be quite involved in their children's lives.

According to the magazine, single fathers could face some of the same issues as their female counterparts and their devotion to their children could be equally as strong. In "Second Wife," published in July 1938, Donalda and Peter were finding marriage difficult because Peter's twelve-year old daughter, Marianne, commanded much of his attention. To reaffirm his commitment to Donalda, Peter planned a vacation to Bermuda for the two of them while Marianne was at summer camp. Upon their arrival, however, they received a telegram that stated that Marianne had been in an accident. They returned immediately. Marianne had been thrown off a horse and was in a coma. Donalda, a former nurse, was quick to call in a favour and get the best surgeon to return from vacation to assess Marianne's condition. Assisted by Donalda, the surgeon operated. Marianne woke up shortly thereafter. For the first time, Peter realized that Donalda cared deeply both for himself and his daughter. He admitted to Donalda: "I thought you didn't care for Marianne. I had the insane notion that if I loved you each separately, I could keep things smooth. ... But now I see what a fool I've been." And then he professed, "Donny, all my life, and beyond that if it's possible, I shall remember what you did today, and worship you for it. ..."[50]

Regardless of how they entered into fatherhood, almost all of *Chatelaine's* modern fathers of the pre-World War Two period were devoted to their children. In "Tin-Tin Twopenny," published in May 1929, the author told the story of so incredible a bond between father and son that it went so far as to almost alienate the mother from the family. "Father and son were inseparable. It seemed almost to Louise [wife/mother] as if Richard [husband/father] had evoked Tin-Tin Twopenny [son] out of his own sentimentalizing, his own romance. ..."[51] One winter, Tin-Tin Twopenny caught a cold but managed to keep an important engagement with his dad to present a purse to the Queen of England. His cold, however, got worse on the trip. Within forty-eight hours Tin-Tin Twopenny was dead. His mother was oddly at peace while his father raged in grief. Richard eventually left Louise to marry his secretary. The new couple had twin boys shortly thereafter.[52] While the story ended with Louise reminiscing about her son, it is clear that for Richard his role as father extended beyond the grave.

Most stories of devoted fathers in *Chatelaine* were not so tragic. For example, In "Disturbing Age" a single father, Dr. Bradley, was pushed by his sister to send his teenage daughter to boarding school so that she could learn how to become a proper young lady – something that a single dad was apparently unable to teach on his own. It was obvious to Dr. Bradley that his daughter was growing up and had become interested in dating and doing things with friends as opposed to solely with him. At the same time, however, she continued to have affection for her father and to include him in her activities. He ignored his sister's advice and father and daughter, one is led to believe, lived happily ever after.

And, according to Dr. Bradley, his daughter was a far better young woman than his niece.[53] This example is particularly interesting because it shows how a father-daughter relationship could exist even in the absence of a nuclear family.

In the late 1920s and 1930s, *Chatelaine*'s modern mother was devoted to her children. They were not expected to be her only interest, however. Husbands were still a number one priority and, as will be discussed further, it was expected that some middle-class wives and mothers would and should work outside of the home. In the early years of *Chatelaine*, however, motherhood, like being a wife, was a job in which success was not guaranteed. Women were not naturally "good" mothers and this arguably allowed fathers to take an active role in parenting.

By the outbreak of war in 1939, the image of the modern mother in *Chatelaine* had begun to change. Women were now considered innately good at mothering. And motherhood took on increased importance during the war and became associated with a new type of nationalism. The survival of a preferred type of Canadian was no longer the sole issue; national survival itself was now deemed to be threatened. Motherhood, as Linda Grant DePauw argues in *Battle Cries and Lullabies*, prioritized how women were seen during the war.[54] Men, often physically removed from their positions as fathers, started in *Chatelaine* to have secondary roles in child rearing.

The war both heightened the importance of motherhood in *Chatelaine* and also connected it directly with nationalism. Indeed, a 1941 advertisement for war savings certificates began, "My children, my loving – trusting – little children ... Mine! God's precious gift to me. Mine to nurture – to guide and to shield. Yes, mine the blessing – but mine the responsibility." The advertisement portrayed a woman on top of a hill protecting a small boy and girl. The picture suggests that the woman was their sole guardian; however, the advertisement continued, "Yet by my bare hands alone I cannot protect my children from the terrors of Nazi barbarism and slavery. I must join with thousands of other Canadian mothers – to provide supplies for the Army, Navy and Air Force – to crush the terror that threatens all free, happy children – and keep the Hitler pestilence from our land." At the end, the woman announced her pledge to her children and to Canada, "I will not fail or falter – I will not weaken or tire – in my efforts to keep my children free – to keep Canada free. I will – I must pledge, and pledge my very utmost, to save and lend. I will keep on buying War Savings Certificates."[55] Motherhood in this case provided a principal reason for women to support the national war effort.

The importance of motherhood was not always limited to those with young children to care for. Mothers of soldiers were also key figures in *Chatelaine*. A March 1943 advertisement for Coca-Cola showed a returning soldier on his way home to a comfortable living room set up for his arrival. The advertisement read in part, "Probably the happiest moment in his life – coming home to his family – his own room – perhaps his dog – and to all of his cherished personal possessions. He has dreamed about this home-coming for months ... His mother always managed to add the touches that gave the place that indescribable atmosphere of home. ..."[56]

On occasion, mothers of soldiers and soldiers' wives were honoured collectively in *Chatelaine* for the support they provided men overseas. The poem Gauntlet published in September 1943 illustrates this point.

War or no war.
Her laughter is gay as it was before.

Her days are full of sharing and
giving.
The richness of love, the joy of
living.

Lipstick and High Heels:

Her home is a shining citadel

Where courage, hope and calmness

dwell.

That's what wives and mothers are

for.

War or no war.[57]

Certainly with the war motherhood took on new significance and *Chatelaine* encouraged women to enter this sisterhood. New images that emerged in *Chatelaine* included women having babies at older ages. For example a May 1940 advertisement for Castoria, "the modern SAFE laxative made especially and ONLY for children," suggested that women as old as thirty-six years would have no problem raising a baby with the help of their product.[58] *Chatelaine* also assumed that most newly married women would soon give birth and this provided a reason to promote early marriages. In a September 1941 article that debated the pros and cons of the increased marriage rate among young people, *Chatelaine* took for granted the fact that there would be an "heir born by the end of the year." The article did suggest that some women might find the strain of raising a baby alone while their husbands' served overseas overwhelming. On the other hand, the author, Adele White, observed that "marriage and motherhood are two of the greatest experiences in a girl's life, and it may be a lot sadder to have no husband and no baby – lap dogs and canaries make poor substitutes." Moreover, it was suggested that marriage and a child would help returning servicemen to establish themselves in the postwar world. White wrote, "A wife, and perhaps a child, provides a strong incentive to get settled in a job."[59] There is no doubt that *Chatelaine* now saw motherhood as an integral part of Canadian womanhood and a crucial part of the war effort. Middle-class women may have been encouraged to have babies in the 1930s; by the 1940s *Chatelaine* insisted that they fulfil this mandate.

Chatelaine also suggested that it was no longer sufficient for some women to be motherly just to their own offspring. "What is this business of being a foster mother?" asked Adele Saunders in a September 1945 article. She explained, "Let's look at it this way. There are some women who make careers of writing or painting; some who choose secretarial work or become nurses or doctors; but in the case of Mrs. Rogers and others like her, childcare is the most important and satisfying job in life. Homemaking and motherhood is not something that merely 'happens'; they deliberately seek it as a career. They can be mothers not only to their own immediate family circles but to a continuous chain of boys and girls. ..."[60] Motherhood could extend beyond bloodlines as the 1931 story about Grace and Evvie suggested. In the 1940s though, *Chatelaine* expected women to have their own children in addition to helping care for less fortunate boys and girls.

At the same time that *Chatelaine*'s modern mother increased in social value her parental counterpart was pushed to the margins. During the war years, *Chatelaine*'s fathers had little to no interest in playing an active role in their children's lives. For example, in the short story "Fathers are Born" that appeared in July 1941, Hariet and John are a recently divorced couple with a young daughter and son. Hariet separated from John because he showed no interest in their children. Following their divorce she began to date David, a man who appeared as interested in her kids as in her. Hariet, however, remained hopeful that John would change. One weekend John asked if he could take the children with him to their grandfather's. Hariet dreamt that this was the beginning of a great transformation. However, when the children returned and said that their father had spent the entire weekend golfing while they went with their grandfather on errands, Hariet knew that nothing had changed. She became convinced that her future, as well as that of her children, was with David. To confirm her beliefs, John admitted that the only reason why he had wanted her back was because he had heard rumours that she was dating David. He had not developed an interest in the children.[61]

Another example of this laissez-faire attitude among fathers in the early 1940s was portrayed in the character of Professor Blakely in November 1943's short story "Step Lively Professor." Professor Blakely was a stereotype of the absent-minded professor as is illustrated in the following scenario taken from the story: "Professor Blakely tapped his book with a pencil. 'And what is your name, young man?' Ben grinned in spite of himself. 'It's Blakely, sir.' 'Well, Blakely, I suppose you've come to complain about my marking or something, well, get on with it!' Ben put his hand on his father's shoulder. 'It's me dad – Ben.'"[62] This type of parental indifference – which in this case was seen as humourous by both son and reader – was, in *Chatelaine*, rarely seen to adversely affect the children.

It was perhaps less drole, yet not necessarily less common, when returning soldiers felt alienated from offspring when they met them for the first time at three or four years of age. Articles in *Chatelaine* empathized with returning war veterans, but they also tried to see the situation from the mother and child's sides as well. In "Going Home" a December 1944 fiction story, Reg, a wounded soldier, was not eagerly anticipating his arrival home. Since his absence, his wife Clare had given birth and raised their son while supporting the family on her wages as a schoolteacher – she had had no choice. When Reg returned home he neglected to bring a present for his son, Tad – as Clare was perhaps too quick to point out. Reg was unaware how to behave around his "new" family. Tad was ecstatic that he finally had a dad but Reg was certainly not as exuberant over the reunion. He noted that "He tried to make friends with Tad, but found a five-year-old a somewhat unsatisfying companion."[63] In the end Reg's fragile condition was revealed when he fainted at a local dance. He and Clare realized their love for each other and they reaffirmed their commitment to one another. There was, however, no mention of Reg committing to fatherhood, a phenomenon that was reflective of many returning veterans who were new fathers. In his social history of Canada during the Second World War, Jeffrey A. Keshen notes that "despite their jubilant welcome home, the road back to civvy street and family life was an arduous one for many Second World War Veterans. ...Many resented wives or girlfriends who had grown too independent, and others could not reconnect with their children."[64]

During the belligerence of 1939 to 1945, *Chatelaine* underscored the importance of motherhood to the home and to the nation. Fathers in *Chatelaine* were often overshadowed by this new powerful image of the innately good mother. Women were mothers and men were soldiers and there was little room in *Chatelaine* for negotiation of these gendered wartime norms, reflecting what many historians argue is a natural occurrence during periods of belligerence.[65] As Jonathan Vance argues, the association of women to motherhood is heightened during periods of belligerence and often solidified in postwar memorials.[66] He notes that some women during the Great War actually envied the mother who had lost her son in battle. He writes that "Such people could not join the band of brothers at the front, but at least they could appreciate the almost magical quality of that select group."[67] Author Linda Grant de Pauw also elaborates on the heightened value attached to motherhood during war. "In a traditional war story" she comments, "the male heroes do the fighting and embody the martial virtues. Their reward for suffering hardship and risking their lives is woman's love, including, in addition to sex, all the admiration, compassion and provision of creature comforts that are associated with the image of wife and mother."[68]

In the postwar years, the image of the innately good mother continued to polarize women and men's parental responsibilities. Largely,

141

Chatelaine's post-1945 modern mother was confined by this role. Like *Chatelaine's* modern wife described in chapter three, some mothers grew frustrated by these constraints.

In the postwar years, *Chatelaine* again reminded readers that babies were essential for happy, lasting marriages and the development of the nation. A happy home was the root of a happy, healthy nation and women lay at the core of this ideal. A May 1946 article encouraged readers not to delay parenthood. The author Ruth MacLacklan Franks, a psychiatrist, cautioned that "Canada has not maintained her population." Franks suggested that "Three children per married couple should be a minimum goal...." She reasoned that "The happiness of the home is dependent on a great many things. The happiness of the home is dependent on the happiness of the country, and likewise the happiness of the country is dependent on the happiness of the home." Franks provided an example of a couple who had married young while the husband was completing his education. The newlyweds had promised their parents to delay parenthood for five years in exchange for their blessings and some financial aid. The wife desperately wanted a child to help her through the lonely hours. She contemplated getting a job, but her husband was appalled by the idea and expected his wife to be content with housework. The couple kept their promise to their parents. But once the husband was finished school, their efforts to have a baby failed. The wife was no longer young and they remained childless for several years. Eventually the couple had a son, but he was destined to be an only child. This situation was, according to Franks, unfortunate for all. The son was overprotected and his parents had a continuous fear that something would happen to their only offspring. Franks implored readers not to allow this to happen to them. She could see no reason for people to delay "their greatest opportunity for investment in happiness for the future – a baby."[69] Indeed, in postwar Canadian society the average age of women and men at their first marriage was declining and women were having more children at younger ages than during the depression.[70] *Chatelaine* obviously encouraged its readers to be part of these new statistics as the postwar "baby boom" got under way.

Additionally, *Chatelaine* projected the belief that motherhood helped to transform women for the better. For example, a June 1948 article in *Chatelaine* told the story of Mrs. Douglas Hyde of Wimbledon, England. Mrs. Hyde had flirted with communism for several years in her youth and married the editor of the British communist paper *The Daily Organ*. Mrs. Hyde first started to question her new ideology when her daughter was born. As the article noted, "this was when Mrs. Hyde first began to see the 'salvation of the world' not as a question of mere belief in doctrine, but characteristically as a mother, a question of service and sacrifice." When her daughter started school at a local communist-run daycare, Mrs. Hyde admitted to her husband that she was no longer as enamoured with communism. They also had an infant son to think of. The Hydes were beginning to see that "the god of Communism was really Russia, and while that might be all right for the Russians – it wasn't England's cup of tea." Their two children were baptized in the Roman Catholic faith and the Hydes also returned to their former religion. Mrs. Hyde announced that she had rejected communism because she was a "woman, wife and mother – not a pseudo-masculine cog in a party machine." Specifically, she rejected the ideology for the good of her children. She remarked that "Communism is a power philosophy. Motherhood needs no philosophy."[71]

The Cold War, as many authors have argued, provided an opportune setting for the "cult of domesticity" to flourish and for feminine and masculine roles to be redefined around traditional middle-class ideals that valued democratic family relationships within gendered spheres.[72] As Doug Owram notes, "Postwar experts insisted that the modern family must reflect the practices and values of a democratic people."[73] However, this imagery, as Mona Gleason argues, represented a middle-class ideal, not the Canadian postwar reality. She notes, "In the conventional imagination, the 1950s family is stereotypically white and middle class. The attractive young husband and wife live in the suburbs and have two bright children – a boy and a girl." She continues, "The father works in an office in the city to which he drives in the family station wagon. The mother, perpetually clad in dress, high heels, pearls, and lipstick, runs the household and cares for the children. ..."[74] *Chatelaine*, with little deviation, directly spoke to and about this white, middle-class Anglo-Saxon ideal.

In spite of this idealistic image, after 1945 *Chatelaine's* modern mother often felt trapped in the role that increasingly defined and limited her. An August 1952 article which discussed the many lives of modern women noted that: "It is only after today's young woman has married and had a child or two that she begins to wonder whether the 'choice' offered her wasn't an illusion or a downright fraud. After all the study, the training, all the dreaming and planning, she now finds herself in the confining world of marketing, cooking, cleaning, and baby-chasing; and she sees no relief ahead." Part of the problem, according to the authors, was that modern mothers doted too much on their children, something that had been avoided in the past because large families and rural conditions did not permit it. Their advice was for women to take some time for themselves outside of their roles of wives, mothers and home-makers.[75] The next month the authors asked women if they were "crazy about [their] kids, but feeling trapped?" This time they addressed the isolation of mothers in suburban homes and again encouraged women to take time for themselves and to participate in group activities with other mothers who were similarly secluded. The authors commented that "From the point of view of the women themselves, or from the point of view of society, is it necessary – is it wise – to make them choose between being mothers and developing as human beings." They declared, "mothers can be human."[76] What they meant by this comment was that women could have a life outside the confines of motherhood–something that was becoming somewhat of an anomaly within the pages of *Chatelaine*, yet, as Veronica Strong-Boag points out, could be a reality in Canadian suburbs.[77] It was also reflective of a growing movement towards liberal individualism.

By the postwar period, *Chatelaine* was also blunt in its assessment of father-hood. The title of a May 1947 article asked boldly "What's the Matter with Father?" And announced: "He's NOT all right!" The problem, according to the article, was that fathers were not taking an active role in rearing their children. The article noted that "… in too many cases the male parent has become merely that man who earns money, pays the bills, and comes home evenings and week ends [sic]. A conscious, responsible fatherhood – in the way that we think of dedicated mother-hood – is a rare phenomenon."[78] The solution, written by a father himself, was that men needed to learn how to become better, more active parents. "The catch" of course, as the author stated, was "that it [being better fathers] meant work." He confessed, "… I wasn't consistently in the mood for Timmy's breathless chronicles of his day. I kept on, though; because that or some similar planned co-operation is absolutely essential. Hit-or-miss won't do. The most we fathers can give is never quite enough; but there is nothing to keep us from doing our best, and from doing it better all the time – nothing whatsoever. … Except, of course, ourselves."[79] And somewhere along these lines *Chatelaine's* reluctant father figure of the late-1940s/1950s was born.

The author of a July 1950 article admitted in the opening lines, "I am a father – but I don't like babies."[80] But he was also quick to add "Before the women go off the deep end let me make myself very, very, clear. CHILDREN I like. BABIES I can do without!"[81] As a devoted husband he tried to have an interest in his infant son. He was unsuccessful in pulling off the illusion, however, and his wife asked, "Just when do you think Bobby changes from a baby to a child? WHEN will you start taking an interest in him?"[82] He had no answer for her. Luckily for this trio their story ended happily. The author, however, insisted on cautioning women from pushing men into active parental roles. In his conclusion he asserted, particularly to mothers, "… don't push us fathers. Let us take our time to know our sons and daughters. And don't go into a snit when we don't come up to your specifications in the parent field." As proof of his reasoning he described his own familial situation: "Today our son is two years old and we are pals. He likes me and I certainly like him. My wife agrees I am his favourite and she says now her predictions that he would turn from me because I didn't dote on him in his early months are unfounded."[83]

A similar casual attitude about fatherhood was expressed in the 1953 article "Reluctant Father." In this story Alec was not interested in having an active role in his infant daughter, Butch's, (Alec had wanted a boy), upbringing. He was bored by conversation about babies and asked his wife Peg the rhetorical question: "Just because we have a baby do we have to act like nitwits?"[84] After being forced to spend the day with Butch because Peg had a previous commitment and the sitter was suddenly unavailable, Alec began to be quite attached to "daddy's little girl." Moreover, he and Peg agreed that conversations about babies should be limited and that they should continue to have "adult conversations" that did not confine them to the roles of mother and father. Not only had Alec come to terms with being an active father, by the end of the story he was even looking forward to being a father again. Peg's appointment had been with an obstetrician.

Not all stories of reluctant fathers in *Chatelaine* had happy endings, however. "The deserted family suffers greater misery than one broken by death or divorce," was the caption of a January 1951 article about "Runaway" husbands. It was predicted that in 1951, 2,000 Canadian wives would be deserted in this way.[85] This loss would leave these mothers to fend for themselves and for their children. The economic strain that these families would face was obvious. Perhaps less apparent was the fact that the children were also usually left without the presence of a strong male role model.

Notably, the reluctance of *Chatelaine*'s modern father of the post-1945 period is different than the picture of fatherhood that historian Robert Rutherdale paints. Rutherdale argues that "As a revamped cultural ideal, masculine domesticity took shape in the first two decades following the Second World War within an expanding consumer economy that privileged fatherhood by valorizing a variety of home-centred and family-based pursuits from the backyard gardener to the Scout leader or hockey coach." Rutherdale continues, "Respectable manhood translated into companionate marriages and involved parenting...." For the most part, Rutherdale's oral histories confirm these "ideals of family consumption."[86] Generally, however, the image of involved fathers was absent in *Chatelaine*'s post-World War Two discourse.

In a way, the post-World War Two period provided an opportunity for men and women to re-negotiate their parental roles. *Chatelaine*'s modern mother maintained her innate ability and heightened importance bestowed upon her during the war, but she now sometimes questioned the confines that this role placed her in. From the outskirts, *Chatelaine*'s modern father re-entered the picture but his literal and figurative absence from 1939 to 1945 was not always easily overcome. *Chatelaine* encouraged women to give their men time to find their place in the family unit. The magazine was less generous to its female readership. *Chatelaine* acknowledged that some mothers challenged the confines of motherhood, but it did little to provide them with an alternative to hearth and home.

Hearth and home were, according to *Chatelaine*, the responsibility of women. Women may not have enjoyed all aspects of housework but, regardless of her other occupations, women were expected to take care of the home. Husbands were expected to provide their wives with the economic means to accomplish these tasks. Part of a woman's responsibility included raising offspring. Motherhood in *Chatelaine* was always considered to be of paramount importance to the modern woman. In the 1930s, *Chatelaine*'s encouragement of its readers to have babies can be viewed as an attempt to sustain a white, Anglo-Saxon, middle-class norm in Canadian society and speaks to the middle-class tone that filled the magazine. *Chatelaine* did not suggest that women would be innately good at raising their offspring and the magazine provided mothers with advice from a growing field of experts. In the end, some mothers would be successful, some would not, and all would have to work hard to be their best. Canadian women were not expected to devote all of their time in this pursuit, however. They were allowed to take time for themselves and to socialize with their husbands. Fathers too in *Chatelaine* throughout the 1930s took pleasure in actively raising their children. But the war created a literal and figurative distance between *Chatelaine*'s modern father and his offspring that proved long lasting. Simultaneously, the war elevated the social status of motherhood and linked it directly with the survival of the nation, a phenomenon that Susan S. Grayzel argues occurred for British and French women during the Great War.[87] Women were now somehow expected to be innately good at this role. Moreover, at a time when women were readily working outside of the home to support the war effort, *Chatelaine* suggested that raising children should be a full-time occupation. These changes carried into the postwar years and caused some women to question their choices.

The most noticeable change to motherhood from 1928 to 1956 was the new belief in *Chatelaine* that emerged in conjunction with the Second

World War that women had a natural ability for this role. Expert advice did not disappear from the pages of *Chatelaine*, but there was far less critique of mothers or questioning over whether a woman would make a good mother. The wartime rhetoric was that if she was a woman, then she would be a good mother – national survival depended on it. This change occurred with the war and not in the 1936/37 timeframe. Motherhood was already associated with national survival before 1939 – albeit a very specific type of national survival prioritizing middle-class, white, Anglo-Saxon Canadians – thus there may have been less need to channel this association prior to the war. There is no doubt, however, that the association forged in *Chatelaine* in 1939 between motherhood and national survival was more direct and overt than what had previously appeared in the magazine.

The most interesting conclusions that can be drawn from this chapter concern the changing roles of fathers from 1928 to 1956. *Chatelaine's* pre-war dad was active and engaged in the upbringing of his children regardless of whether they were his biological offspring or adopted. But when war arrived in 1939, fathers were noticeably absent from their children's lives. In a large part this was but a reflection of a wartime reality. Many Canadian fathers were in uniform fulfilling that most "natural" manly role of defender of hearth and home. But in Canada, as elsewhere, war also heightened the differences between men and women, the masculine and the feminine. Common sense dictated that men, largely by default, were away as fathers. Their absence opened up opportunities for women in public life and this, to some degree, as the next chapter shows, also affected *Chatelaine's* changing understandings of women's relationships to paid employment.

Endnotes

1   Helen Shackleton, *Chatelaine*, September 1931, 42.

2   Willard Temple, *Chatelaine*, July 1950, 10-11, 33-34, 46-48.

3   This phenomenon has been well documented with regard to Canadian society at large in the mid-twentieth century. See for example, Alison Prentice et al.'s discussion of the "educated housewife" of the 1920s and 1930s in Alison Prentice, Paula Bourne, Gail Cuthbert Brandt, Beth Light, Wendy Mitchinson and Naomi Black, *Canadian Women: A History* (Toronto: Harcourt Brace Canada, 1996), 281-282; Veronica Strong-Boag, *The New Day Recalled: The Lives of Girls and Women in English Canada, 1919-1939* (Markam: Penguin Books, 1988), 19-20; and for a discussion of gender biases in the education system in the 1950s see Doug Owram, *Born at the Right Time: A History of the Baby Boom Generation* (Toronto: University of Toronto Press, 1996), 130-131.

4   Frances Lily Johnson, *Chatelaine*, March 1929, 25.

5   Helen Palmer, *Chatelaine*, June 1952, 22, 29, quote, 29.

6   Strong-Boag, *The New Day Recalled*, 113.

7   Eric Shepherd, *Chatelaine*, November 1931, 37.

8   E.G. , *Chatelaine*, May 1931, 17.

9   Geraldine McGeer Appleby, *Chatelaine*, July 1933, 13, 30,37.

10   This connection even existed into the 1950s. As historian Doug Owram notes, the 1950s was, paradoxically, a decade in which Canadians wished to dispel the myth of women as weak and frail while at the same time the age was "overwhelmingly domestic in its orientation, and part of that domesticity included strict separation of career roles." Owram, *Born at the Right Time,* 131.

11   Helen G. Campbell, *Chatelaine*, March 1938, 59.

12   Veronica Strong-Boag, "'Their Side of the Story': Women's Voices form Ontario Suburbs, 1945-1960" in Joy Parr (ed.), *A Diversity of Women: Ontario, 1945-1980* (Toronto: University of Toronto Press, 1995), 61.

13   This connection is particularly interesting considering the rise of the "expert" in the lives of twentieth century Canadians. This theme will be picked up in the discussion of women as mothers.

14   *Chatelaine,* April 1948, 40.

15   Valerie J. Korinek, *Roughing It in the Suburbs: Reading Chatelaine Magazine in the Fifties and Sixties* (Toronto: University of Toronto Press, 2000), 195.

16   Jean Pringle, *Chatelaine*, May 1948, 34.

17   Mary Evans, *Chatelaine*, May 1948, 34-35.

18   Helen Stewart, *Chatelaine*, May 1948, 35.

19   *Chatelaine*, April 1947, 64.

20   *Chatelaine*, June 1947, 6.

21   Ibid.

22   Ibid.

23   Mariana Valverde, "'When the Mother of the Race Is Free': Race, Reproduction, and Sexuality in First-Wave Feminism," in Franca Iacovetta and Mariana Valverde (eds.), *Gender Conflicts: New Essays in Women's History* (Toronto: University of Toronto Press, 1992), 3.

24   Valverde, "'When the Mother of the Race Is Free',"3.

25   Alison Berg, *Mothering the Race: Women's Narratives of Reproduction, 1890-1930* (University of Illinois Press, 2002), 1.

26   Berg, *Mothering the Race,* 5.

27   Mariana Valverde, *The Age of Light, Soap, And Water: Moral Reform in English Canada, 1885-1925* (Toronto: McClelland & Stewart Inc., 1991), 104.

28   Prentice, et al., *Canadian Women: A History*, 295.

29   Valverde, *The Age of Light, Soap, and Water*, 33.

30   Strong-Boag, *The New Day Recalled*, 149.

31   The same rhetoric was being delivered to French Canadians, with arguably more success given the high birth rate among French Quebecois. Among the working-class, however, motherhood was often rejected. Andree Levesque, translated by Yvone M. Klein, *Making and Breaking the Rules: Women in Quebec, 1919-1939* (Montreal: Les Editions du Remu-Menage, 1989), 23-52, 81-100.

32   Isabel Sampson and Agnes Thomas, *Chatelaine*, May 1933, 26.

33   Strong-Boag, *The New Day Recalled*, 150.

34   Isabel Sampson, *Chatelaine*, May 1933, 26, 70.

35   Angus McLaren and Alrene Tigar McLaren, *The Bedroom and the State* (Toronto: McClelland and Stewart Limited, 1986), 68.

36   Prentice, et al., *Canadian Women: A History*, 293-295; and Strong-Boag, *The New Day Recalled*, 88-89. Denyse Baillargeon also argues along these lines in her study of working class housewives in Quebec during the Great Depression. She states, "We can surmise that during these years, the respondent's [a woman who had been of childbearing age during the depression] decision to use contraception had some connection with the economic difficulties of the 1930s. In fact, the majority of couples who tried to control their fertility experienced cuts in wages or had to live on welfare for more or less prolonged periods." Denyse Baillargeon, "'If You Had No Money, You Had No Trouble, Did You?': Montreal

Working-Class Housewives during the Great Depression," in Wendy Mitchinson et al., *Canadian Women: A Reader* (Toronto: Harcourt Brace Canada, 1996), 255.

37   Prentice, et al., *Canadian Women: A History*, 294.

38   Agnes Thomas, *Chatelaine*, May 1933, 26, 70.

39   Deborah Gorham argues that in the late nineteenth century young women struggled with resolving desires for a "modern" existence that involved a career outside of the home and traditional motherhood. Already by this time, in the purview of the middle-classes, "improved education for girls was [considered] the way to improve the quality of motherhood." Yet, "in any contest between the two opposing sets of values, they [educators of Victorian girls] believed that femininity should triumph over purposeful, self-fulfilling achievement." Deborah Gorham, *The Victorian Girl and the Feminine Ideal* (Bloomington: Indiana University Press, 1982), 108.

40   Evelyn Seeley, *Chatelaine*, February 1936, 4, 40.

41   Veronica Strong-Boag, "Intruders in the Nursery: Childcare Professionals Reshape the Years One to Five," in Joy Parr (ed.), *Childhood and Family in Canadian History* (Toronto: McClelland and Stewart Limited, 1982), 178.

42   Strong-Boag, "Intruders in the Nursery," 178.

43   True Davidson, *Chatelaine*, September 1931, 15, 35, 36.

44   Agnes Sligh Turnbull, *Chatelaine*, November 1934, 16-17, 34-35, 46.

45   Charles Bonner, *Chatelaine*, March 1930, 5.

46   Edwin Dial Torgerson, *Chatelaine*, March 1933, 14.

47   Ibid., 41.

48   Maude Radford Warren, *Chatelaine*, September 1934, 41.

49   Cynthia Comacchio "'A Postscript for Father': Defining a New Fatherhood in Interwar Canada," *The Canadian Historical Review* 78 (1997), 388.

50   *Chatelaine*, July 1938, 43.

51   Christine Jope-Slade, *Chatelaine*, May 1929, 4.

52   Ibid., 48.

53   Elizabeth Whiting, *Chatelaine*, July 1934, 14.

54   Linda Grant De Pauw, *Battle Cries and Lullabies: Women in War from Prehistory to the Present* (Norman: University of Oklahoma Press, 1998), 17.

55   *Chatelaine*, May 1941, 65.

56   *Chatelaine*, March 1943, 64. Susan R. Grayzel argues that in the case of Britain and France during the Great War, women were associated to motherhood in the same way that men were to soldiers. Susan R. Grayzel, *Women's Identities at War: Gender, Motherhood, and Politics in Britain and France During the First World War* (Chapel Hill: the University of North Carolina Press, 1999).

57   May Richstone, *Chatelaine*, September 1943, 42.

58   *Chatelaine*, May 1940, 28.

59   Adele White, *Chatelaine*, September 1941, 9.

60   Adele Saunders, *Chatelaine*, September 1945, 16.

61   Helen Bullard Rydell, *Chatelaine*, July 1941, 14.

62   Philip Cyrys Gunio, *Chatelaine*, November 1943, 15.

63   Elsie Fry Laurence, *Chatelaine*, December 1944, 40.

64   Jeffrey A. Keshen, *Saints, Sinners and Soldiers: Canada's Second World War* (Vancouver: UBC Press, 2004), 8.

65   See for example: Grayzel, *Women's Identities at War*; De Pauw, *Battle Cries and Lullabies*; Jonathan F. Vance, *Death So Noble: Memory, Meaning and the First World War* (Vancouver: University of British Columbia Press, 1997); and Deidre Beddoe, *Back to Home and Duty: Women Between the Wars, 1918 – 1939* (London: Pandora Press, 1989).

66   Vance, *Death So Noble*.

67   Ibid., 126.

68   De Pauw, *Battle Cries and Lullabies*, 17.

69   Ruth MacLacklan Franks, *Chatelaine*, May 1948, 29.

70   Prentice et al., *Canadian Women: A History*, 379.

71   Jodi Hyland, *Chatelaine*, June 1944, 26–27.

72   See for example: Owram, *Born at the Right Time*; Mona Gleason, *Normalizing the Ideal: Psychology, Shooling, and the Family in Postwar Canada* (Toronto: University of Toronto Press, 1999); and K.A. Cuordileone, *Manhood and American Political Culture in the Cold War* (New York: Routledge, 2005).

73   Owram, *Born at the Right Time*, 45.

74   She also argues that this ideal was what the experts prescribed as normal and what new Canadians and others who did not fit the prescription tried to emulate. Gleason, *Normalizing the Idea*, 6. Nancy Christie and Michael Gauvreau also argue in their revisionist account of Canadian culture in the post-World War Two period, that Canadian family life in the 1950s was much more complicated than Owram suggests. Nancy Christie and Michael Gauvreau (eds.), *Cultures of Citizenship in Post-war Canada, 1940-1955* (Montreal: McGill-Queen's University Press, 2003), 4.

75   Sidonie M. Gruenberg and Hilda Sidney Krech, *Chatelaine*, August 1952, 16-17, 48-49, 50-54.

76   Ibid., *Chatelaine*, September 1952, 12-13, 50-52, 54-55.

77   Veronica Strong-Boag, "Home Dreams: Women in the Suburban Experiment in Canada, 1945-1960," in Chad Gadffield, *Constructing Modern*

Canada: Readings in Post-Confederation History (Toronto: Copp Clark Longman Ltd., 1994), 477-505; and Strong-Boag, "'Their Side of the Story'," 46-74.

78   Timothy Fraser, *Chatelaine*, May 1947, 10.

79   Ibid., 82.

80   Anonymous, *Chatelaine*, July 1950, 4.

81   Ibid.

82   Ibid., 60.

83   Ibid.

84   Nancy Cardozo, *Chatelaine*, September 1953, 15.

85   Fred Bodsworth, *Chatelaine*, January 1951, 12.

86   Robert Rutherdale, "Fatherhood, Masculinity, and the Good Life During Canada's Baby Boom, 1945-1965," *Journal of Family History* 24 (1999), 369.

87   Susan R. Grayzel, *Women's Identities at War: Gender, Motherhood, and Politics in Britain and France During the First World War* (Chapel Hill: the University of North Carolina Press, 1999).

Chapter Five

From Female to Feminine: Images of Women at Work

Oh mother … it will be all right. This is my generation. Yours earned the right to careers. And it − it was a bit swamping for mine. Girls felt they simply had to go to work and have a career, just like the boys. But with the war we have gone one farther. We've earned the right not to have a career, if we don't want it. If we want to get married and have children and darn a man's socks, surely we're entitled to it? Some of us want just that. If we don't want it, we can be anything, but if we do want it … why, I've fought for my home and my children! I stuck it out there [in the women's army] and looked at death so close I saw the whites of his eyes. … Mother, darling, I'm going out tonight and get me that little house and those children if I'm lucky!

Veila Ercole

Chatelaine, November 1945[1]

....Lest you think I am forgetting the importance of homemaking as a career for women, I wish to state that in several centres in Canada a special course of training in Home-making and family living has been designed for ex-servicewomen. I am glad to be able to announce that in some centres evening classes in this subject are also being provided for those men who recognize that they too need training. …

Lipstick and High Heels:

I am very much aware of the importance of homemaking, but let us not forget that women have demonstrated their ability to perform all sorts of tasks hitherto not open to them, and we should see to it that opportunities for them to use their talents to the full are never closed again.

Olive Russell,
Superintendent of Women's Rehabilitation,
Department of Veteran Affairs,
in a CBC interview,
Vancouver, 25 March 1946[2]

In its inaugural issue of March 1928, *Chatelaine* published a short story about the fictional character Nora Brady and her quest for happiness. Nora Brady was a plain young woman who possessed, of her own admittance, no physical beauty. Assuming that her physical appearance had eliminated her option to marry, Nora looked for a job. She found one as a personal secretary for an elderly wealthy man, Mr. Millen. Mr. Millen quickly became a pseudo-father for the homely Ms. Brady. He admired his young employee, explaining that "She's not like the rest of the senseless hussies, forever titivating [sic] before a mirror, powdering their noses. Bah! Takes an interest in her work instead of calculating the effect she's having on the man she's taking dictation from. There's something about her – "

When a stroke paralysed Mr. Millen, it was Nora who he sent for to take care of him. In the evenings, Nora would go to the local park and watch the ships pulling into the harbour and daydream about the treasures that they carried. On these journeys she often ran into Michael, a handsome acquaintance who had recently been rejected by his beautiful fiancée. Soon she and Michael fell in love and married – although Nora always questioned why Michael was attracted to her. When Nora told

Mr. Millen of her elopement, he was appalled. "The first foolish thing I've ever know you to do," he barked from his deathbed. He asked, "What are you throwing yourself away for on a bond salesman?" And he described how he foresaw her future, "Squalling kids and a garret – hot in summer, freezing in winter." "Couldn't you have chosen better?" he asked, while warning her that her husband would leave her for "the first pretty face he sees." He concluded, "you're not pretty Nora, but I thought you had brains."

Shortly after the tirade Mr. Millen died. He bequeathed his entire estate to Nora with the caveat that no husband should ever touch her fortune. Nora convinced Michael to quit his job and travel the world with her. Mr. Millen's last words remained dear to her heart, however, and Nora continuously accused her husband of being interested in "pretty girls."

Eventually, Michael announced, "I can't stick it any longer. I'm going home. Going back to my job. I'm losing my self respect. I've got to get back to work." With her husband gone, Nora was miserable. She saw her inheritance as the root of her problem. Nora returned home and gave the remainder of the fortune to Mr. Millen's family, (who had all along felt that they were the rightful heirs). Once back, she returned to work as a secretary. She wondered, "What else for the Nora Bradys of this world?" Slowly her health failed her and her landlady, discovering Michael's address on a crumpled piece of paper, sent for him. Michael rushed to his wife's side and professed his unconditional love. He convinced her that when she was at his side he had never even noticed another women. The false accusations, however, had broken his spirit and he had felt compelled to leave. Nora saw the error of her ways and her strength returned.[3]

Nora's story exposes many of the complexities of *Chatelaine*'s modern woman and the relationships forged between marriage, work and womanhood in the magazine. For the most part, marriage was a woman's destiny. After the ceremony, husbands generally provided for their wives, while home and children became women's primary concerns. Yet, for those women, like Nora, who feared that marriage might not materialise, work could be a viable alternative to remaining in their childhood home. Certainly, for a growing number of middle-class women, in the 1930s and 1940s a brief period of paid employment was beginning to bridge the move from the familial to the conjugal home. Most jobs for women, however, enforced male dominance – remember it was Nora who took dictation and acted as an assistant to her male boss, a position that could take on parental overtones. Equality in the workplace, as in marriage, was generally an elusive concept. For working wives, this struggle was even more difficult. Indeed, having "tasted the good life," Nora was apparently no longer fit for the rigours of a nine-to-five job.

While still stressing gendered roles for men and women, particularly for husbands and wives within public and private domains, the working woman was a commonplace image in *Chatelaine* from 1928-1956. In the late 1920s and early 1930s, without posing a threat to the preference for home and family that most middle-class women were assumed to possess, the modern wage earning woman, whether married or single, was considered quite normal and acceptable in *Chatelaine*. Indeed, 1930s editor, Byrne Hope Sanders was a wife, mother and career woman.

The acceptance of working women that characterised the early part of the 1930s began to change towards the end of the decade, however. The recognition of the competence and ability of women workers in *Chatelaine* was replaced, by the late 1930s, with an increased emphasis on their femininity. Moreover, after the coming of war in 1939 when, irre-spective of marital status, an unprecedented number of women entered the paid workforce, *Chatelaine* projected the belief that once the war was over middle-class women would return to the family hearth. Indeed, despite Olive Russell's optimism about the postwar working opportunities for women noted in the epigraph of the 1946 interview, it was not until the mid-1950s that wage working women were again treated as normal and acceptable in *Chatelaine*. In the 1940s and early 1950s the case of working wives presented unique difficulties. And, as the 1945 story quoted at the beginning suggests, some modern women of the 1940s wanted to return to the home.

Some women's historians have posited that by the 1920s there was a growing acceptance in Canadian society of single, middle-class women working for wages. The majority of men and women assumed, however, that women would leave the working world on marriage.[4] As historian Paul Axelrod notes, in the 1920s many Canadian women were optimistic about their job opportunities. Their contributions to the war effort of 1914-1918 and their recent enfranchisement allowed them to look favourably on future employment possibilities. However, the social and economic upheaval after 1919 caused many of these ambitions to be stunted. Following the Great War, as a group, women were marginalized to low paying jobs in manufacturing and clerical work. Those women who chose "professional" careers were for the most part nurses and teachers and continued to struggle for proper recognition in terms of status and monetary rewards. While the situation was not ideal for either single or married women, the position of married women in the workforce was particularly difficult. In the 1920s, for example, women employed in the federal civil service – positions that had been only opened to their sex in the first decade of the twentieth century – were forced to resign from their positions upon marriage.[5]

In their general history of Canadian women, Alison Prentice, Paula Bourne, Gail Cuthbert Brandt, Beth Light, Wendy Mitchinson and Naomi Black conclude that, "If the 1920s were difficult years for women workers, the 1930s were disastrous."[6] Veronica Strong-Boag echoes this sentiment in *The New Day Recalled.* She cites provincial and federal laws that limited the employment of women and specifically targeted married women as unemployable.[7] In 1930s Canada, men and women were treated differently in the employment market and by federal and provincial relief agencies. While there is little consensus among historians as to the appropriate weight that gender, class, race and ethnicity should be given when analysing attitudes towards women's employment during the Great Depression, few would disagree that gender was an issue.[8]

There is no doubt that the realities of women's working lives in the interwar period were complex and multifaceted. Some of this diversity was reflected in the pages of *Chatelaine. Chatelaine,* however, was a magazine that generally expressed middle-class ideals of Canadian womanhood. Interestingly, for the most part, *Chatelaine*'s modern woman of the 1920s and 1930s often "worked," even though frequently she was married. *Chatelaine*'s working woman was usually relatively well educated and she was generally capable and confident. While work did seem to be a reality for *Chatelaine*'s modern women, more often than not these women held "jobs" outside of the home; few had "careers." The women in *Chatelaine* who aspired to careers in addition to marriage and motherhood usually realigned with middle-class ideals by (re)turning to full-time domesticity.

According to a number of articles in *Chatelaine,* one of the attributes of the modern woman of the late 1920s and early 1930s was that she was intelligent and capable of a university education.[9] In September 1929 *Chatelaine* ran an article about sending daughters off to college. In discussing the economics of this venture, the article read: "To the thoughtful parent, one of the encouraging signs of the age is that [waged] labor has become not only a fashion but a passion."[10] More middle-class families could now pursue this venture because of their daughters' earnings and this was an option that *Chatelaine* implicitly encouraged. Although such opportunities would not have been open to all readers, *Chatelaine* did assume that girls, as well as boys, should have the opportunity to go on to higher education. Space was also devoted to columns about educated career women. For example, in July 1929 a column entitled "Our Women Magistrates" was published and regular columns such as "The Family Budget" that began in 1931 and "Women in the World," which was started in 1932, were written for and about capable, competent women and proved to be long lasting features of the magazine.[11]

In reality, the educational opportunities afforded to women in the 1920s and 1930s were not that liberal. As Paul Axelrod notes in *Making a Middle Class*, university students in the 1930s were a select group of individuals who hoped that "university education would secure their place within the middle class."[12] He stresses, however, that there were far fewer opportunities afforded to women compared to men. Axelrod reasons that "…women were still expected to become full-time wives and mothers, and they received little support and faced many barriers if they challenged this destiny."[13] As Veronica Strong-Boag notes, most women who attended university selected an Arts major which prepared them for occupational opportunities open to their sex: "teachers, social workers, librarians, clerical workers, saleswomen, and wives." She also remarks that "To an important degree, higher education in general for middle-class girls was acceptable because it did not fundamentally threaten the primacy of the family headed by the male breadwinner." Some parents, particularly fathers, could be proud of their daughters' university education because, as the dad of a household science major put it, "They say you know that when a girl finishes that course, she gets her M.R.S."[14] Canadian middle-class women with a university education were still expected to embrace domesticity and be full-time wives and mothers.

But, *Chatelaine's* modern woman did not "need" a man. All women were still expected to want marriage in the future, but there was no longer the assumption that women would go directly from the parental home to the conjugal home. For example, in a 1929 article that addressed women in need of a New Year's resolution, the author of "Starting Over Again" suggested to a recently jilted stenographer that:

> Even if love never comes your way again there is much in the world for you to see and do and enjoy. This is not the Victorian age when maidens were supposed to go into a decline or at least be "sicklied o'er" with the pale cast of melancholy because of a broken engagement. The modern woman girds herself afresh for the combat and steps out to make her own place in the sun, dependent on no man.[15]

The young stenographer was clearly a woman of the new age. She was independent; instead of relying on a man, she appears to have spent much of her free time with other, presumably single, businesswomen.

"Starting Over" gave quite different advice to an already married middle-aged invalid. She was directed to increase her interest in her husband and children's activities, to stop complaining of her aches and pains and above all to wear "becoming negligees" and keep her hair, skin and hands carefully groomed. Her primary goal, according to the columnist, should be to keep her husband. Whether consciously or unconsciously the author was helping to define the "new" modern young woman in contrast to women of a previous generation. As was shown in chapter three, *Chatelaine's* modern young woman of the early 1930s married on her terms, if and when she wanted to. Husbands were not a necessity. Many older women may have had trouble grasping this new attitude and perhaps they were not in the position to exercise this choice.

With the depression of the 1930s, unemployment among men and women grew and this prompted many to question having women in the labour force. The general view in the middle-classes was that women were economically dependent on fathers or husbands. Those who worked did so for luxury items. Consequently, women were urged to give up their paid employment and return to the home. As US historian Alice Kessler-Harris records, this view was expressed in most popular American magazines of the 1930s. Particularly vulnerable were working wives because many assumed they were contributing to a double-income family while other families survived (or did not) solely on relief. As Kessler-Harris notes, the public pressure in the fight for women to leave paid employment in the US seemed to be initially successful. For example, in the first few years of the depression twice as many women lost their jobs as men. This trend was short-lived, however; some employers preferred to hire women because they could pay them less and they were less likely to demand a raise or improved working conditions. Additionally, the stratification of jobs into male and female sectors continued to alienate men from being secretaries, stenographers, typists, and clerks. In fact, Kessler-Harris concludes that the depression actually pulled married women into the labour market as well as increasing the percentage of single women who worked for wages.[16] In the Canadian context too, as Veronica Strong-Boag notes, the misogyny of the 1920s was exacerbated by the depression of the 1930s. But, like Kessler-Harris, Strong-Boag concludes that the depression ultimately confirmed a place for women in the workforce.[17] The popular view, however, as Alison Prentice, Paula Bourne, Gail Cuthbert Brandt, Beth Light, Wendy Mitchinson and Naomi Black articulate was that married women should vacate paid positions and "the appropriateness even of single women working for wages widely conceded during the 1920s was called into question."[18] The unemployment insurance debates of the mid-1930s Ruth Roach Pierson argues reveal that the Canadian federal government also assumed women were dependent on fathers or husbands.[19]

Chatelaine, however, did not simply project "popular" assumptions about women and work. In the 1930s, *Chatelaine* did not suggest that Canadian women should leave the workforce. It was assumed that women were first and foremost wives and mothers – and given the economic hardships of the business world, many considered the "job" of wife to be the best position a woman could have. There was, however, a growing demand expressed by women in *Chatelaine* to support those women who worked for wages. Indeed, in the "Reader's Last Word" column of the March 1934 issue a reader in Ontario stated explicitly "To Canadian women who belong to the business world, Canada makes one call. We homemakers should at all times be sympathetic and loyal to those women."[20] This article expressed a desire for solidarity among all women, working or not, to uphold (or indeed to establish) the gender-less right of women to paid employment. While sympathy may have been bestowed upon women who had to work for wages, at least some of *Chatelaine*'s readership felt that middle-class women's right to employment should be distinct from marital status.

High unemployment of men because of the depression nonetheless brought the issue of working women, particularly working wives, to the forefront.[21] There was some debate in the pages of *Chatelaine* during the depression about women working for wages. In an argument that was reminiscent of Byrne Hope Sanders' appeal for "bachelor girls" to leave the workforce, in the article "Go Home, Young Woman!" that appeared in September 1933, the author encouraged women to leave the paid labour force and return home. Too many men were out of work for women to be taking their place. While acknowledging that it would be "fantastic" to think that a law could pass through Parliament that would regulate the employment of women, the contributor stated that: "Today, I earnestly believe that there is a new patriotic call to women – a call to leave their jobs in industry and commerce – a call to sit down in favor of the million or so men in Canada who are out of work."[22] Notably, the accompanying pictorial suggested that it was working-class women who should leave their jobs.

Not all readers agreed, however, and this article provoked a series of vehement responses. Published two issues later they were appropriately grouped under the heading "Can You Shackle Women Again?" The majority of the respondents were infuriated by the suggestions made in the September article and the overwhelming answer to the question of whether women should be kept out of the paid labour force was an emphatic "no!"[23] One reply suggested that the author of "Go Home" was "backwards" in his thinking because he was a man, and a Quebecer – thus there existed the suspicion that he was not an English, Anglo-Saxon. Such stereotypical gender divides were regularly expressed in *Chatelaine*. These issues often developed into a "man" versus "woman" theme and could be carried through several months. But the reference to the author's provincial origin was unusual.[24] Another respondent to "Go Home" was also horrified by the proposal. She noted that in the past women had had to find a husband for the same reason that men looked for work: to support themselves. In no way would she support a return to such conditions.

However, there was one notable response from a self-styled "Victorian" that differed from the majority. This contributor, who, by deduction, obviously considered herself too old to be a modern woman of the 1930s, linked women leaving the job market with women's patriotic duty during the Great War. The "Victorian" stressed that if women did go "home," then men had to share their earnings with them. In no way, however, did the "Victorian" support a return to a scenario where women were economically dependent on men. And she recognized that, "...since women have tasted the sweets of independence, it will need great sacrifice and self-denial to step down."[25]

Such direct comparison of women's positions during the depression and their experiences in war was common in *Chatelaine*. Among other things, it served to connect women of different generations. At the same time, however, the modern woman of the 1930s was different from her mother and grandmother. It was also clear that there were fundamental differences between the wartime conditions of 1914-1918 and the 1930s.

A number of contributors to *Chatelaine* recognized that the depression did create unique problems for single working girls, particularly if their beaus were unemployed. An article "They Won't Let the Woman Pay!" that appeared in March 1934, chronicled a conversation between a young working woman and her older aunt. The young woman was upset because her boyfriend would not allow her to pay for them to go out. Once again generational differences were underscored. The young woman complained about her boyfriend: "He's got a bad case of unemployment, with complications of pride, stubbornness and general mulishness. ..." Her aunt counselled: "It's the war-time position all over again. You were playing dolls and your generation didn't worry about keeping up the morale of men. But your generation has the task at hand now, without the aids of excitement, mob emotion, and the fortifying feeling which the men had that they really were doing a big job." During the Great War women took jobs because of a shortage of "man" power. Their employment was considered viable only so long as that emergency lasted. Women who worked for wages in the 1930s were not responding to a national emergency. They were a fact of life. In this scenario, the aunt suggested her niece partake in free activities, such as going for a walk, with her boyfriend. The young woman took her aunt's advice. In the end there was no mention of her leaving her paid position, but she concluded: "Evidently it does something to a man when the girl makes grand gestures instead of him. And I guess we girls still react to caveman stuff. We like a boy who puts us in our place, and won't let himself be wheedled."[26] The message was mixed. Women still wanted their man to be the more assertive of the couple, yet they were hesitant to leave jobs that offered them a degree of economic independence.

Reflecting the situation in Canada, many of the working women who appeared in *Chatelaine* were not necessarily in the labour force by choice. They were there because they had to support themselves or their families. Veronica Strong-Boag notes, "Girls of all classes were especially susceptible to the economic claims of family"; as the old song goes, "A son is yours until he weds; a daughter is yours forever."[27] *Chatelaine's* November 1929 editorial noted that daughters' contributions to supporting parents and extended family were often much greater than those of their brothers. Editor Byrne Hope Sanders offered the example of a female acquaintance who had both a daughter and a son. The son had left home to work in the city and save for a family of his own. The daughter stayed home and kept her "pernickety little job" because she felt her mother would be lonely without her. The financial burden of supporting the mother fell mostly on the daughter. However, as the editor put it: "...it is the son of whom the mother speaks constantly and pridefully. The daughter is just ... a good girl. But when the son's roses come on Mother's Day, the whole town is told of his wonders and his thoughtfulness and his kindness to an old mother."[28] Despite this discrepancy, and Sanders' obvious sympathy for the neglected daughter, she concluded that women should be honoured to serve their families because without obligations toward others, life would be meaningless.

Women who worked to support themselves or to support their families were not always single. The cover of the March 1930 issue of *Chatelaine* asked "What of the Wage Earning Wife?" There was some concern about the potential conflict between one's responsibilities as a wife and mother and working for wages. As Veronica Strong-Boag notes, "it was difficult" for women in the 1920s and 1930s "to know how to combine marriage and family with life in the paid labour force."[29] The author of *Chatelaine's* lead article, Helen Gregory MacGill, M.A., a female juvenile court judge, proposed that the new attention that this group was receiving was due to the increasing number of middle-class women in the workforce. MacGill was responding to the popular debates about barring women from paid employment that were being voiced in many circles of Canadian society.[30] She noted that women had always worked even though they had not always received formal remuneration for their efforts. She argued that wage earning middle-class wives had brought the issue to the forefront because they represented the biggest challenge to traditional gender norms.[31] As Strong-Boag notes, women of ethnic minorities and poor women had been working for wages for generations, often while maintaining a family. But, in the Canadian middle-class, women were still expected to leave work upon marriage.[32] However, MacGill remarked that, "Employers often do not appear to share the same objection to the married woman employee or they would not engage her. On the contrary, in some of the Minimum Wage investigations, employers had asserted that they were glad to engage married women as they were 'more reliable and steadier on the job'."[33] Lobbying for the right of all women to take paid employment, she further suggested that there were many categories of married women. For example, she wondered if the term should be restricted to those with homes and husbands. And she asked whether deserted or divorced women with children, or women with sick, incompetent, or incapable husbands should be considered as married women. She also singled out the critics of working wives: single women and women with unemployed husbands. The author concluded that, "Being married or unmarried may be a sign of a certain attractiveness to or for the other sex, but it is not always an evidence of greater or lesser competence. ...The employer, if a good business man, looks for competence."[34]

The topic of working wives was further elaborated in that month's editorial. There the editor addressed what she called the "Modern Problem." Fuelled with facts gathered from a *Chatelaine* survey of a selected group of three hundred married women in business, Byrne Hope Sanders concluded: "the problem is a reality, and will be solved in spite of bitter prejudice!" While the message from the editor was short, it was to the point. In March 1930, Sanders approved of working wives.[35]

A section called "Women in the World" that appeared in March 1932 again debunked the myth that married women entered the workforce for pleasure. Most needed the income. The case of women working at the University of Toronto was given as an example. *Chatelaine* reported that three years earlier, the university had decided to dismiss all of the married women on its staff except for those who were the sole support of families, wives of disabled husbands, or special experts. The results were that "out of the hundreds of women on the staff, just ten were affected."[36]

Images of women at work were common in *Chatelaine* in the late 1920s and early 1930s and projected the female labour force as competent and capable. The magazine often coupled these images with the expressed economic needs of women to support themselves and their families. The types of jobs described for women – as secretaries, stenographers and office workers for example – suggested that while these women may have worked for economic need, they were nonetheless middle-class. The question of the wage-earning wife was more controversial than that of single women. Working for pay outside of the home had been traditionally viewed in Canadian society as detrimental to women's "primary" positions as wives, mothers and homemakers.[37] *Chatelaine* challenged this. The magazine published material that highlighted the unique difficulties faced by working wives and mothers and, for the most part, ultimately reinforced the traditional belief that a wife's place was in the home. However, those articles also aired the frustrations faced by women torn between the duties of being a wife, and more often than not a mother, and their desire or need to have a job outside of the home. *Chatelaine* sympathized with these concerns.

Chatelaine's acknowledgement in the early 1930s that some women – occasionally even wives and mothers – wanted careers was exceptional for the period. In most cases *Chatelaine's* modern working woman was employed in a nine-to-five "job." There were, however, exceptions and these again speak to the middle-class nature of the magazine. Interestingly, the images of working women, particularly "career" women, found in *Chatelaine* are somewhat at odds with Deirdre Beddoe's conclusions about the images of British women in the interwar period. Beddoe suggests that: "Only feminist magazines [in Britain] advocated the role of career women, and although such small publications celebrated women's achievements and triumphed at each new step forward, it was as though they were whistling in the wind and their thin voices drowned out by the roar that 'women's place is in the home'."[38] While *Chatelaine* was by no means a small publication by Canadian standards, the maternal feminist views of its editors were evident in its content, particularly with regard to career options for women. Moreover, during the depression, to underscore the fact that women could (and should) work for personal fulfilment rather than out of economic necessity was suggestive of equality based feminism.[39]

For example, in July 1928, *Chatelaine* ran an article called "Only a Super-Woman can Juggle Both a Family and a Career." The article told the story of a new bride struggling to keep up with her writing career and trying to balance this with her new duties at home. Before she had married, this young woman had felt quite superior when she thought of the married women who had faded from the workforce. "Yet we sometimes look askance when some young woman whose work once showed promise sinks quietly beneath the waves of matrimony. 'Spineless,' we [single working women] think secretly, and we feel perhaps a bit superior that we are single and splendidly carving out our lives." In 1928, as a newlywed, the author was now more perceptive to the plight of working wives. She noticed that when a working wife "found her strength unequal to two jobs, she gave up the least important and died from the professional world with no one to blow Last Post over her but her family and a few close friends."[40] Careers were decidedly secondary to family. The author, however, initially refused to allow her new position as a wife to derail her from her dream. But as she came to realize, working wives faced significant challenges. Balancing work and maintaining a home and family was difficult. Working wives were also at a disadvantage compared to single women and men in the workforce. Married women were expected to complete all of the household duties in addition to working for pay. An article that appeared in 1934 put it quite succinctly: "one of the chief handicaps of women in business is that they have no wives."[41]

The situation was made even more difficult when a working wife was also a mother. In February 1932, *Chatelaine* ran a short story called "A Woman's way." In the story, the protagonist, Iris, married and continued to work. But she then discovered that she was pregnant and had to decide what to do. As Iris explained it to her husband Bob: "I want a baby, now that it has come to us. ... It isn't right to dodge it."[42] At the same time she also had her career. She continued, "Since I have gone so far and have so many years of education and am, as I stand now, such a highly developed product with such a large investment of time and capital in me, I am more important by far than a life just beginning on a purely instinctive basis."[43] Iris knew that they could not be an old-fashioned family. The couple decided to hire a professional caregiver to look after their son and Iris would continue with her career in advertising. The dilemma continued, however. When the child became ill, Bob suggested that Iris stay home and take care of him. She retorted: "Why don't you do it? You are his father? I gave nearly a year absolutely out of my life to bringing him into the world and getting him started, it's your turn."[44]   In the end, and to her chagrin, Iris who was even referred to as 'Miss' Newman professionally, became a stay-at-home wife and mother. Yet the final lines captured Iris' continuing dissatisfaction. Iris said to her son: "Mother loves you better than her life. But oh my own, grow up, grow up, grow up fast, so that mother can have another chance before she dies."[45]

For the first eight years of its existence *Chatelaine* treated the modern wage-earning woman as normal and acceptable, irrespective of her marital status. She was independent and relatively well educated. During the depression, at the same time that many in Canadian society challenged the position of women as wage earners, the magazine underscored women's need and right to support themselves and their families.

In the latter half of the 1930s, the images of modern Canadian working women in *Chatelaine* began to change. An increasing portion of the news printed in the magazine covered the deteriorating situation in Europe. *Chatelaine* began to project the belief that another world war was inevitable. Not surprisingly, the magazine highlighted the role of women in maintaining the peace. The magazine also began to emphasize the importance of women's volunteer work over their paid employment. This may have been a result of the decreasing opportunities available for women to find waged work. Noticeably, however, volunteer work was traditionally the purview of middle-class women and may also have served to reinforce traditional gender norms during a time of growing national anxiety. When the wage-earning woman appeared in articles and commentary, the magazine now concentrated on her "feminine" qualities and it also began to suggest that some jobs were unsuitable for their sex.

With the heightened political tensions in Europe, *Chatelaine* pushed its readership to take an active role in working for the nation. As wives, mothers and homemakers, women were encouraged to "work" for peace largely from the private sphere and generally as volunteers. An article that appeared in June 1936 asked the question: "Do you think modern women live in a futile round of pleasure?" The article described middle-class women who had lived a half-century earlier and had felt the need to spend their free time in idle pursuits to prove that they did not need to work. But times had changed and now *Chatelaine*'s modern woman was no longer defined purely by economic independence like those of an earlier time. Indeed, some middle-class women needed to work for wages in the 1930s to support themselves and more often than not their families.

Middle- and upper-class Canadian women continued to join clubs, how-ever. In the 1930s, women's clubs were often more than just social milieus. Many women, witness to the devastation of the depression, were driven by the objective of bettering their communities, their country and the world.[46] Many club members were maternal feminists. For some women club work was their sole pursuit; others did it in addition to paid employment.

An explicit connection between the value of women's clubs and the deteriorating political situation in Europe was presented in *Chatelaine* in the opening lines of the 1936 article: "A Hitler couldn't send Canadian women 'back to the kitchen' and lock the door on them. He would find himself faced with opposition from some 500,000 women organized in 1,800 clubs..."[47] The article underscored the value of women's volun-teer organizations, traditionally the purview of the middle and upper classes. It cited the accomplishments of women's clubs that grew from the desire "to further the application of the Golden Rule to society, custom and law."[48] As the article stated, women could work together in volunteer organizations to further the interests of their sex and society at large. This article was a clear expression of 1930s maternal feminist beliefs.

Parallels in *Chatelaine* were also sometimes drawn between women's work in the house as wives, mothers and homemakers, and the more male dominated field of international relations. Women were assumed to be expert "diplomats" and "strategists" of the home. Indeed, an October 1936 article by Helen Campbell began: "The real diplomats of the world are not those exalted statesmen who manage the affairs of nations." "No sir," Campbell continued, "they're the mothers of families who bring up their children in the way they should go, and keep peace in the house while they are doing it."[49] Certainly, as the vocabulary of this article suggests, women were expected to raise the nation to be peace-minded and this started in the home.

If peace eluded them, however, women were expected to band together and fight for national survival. In "Women at War" that appeared in January 1938 the author, Lieutenant-Colonel (LCol) Fraser Hunter described the military training that many women were going through in China and Japan. Hunter asked if Canadian women would be so prepared and able if their homeland was invaded. For the time being, however, Canadian women needed to concentrate even harder on maintaining the peace. As the LCol wrote, "With so many women fighting for their lives and protection of their homes throughout the world today, is it not more imperative than ever that women should determine to fight tenaciously for peace?"[50] To best fulfil this task women were expected to organize themselves into clubs and volunteer their energies in this pursuit. Men were absent from this apparently crucial and imperative struggle.

Surprisingly, the images of women and work that appeared in *Chatelaine* from 1936 to 1939 foreshadowed those of the war years when women entered the paid labour force in unprecedented numbers. Between 1939 and 1944, the number of women working for wages swelled from 22.7 per cent to 33.1 per cent of the non-institutionalised female population fourteen years and older. [51] Some women even entered occupations previously restricted to men, such as operators of heavy machinery; many women worked as labourers on farms; and some joined the women's auxiliaries. Ruth Roach Pierson remarks that "By autumn 1944 the number of women working full-time in Canada's paid labour force was twice what it had been in 1939, and that figure of between 1,000,000 and 1,200,000 did not include part-time workers or the 800,000 women working on farms." She continues, "furthermore, most of Canada's three million adult women were contributing volunteer labour to the war effort. And by war's end, nearly 50,000 had served in the Women's Services of the Canadian armed forces."[52] Nonetheless, *Chatelaine*'s modern working girl of the war years was in many ways far more traditional than her depression era sister. Volunteer work was often prioritized over paid employment for women and *Chatelaine* gave little attention to rural work. Moreover, during the Second World War, being physically attractive became of paramount importance, particularly for the working woman. Indeed, attractiveness and work ability became directly linked in *Chatelaine*. From 1939 to 1945, women were also given the responsibility of keeping up men's morale. Jeffrey A. Keshen suggests that these changes helped to reassure the Canadian population "that as women moved into new social roles ... very little was in fact changing."[53] Certainly, in the case of Great Britain scholars like Gerard J. De Groot for example, conclude that "The message was clear: [British] women might do men's jobs, but they remained women."[54]

An article titled "What Can I do Now," that appeared in November 1939, suggested areas where Canadian women could help in the war effort. For the most part these grew out of traditional roles and skills: knitting and sewing; home nursing and first aid; lorry and ambulance driving; and keeping up morale. It was even remarked that "the greatest job of every woman at the moment is to see that her own house is in order."[55] The question of going overseas did come up, however. The author predicted that registered nurses would be among the first group of women in demand. Although Lotta Dempsey, a regular contributor to *Chatelaine* and short-term editor in the 1950s, suggested that women might be invited to join in the Army, Navy and Air Force auxiliaries in England "as they were before," the bottom line was that men had the immediate situation under control.[56] Yet, despite these obvious gender divides, the article concluded: "Today women share and share alike with men ... in war as in peace...."[57]

On one hand, *Chatelaine* defined the modern working woman of the 1940s as equally capable as her male counterpart. This was partially in response to the war emergency, but it also represented a natural growth of the modern working woman of the 1930s. Simultaneously, however, the magazine portrayed the modern working woman of the 1940s as subordinate. Herein lay the paradox; in *Chatelaine* a working woman was somehow both equal and inferior to a working man. The jobs that women performed stressed their equality to men in terms of ability, but the emphasis that the magazine placed on their appearance and the temporary nature of their jobs suggested that they were not being evaluated in the same way as men.

To the readers of *Chatelaine*, it seemed that of most importance for single girls during the war was to be attractive to boys in uniform. This point was exemplified in the opening paragraph of the March 1942 article "Bright Girl." The article reported on the lives of working women. It began: "'Look,' said the boy in air force blue, one foot just inside my office door. 'Will you say a word or two to a lot of nice girls who think that because they're being useful these days they ought to look that way, too? ..."[58] The article suggested that working women were a novelty, and it recommended that women should continue to dress attractively for men, irrespective of practicality. A few months later *Chatelaine* gave fashion advice to war workers in its "Fashion Shorts" column. Admitting that slacks were necessary for war work, it continued: "When a gal is out from the factory she wants a pretty dress to go places and do things. ..."[59] Indeed, in *Chatelaine*, women's work clothes were often described as necessary evils to be counterbalanced at every opportunity with distinctly feminine attire.

By 1942, the question concerning women's war clothes was grave enough for the Department of Munitions and Supplies for Canada to run an advertisement in *Chatelaine* featuring a young woman in trousers and two middle aged onlookers, with the caption "Please Don't stare at my Pants: Brave men shall not die because I faltered!" The advertisement asked, "Would you like to know why I wear trousers like the men when I go about the streets?" And answered, "Because I am doing a man's job for my country's sake." It explained that working women demonstrated "the revival of the heroic spirit of the pioneers who laid the foundation of our country. The women folk in those days stood shoulder to shoulder with their men. ...Today these women are again standing behind their men..."[60] Through keeping a distinction between men and women's work and establishing an historical precedent for exceptions to this gendered division of labour, this advertisement tried to make women war workers acceptable.

While most Canadians applauded all contributions to the war effort, women workers who challenged traditional gender norms might not be as warmly welcomed, especially by those of an older generation.[61] Indeed, the middle-aged onlookers illustrated a generational difference between the young women of 1940 and those who had come of age during the interwar period. The two bystanders were probably old enough to remember and appreciate the experiences of the Great War and their ideas of gender norms had been constructed in an earlier decade. Their presence also highlighted the challenge that women war workers were making to social norms. Moreover, the mere existence of the advertisement highlights the pervasiveness of the question of middle-class women in outfits appropriate for manual labour. For *Chatelaine*, a common way to resolve the issue of women workers and their proliferation into the workforce was to emphasize their femininity and subordination to men. It is interesting to note that the pioneer women referred to in the advertisement stood "shoulder to shoulder with their men" whereas the Canadian women of World War Two were standing behind their men.

As Ruth Roach Pierson argues, Canadians found women in military uniform particularly jarring. She suggests that despite the apparent "gains" made by women during the war, the popular press emphasized women's femininity. According to Pierson, this association rested on beliefs formed in pre-war Canada in which masculinity included the military traits of hardness, toughness, action, and brute force; femininity on the other hand was definitely unmilitary and included attributes of softness, fragility, passivity and gentleness.[62] Jeffrey Keshen, however, cautions readers about drawing false conclusions concerning the wartime images of women at work and the emphasis on their femininity. He states that "Such messages could certainly be viewed as trivializing women's work by suggesting that women's feminine traits were more important than their abilities." But, he continues, "they could also be interpreted as reassuring a woman that she need not sacrifice her sexual appeal by taking on physically demanding, typically male jobs; in other words, this was not an 'either-or' proposition."[63] Yet, in his discussion on the images of women in the military, Keshen is quick to add that there was a noticeable concern that "women in uniform would become masculine in appearance or temperament." Even more so than for female civilian workers, an emphasis on femininity was often used to counterbalance the fear in Canadian society that women in the military would become masculine.[64] Many historians have argued that this was also the case in Britain and France.[65]

Indeed, to *Chatelaine*, and to many in Canada at the time, the image of women in uniform seems to have been particularly jarring. Rather than highlighting their competence, many articles and advertisements emphasized military women's femininity. For example, in November 1943, one article remarked that: "Prize-winners in health and beauty, these days, are the girls in the Services. Just watch them as they swing down the street, trim, smart and clear-eyed."[66]

With the United States entering the war in December 1941, American advertisements in *Chatelaine* increasingly dealt with war-related topics and women's femininity was often a central element of the campaign. In 1944, the American cosmetics company Tangee ran an advertisement for lipstick with the heading "We are Still the Weaker Sex" over the backdrop of seven wallet-sized pictures of women in uniform. The advertisement continued: "Many of us may be serving shoulder to shoulder with America's fighting men – but we are still the weaker sex... It's still up to us to appear as lovely and as alluring as possible. ..."[67] *Chatelaine* suggested that women were expected to be interested in meeting men and men were presumed to be attracted to those who took great care with their appearance – often heavily made up and carefully dressed. Women needed to focus on their appearance to "catch" a man, whereas men were free to devote their time and energy to their work. Furthermore, describing women as the weaker sex explicitly subordinated them to their male counterparts.

Material concerning the roles of military women would also sometimes stress traditional female tasks. In November 1943 an announcement appeared with the caption "Wanted: 1, 000 Girls...." The segment continued: "There's woman's work to be done for the Navy... It's cooking, and laundering, and waiting on the men of Canada's navy... It's keeping them well fed, clean and comfortable... They want eager, ambitious young women who enjoy homemaking and housekeeping. ..."[68] The subordination of women to their male counterparts was blatant. So too was the reinforcement of traditional gender roles in the kind of work women were asked to do – a phenomenon that had been equally apparent during World War One.[69] Indeed, the distinction between "women's work" and "working women" was often blurred. Moreover, this advertisement called for young women, not mothers. Motherhood was often associated with the ability to be a good nurse and caregiver, but the Canadian government recruited young, single women to serve in its auxiliaries.

In *Chatelaine*, it was not enough for the modern working woman of the early 1940s to be attractive; she had to be cheerful and keep up morale too. During the war women were encouraged to support each other while their men were away. They were also expected to supply the men overseas with cheerful news from home and accounts about how well they were doing. However, simultaneously they were supposed to maintain their dependence on the opposite sex. The images of working women in *Chatelaine* in feature articles, advertisements and fiction during the war demonstrate all of these qualities, despite their seemingly contradictory natures.

In a quarter-page section on women's war work that appeared in September 1940, the message to women was to spread cheerfulness. It read: "Don't spread rumors but do spread cheer. 'Chins up, keep smiling,' is the message our Canadian soldiers often send to their best gals. These men know the value of a smile and a cheerful word and how such small things can help the morale of the people."[70] In September 1943, *Chatelaine* published an advertisement encouraging women to write cheerful letters to the men overseas. In part, it read:"…letters from home are treasures! Make sure he gets those letters. Newsy letters, happy letters, cheerful letters, from you, and from every member of the family. He cannot get too many! They cannot be too cheerful!"[71] There was no mention of writing to the women overseas – a silence that was also apparent in the April 1944 editorial that dealt with the same subject.[72] The editor discussed the morale of fighting "men" and educated women about what types of parcels and letters to send to them.

The readers of *Chatelaine* were well aware, however, of the work that women were doing during the war. For example, to assist women, the magazine offered a regular feature section called "Meals of the Month" which offered menus for each day of the month; in 1942, this section temporarily became a brown-bag lunch planner for working women. Moreover, a semi-regular column from 1939 to 1945 called "Women's War Work," featured several women each month contributing to the war effort. In November 1940, for example, a collage of pictures of women working for the war effort appeared under the caption:"Sew, shoot, drill, study, save – so run some of the verbs at the core of the 'doing sentence' of Canadian women at war. With a steadily rising sense of efficiency, women are finding a multitude of ways in which to prepare themselves to be of service to their country…."[73]

Recognizing the growing numbers of married and single women in the workforce did not mean that *Chatelaine* portrayed these women as completely independent or autonomous. Despite the title of the July 1942 article "Dear Men: We Miss you but We're Doing All Right…" the content underscored women's dependence and "need" for a husband, (as chapter three argues). The general theme was that women should

"...work out our own well-balanced pattern of life for the duration, so that when peace and victory bring our husbands back again, we (and they) can count on picking up the threads of a normal, happy marriage."[74] Wartime work for women was clearly being interpreted as an anomaly. The article continued with descriptions of what individual women were doing for the war effort, like working in munitions factories, yet it ultimately reinforced their roles as wives and mothers. The reader was introduced to one young munitions worker, "still a slip of a girl, though she has been married for nine years," as if there was a connection between a woman's size and the number of years that she had been married. Although the young woman was proud of the fact that she was able to take over a man's job, the author made it clear that, all the while, this young mother dreamt of the return of her husband, moving to a bungalow and of having another child.[75] All of her ambitions reinforced traditional gender roles for women.

During the Second World War it was undeniable that women were in the workforce in a higher concentration than ever before and this led some contributors to question what would happen at the end of the war.[76] This topic was broached in *Chatelaine's* September 1944 editorial. The wartime editor, Mary Etta Macpherson, asked: "...when the emergency has passed, and peace is established, what will happen to this great mass of voluntary womanpower?" She queried, "Will it be permitted to dissolve and scatter quickly back to the interminable bridge parties of pre-war days, and to the club groups with their 'papers' on Elizabethan dramatists and their succession of tea hostesses at flower-decked tables?" Macpherson obviously feared that the peace activist club days of 1936 might be replaced in the post-World War Two period by a return to Victorian standards. Alternatively, however, she asked, "Or will the present hard-won sense of responsibility and discipline, and the proved capabilities at a score of jobs, be utilized and further developed?"[77]

The women who filled wartime positions represented a different group of women than those of the previous generation. They did not work only because of a need to support themselves. They were working for their country. They had more employment opportunities than their mothers had had and they had learned a lot. But there was no certainty that the situation would continue in the postwar years.

Macpherson acknowledged that only women themselves could answer the above question and their choices would have "repercussions down the years in this Dominion." In line with maternal feminist beliefs, she suggested that women's postwar energies should be focused on community work. As she described: "the cultural study groups have a virtually unscratched field of opportunity in community beautification: the elimination of local ugliness ... can do more for the spirit and mental contentment than a hundred sterile discussions of poetry."[78] The editor did not broach the subject of women and paid labour in the postwar period. She described the unprecedented gains that women had made during the war in the field of paid employment; but she also encouraged her middle-class readers to concentrate their postwar energies in volunteer work, specifically community work.

Chatelaine's modern working woman of the war years was first and foremost a woman. She was feminine. She was also often a wife and a mother. And she worked to fulfill her patriotic duty. In the postwar period a new idea of modernity emerged. After five years of hard labour, some middle-class women questioned the appeal of wage work. They had not worked to challenge gender norms, they had worked out of a sense of patriotic duty. Many considered that their war work was temporary, a conclusion that Alison Prentice et al. share in the "Bren Gun Girl and the Housewife Heroine,"[79] as does M. Susan Bland in her study on images of women in advertising in *Maclean's*.[80]

As the wartime need for female labour eased, women were split about where their place in society should be and what type of access they wanted to the workforce. There were many issues concerning the employment of women in the postwar period. Some women were determined not to completely lose access to this domain; however, they were also paradoxically trying to create the "ideal" middle-class world for which men had died.[81] According to *Chatelaine*, this world, more often than not, included traditional gender norms that limited women to the home and to volunteer positions while encouraging male dominance of the workforce. Alison Prentice, Paula Bourne, Gail Cuthbert Brandt, Beth Light, Wendy Mitchinson and Naomi Black, however, argue that throughout the 1940s in Canada, "more and more women entered the public realm previously identified as male, while the confinement of adult women to the home lessened."[82] But not all historians are convinced that women's place in the workforce was immediately improved as a result of their wartime contributions to the labour market. For example, Jeffrey Keshen argues that while women proved their ability in the workforce between 1939 and 1945, it was still several decades before their gains would be recognized by legislation such as "equal pay for equal work."[83] Pierson also points to the fact that women's participation in the paid workforce began to plummet in 1946 and only climbed back to its 1945 level in 1966.[84] However, she does observe that in spite of the reduced overall size of women in the workforce, married women continued to represent a large proportion of the female labour force.[85] Married women who worked for wages, particularly if they were also mothers, nonetheless faced many challenges. As Joan Sangster notes, "For women in the 1950s June Cleaver remained the dominant popular image of motherhood, despite its incongruity with many women's lives."[86] Doug Owram states it boldly in the case of middle-class Canadians: "Married women with children were not supposed to work."[87] How World War Two affected the employment and image of working women remains debatable;

in *Chatelaine*, that the war changed the image of modern working women is undeniable.

In the postwar years, *Chatelaine* appeared to return to its interest in and support of the modern working woman that had characterized the pre-war years. There remained the assumption that women would voluntarily leave paid employment, especially if married and the importance of volunteer work continued to be stressed. For those women who continued with waged work, the "double day" was still a reality. However, being modern no longer meant having or wanting to have a profession or to work for wages. As the young woman had noted to her mother in the epigraph at the beginning of this chapter, "This is my generation. Yours earned the right to careers. ... [Ours] earned the right not to have a career, if we don't want it."[88] After the Second World War, the images of the modern working woman in *Chatelaine* continued to be complex and the messages about and to this group of women remained mixed.

The editors and contributors to *Chatelaine* in the postwar period were not sure what they thought of the working wife. In the November 1947 editorial, "Husband's Jobs and Working Wives" the topic was addressed from the perspective of working wives taking jobs away from deserving husbands. The editor suggested that this "depression era fear" was no longer warranted. Byrne Hope Sanders explained that the position of the working wife was in no way enviable. Following business hours she was expected to do all of the housework too.[89] For some, this led to assumptions that, as in the 1920s and early 1930s, girls would leave the work force shortly after their marriage. However, in her editorial six months later, titled, "Unhappy Wives," Sanders lamented that: "Progress has given our girls a chance for education in the professions; in the arts; in business. Women make brilliant students in all those phases of work." But she concluded that: "at marriage the majority must put this promise of personal expression away, and turn their talents into housework."[90] The editor seemed saddened by this fact. But, once again the message was mixed. Women were reminded of the career opportunities open to them. It was also assumed that women would marry and that they would then leave their profession.

Within two years, however, not only did Sanders take it for granted that wives were increasingly in the workforce she apparently saw no problem with this development. In her column in July 1950, Sanders remarked that more women were working after marriage. She stipulated that the "modern way of life" held such a high material standard that two wage earners were needed to support a family. She did, however, add two caveats: women should work only if they could manage both a home and a career; and only if they wanted to work.[91]

These changing views by a single editor over the course of only two years illustrate the fluctuating image of modern working women, especially working wives, during the post-Second World War period. *Chatelaine's* readers no longer worked to provide for necessities as they sometimes had in the 1930s. They now apparently worked for luxuries. As Alison Prentice, Paula Bourne, Gail Cuthbert Brandt, Beth Light, Wendy Mitchinson and Naomi Black note in relation to post-World War Two working conditions for women, "…most married women in the paid labour force could not choose to quit their jobs. It was essential for them to work to maintain their families' standard of living in an increasingly consumer-oriented society."[92] *Chatelaine* reminded women in January 1947 that "Two Careers in One Family? It <u>Can</u> Be Done." The precedent had been set: "Thousands of Canadian women did double duty on home and career fronts during the war years. Today many of them (especially those with professional training) are carrying on – competently, happily, profitably."[93]

12

Yet, the wartime conditions of women and work did not always fit postwar ideals regarding working wives. Even for the working woman, home and family were still the most important things in their lives. But at least some could balance both. An April 1948, article titled "$25,000-a-Year Girl" described the life of real estate saleswoman named Muriel May. Although hardly a girl at thirty-two years of age, Muriel was considered exceptional because of her high income. When discussing her career, "Mrs. May disclaims any suggestion that she uses her looks or femininity to sell to the male half of the partnership. 'It wouldn't work', she says bluntly. 'I know it is a bit of a shock at times when people come into the office and meet a female salesperson, but no man is going to be glamourized into buying a home. I sell to [married] women. ...."[94] Men may have, by and large, been the bread winners, but often their wives controlled the purse strings concerning matters of hearth and home. Perhaps this stated separation from traditional gender roles and the fact that Muriel did not use her femininity to sell homes made the author feel it was necessary to note that: "In spite of a busy social life, which takes in just about every smart party in Vancouver, Mrs. May has had time to teach her teen-ager [fourteen-year-old daughter] to cook and learn the many angles of housekeeping and hostessing."[95] Constant attention was drawn to her marital status in order to assure readers that although *Mrs.* May was an exceptional career woman, she was also a good wife and a mother.

The single working girl also had a high standard to maintain. In the February 1948 article "Would You Be Hired or Fired," a businessman is quoted as having said: "Of course, we couldn't run the office without our little Miss Nimblewit" in reference to his private secretary.[96] While the term "nimblewit" (as opposed to "nitwit") suggests that the businessman valued his secretary's intelligence and ability, this was not clear in the rest of the article. Encouraging women to become a "Little Miss Nimblewit" themselves, the author provided readers with a list of "dos" and "don'ts" needed to become a good office secretary. Notably, the subject of appearance came third on the list, only behind carelessness and incompetence and, remarkably, before unpleasant personality, unnecessary absence, dallying on the job, trouble making and lack of loyalty.[97]

For modern working women in the postwar years, appearance was obviously still very important. In the article "Best Look Forward On Your First Job," May 1955, the issue of what to wear while at work was foremost: "Until now it hasn't mattered too much if your sweater sagged and your shoes are scuffed, but from this day forward you will, we hope, leave all the fine, free carelessness of your high school days back in the classroom. ..."[98] The transition from girl to young woman was apparently partially marked by how one dressed while at work.

This connection is not surprising given that "catching" a husband was sometimes identified as the driving force behind women working for wages. According to *Chatelaine* this was particularly true for women in the military.[99] The March 1953 article titled "The Air Force Puts Romance First" is a good example. The author, Mac Reynolds, described the women's training: "During these two months they have learned how to dance the Samba and how to make a wedding dress. They have been given a lingerie allowance and issued with deodorants." He also noted that: "...their barracks will boast cozy beaus' rooms where the airmen may court them... They are surely the most emancipated service women in history, for the Air Force has discovered that sex – the nice kind, mind you – can do more for service morale than all the tumbling for physical fitness in the curricula. ..."[100] This article neglected to report on any of the serious jobs that women in the Air Force were doing. Instead, in this piece on women and work, femininity and marriage were central. Of course this article was not immune to criticism. In May 1953 two readers' responses on the subject were published. One respondent wrote: "...The tommyrot you wrote may be true in rare cases, but the majority of us did not join up to rope a man, but to wear Her Majesty' uniform with pride, and to find security, adventure and most important, a career to be proud of."[101]

Chatelaine's modern working woman of the postwar years was largely a continuation of the magazine's working woman of the late 1930s and war years. Volunteer work was considered particularly important. Middle-class wives were not expected to work for wages unless, as was the case from 1939-1945, it was for a national emergency. The working mother was especially vulnerable to scrutiny. Whatever may have propelled a woman to work for wages after the Second World War she was expected and encouraged to look feminine and attractive while at work. After all, she just might "catch" a man.

Between 1928 and 1956 three broad images of modern working women were presented in *Chatelaine*. These images loosely coincide with the depression years, the Second World War and the postwar period. In its initial phase the magazine displayed working women as normal and highlighted their need for waged labour regardless of their marital status. Additionally, during the early 1930s, some images that *Chatelaine* published of working women further challenged traditional gender norms: women were not assumed to be content being only wives, mothers and homemakers. Some middle-class women pursued careers. More often than not, however, for these women home and family eventually overshadowed employment ambitions.

By 1936/1937 the magazine was already presenting a more traditional image of working women. Not just war but even the threat of war appears to have encouraged the Canadian popular press to publish more traditional images of women and their place in the world. In the late 1930s in *Chatelaine*, the value of volunteer work was underscored and, by 1939, femininity was emphasized over productivity in the workforce.

These changes lasted throughout the war despite – or perhaps because of – women entering the labour force in unprecedented numbers. Indeed, as M. Susand Bland argues, the housewife heroine remained an important image throughout the war years.[102] Between 1939 and 1945 *Chatelaine* considered the paid employment of middle-class women temporary. The ideal Canadian middle-class woman of the 1940s was a full-time wife, mother and homemaker and *Chatelaine* supported this image. This new image of working women in the early 1940s proved long lasting. Up to 1956, *Chatelaine* continued to stress the femininity and not the professionalism of working women. These emphases were particularly true in the case of working wives and mothers.

Endnotes

1   Veila Ercole, *Chatelaine*, November 1945, 38-39.

2   Reprinted in Jean Bruce, *Back the Attack! Canadian Women During the Second World War – at Home and Abroad* (Toronto: Macmillan of Canada, 1985), 166.

3   Beatrice Redpath, *Chatelaine*, March 1928, 20-21, 48, 50.

4   Deborah Gorham, *The Victorian Girl and the Feminine Ideal* (Bloomington: Indiana University Press, 1982); Mary Vipond "The image of Women in Mass Circulation Magazines in the 1920s," in Susan Mann Trofimenkof and Alison Prentice, (eds.), *The Neglected Majority: Essays in Canadian Women's History* (Toronto: McClelland and Stewart, 1977), 116; Katrina Srigley "In case you hadn't noticed!' Race, Ethnicity, and Women's Wage-Earning in a Depression-Era City" *Labour/ Le Travail* 55 (2005), 69-105; Paul Axelrod, *Making a Middle Class: Student Life in English Canada during the Thirties* (Montreal & Kingston: McGill-Queen's University Press, 1990), 37; and Veronica Strong-Boag, *The New Day Recalled: The Lives of Girls and Women in English Canada, 1919-1939* (Markham: Penguin Books, 1988).

5   Axelrod, *Making a Middle Class*, 37. Alison Prentice, Paul Bourne, Gail Cuthbert Brandt, Beth Light, Wendy Mitchinson and Naomi Black, *Canadian Women: A History* (Toronto: Harcourt Brace Jovanovich: 1996), 224-225. Some couples even kept their marriages a secret so that both partners could continue in federal employment.

6   Alison Prentice et al., *Canadian Women: A History*, 264.

7   Veronica Storng-Boag, *The New Day Recalled: Lives of Girls and Women in English Canada, 1919 – 1939* (Markham: Penguin Books Canada Ltd, 1988), 47-48.

8   For a summary of debates on this topic that were published in *Gender & History* see Katrina Srigley, "In case you hadn't noticed," 73-74. In this article Srigley outlines the debates: American historian Alice Kessler-Harris suggests that gender is given too much of a priority in evaluating discourses of working women in the 1930s; her Canadian couterpart, Margaret Hobbs, conversely argues that much of the rhetoric concerning the nature of women's employment in the 1930s came from a stress on women's domesticity, thus making gender of central importance to the debates. Ruth Roach Pierson also suggests that gender – and the preference for female domesticity – were at the heart of the unemployment insurance debates in Canada. See Ruth Roach Pierson, "Gender and the Unemployment Insurance Debates in Canada, 1934-1940," in A.D. Gilbert, C.M. Wallace, R.M. Bray, *Reappraisals in Canadian History, Post Confederation* (Scarborough: Prentice Hall Canada, Inc.), 336-367.

9   This could involve a formal university education for some, but certainly an informal interest in learning was assumed to exist within the readership. For example, a section called "educational" was created in June 1928 with the series "the Settling of Canada," by M.O. Hammond. An "Art" section also appeared early on that featured paintings by up and coming Canadian artists. (The "Educational" section disappeared in early 1929, and "Art" was removed in January 1931.)

10   Constance K. Seton, *Chatelaine*, September 1929, 26.

11   Anne Anderson Perry, "Our Women Magistrates," *Chatelaine*, July 1929, 11.

12   Axelrod, *Making a Middle Class*, 37.

13   Ibid., 36-37.

14   Strong-Boag, *The New Day Recalled*, 24-25. In 1930, women represented 23.5 per cent of undergraduate enrolment and 26.1 per cent of graduate. For data on university enrolment by sex in Canada see Ibid., 24.

15   Nancy Leigh, *Chatelaine*, January 1929, 34.

16   Alice Kessler-Harris, *Women Have Always Worked: An Historical Overview* (Old Wesbury: The Feminist Press, 1981), 138-141.

17   Strong-Boag, *The New Day Recalled*, 44-47.

18   Prentice et al., *Canadian Women: A History*, 264.

19   Pierson, "Gender and the Unemployment Insurance Debate," 337.

20   *Chatelaine*, March 1934, 84.

21   N.E.S. Griffiths writes that in 1935, "the question of married women

working had become a matter of considerable controversy. The debate, at this time, was not about why they worked but whether they ought to be encouraged to do so." N.E.S. Griffiths, *The Splendid Vision: Centennial History of the National Council of Women in Canada, 1890-1993* (Ottawa: Carleton University Press, Inc. 1993), 187,

22   Mederic Martin, *Chatelaine*, September 1933, 10.

23   *Chatelaine*, November 1933, 26.

24   Arguably, Quebec may have been behind the rest of the country in the rights granted to its female citizens, but *Chatelaine* generally tried to underscore Canadian unity and to minimize provincial differences. The reference might be interpreted as being expressive of the virulent way in which some Canadians viewed the rights of women to waged work in the early 1930s.

25   *Chatelaine*, November 1933, 26.

26   Isabel Turnbull Dingman, *Chatelaine*, March 1934, 26, 43.

27   Strong-Boag, *The New Day Recalled*, 48.

28   Byrne Hope Sanders, *Chatelaine*, November 1929, 16.

29   Strong-Boag, *The New Day Recalled*, 49.

30   See for example, Prentice et al., *Canadian Women: A History*, 264-265.

31   Helen Gregory MacGill, *Chatelaine*, March 1930, 8.

32   Veronica Strong-Boag, *"Janey Canuck": Women in Canada, 1919-1939* (Ottawa: The Canadian Historical Association, 1994), 8.

33   Helen Gregory MacGill, *Chatelaine*, March 1930, 8.

34   Ibid., 9.

35   *Chatelaine* often administered its own surveys by eliciting readers' responses to questions published in the magazine. In this instance, the survey results indicated that 80 per cent of working wives lived with their husbands. Of this group, 34 per cent earned more than their conjugal partner. Of all working wives who responded, 35 per cent were working to support themselves whereas 28 per cent were clearly not. Additionally, the survey revealed that 8 per cent of this group of women worked to live more comfortably, 8 per cent to support a mother, 2 per cent to meet liabilities, 13 per cent to assist in the education of the children and 4 per cent worked partly to support themselves. Of all working women, 58 per cent had children living with them, 38 per cent had no children and 5 per cent had children at boarding schools. It was also noted that 52 per cent of the women surveyed did housework after business hours. Detailed reports like this one allowed readers to draw some of their own conclusions from the data. They also provided quantitative evidence to support arguments made in the magazine. Byrne Hope Sanders, *Chatelaine*, March 1930, 16.

36   *Chatelaine*, March 1932.

37   Axelrod, *Making a Middle Class*, 37.

38   Deidre Beddoe, *Women Between the Wars, 1918-1939: Back to Home and Duty* (London: Pandora, 1989), 9.

39   Margaret Hobbs, "Equality and Difference: Feminism and the Defence of Women Workers during the Great Depression," in Wendy Mitchinson, Paula Bourne, Alison Prentice, Gail Cuthbert Brandt, Beth Light and Naomi Black, *Canadian Women: A Reader* (Toronto: Harcourt Brace & Company, Canada, 1996), 213-214.

40   Virginia Coyne Knight, *Chatelaine*, July 1928, 21.

41   Ibid.

42   Interestingly, this quote hints that abortion was a possible option.

43   A. DeFord Pitney, *Chatelaine*, February 1932, 2.

44   Ibid., 46.

45   Ibid., 48.

46   See for example, N.E.S. Griffiths, *The Splendid Vision*, 181-209.

47   Kathleen Ryan, *Chatelaine*, June 1936, 28.

48   Ibid.

49   Helen Campbell, *Chatelaine*, October 1936, 69.

50   Fraser Hunter, *Chatelaine*, January 1938, 11. This theme and article are elaborated on in the next chapter.

51   Jeffrey A. Keshen, *Saints, Sinners, and Soldiers: Canada's Second World War* (Vancouver: UBC Press, 2004), 149.

52   Pierson, *"They're Still Women After All,"* 9.

53   Keshen suggests that this message was prevalent in the public discourse but he does not discuss who might have originated the message. Keshen, *Saints, Sinners, and Soldiers*, 151.

54   Gerard J. De Groot, "'I Love the Scent of Cordite in Your Hair': Gender Dynamics in Mixed Anti-Aircraft Batteries during the Second Word War," *History* 82 (1997), 73.

55   Lotta Dempsey, *Chatelaine*, November 1939, 68.

56   Ibid., 11.

57   Ibid., 68.

58   Carolyn Damon, *Chatelaine*, March 1942, 43.

59   Kay Murphy, *Chatelaine*, November 1942, 31.

60   *Chatelaine*, March 1942, 1.

61   In the British context, see for example, Gerard J. De Groot, "'I Love the Scent of Cordite in your Hair,'" 73-92. In the Canadian Context see M. Susan

Bland, "Henrietta the Homemaker, and 'Rosie the Riveter': Images of Women in Advertising in *Maclean's* Magazine, 1939-50," *Atlantis* 8 (1983), 74-75, 77.

62   Pierson, *"They're Still Women After All,"* 129.

63   Keshen, *Saints, Sinners, and Soldiers,* 151.

64   Ibid., 178.

65   See for example: Beddoe, *Back to Home and Duty*; Pat Kirkham, "Beauty and Duty: Keeping Up the (Home) Front" in Pat Kirkham and David Thoms (eds.), *War and Culture: Social Changes and Changing Experience in World War Two* (London: Lawrence & Wishart, 1995); Gerard J. De Groot, "'I Love the Scent of Cordite in Your Hair': Gender Dynamics in Mixed Anti-Aircraft Batteries During the Second World War," *History* 82 (1997); and Grayzel, *Women's Identities at War.*

66   Adele White, *Chatelaine,* November 1943, 33.

67   *Chatelaine,* August 1944, back cover.

68   Author unknown, *Chatelaine,* November 1943, 55.

69   See for example: Beddoe, *Back to Home and Duty;* and Francois Thebaud, "Work, Gender, and Identity in Peace And War France, 1890 – 1930," in Billie Melman (ed.), *Borderlines: Gender and Identity in War and Peace* (New York: Routledge, Inc. 1998), 397-421.

70   Irene Todd, *Chatelaine,* September 1940, 28.

71   *Chatelaine,* September 1943, 66.

72   Mary Etta Macpherson, *Chatelaine,* April 1944, 90.

73   *Chatelaine,* November 1940, 12-13.

74   Mona Gould, *Chatelaine,* July 1942, 8.

75   Ibid.

76   Pierson wrote, "…The very increase in numbers of women in the labour force, from approximately 638,000 in 1939 to an estimated 1,077,000 by October 1, 1944, was regarded as a temporary phenomenon." Pierson, *"They're Still Women After All,"* 61.

77   Mary-Etta Macpherson, *Chatelaine,* September 1944, 80.

78   Ibid.

79   Alison Prentice, P. Bourne, G.C. Brandt, B. Light, W. Mitchinson and N. Black, "The Bren Gun Girl and the Housewife Heroine," in R. Douglas Francis and Donald B. Smith, eds., *Readings in Canadian History: Post-Confederation,* 3rd edition (Toronto: Hold, Rinehart and Winston of Canada, Limited), 440-462.

80   Bland, "Henrietta the Homemaker, and 'Rosie the Riveter', 61-86.

81   Although I am not forgetting than women also contributed to the war effort at home and overseas, in 1945 the focus in *Chatelaine* and Canadian

society generally, was on the return of the fighting men and an attempt at reclaiming a sense of "normalcy," even if this ideal pre-dated anything experienced in the decade prior to the war.

82   Prentice et al., *Canadian Women: A History*, 319.

83   Keshen, *Saints, Sinners, and Soldiers,* 170-171.

84   Pierson, *"They're Still Women After All,"* 215.

85   Ibid., 216.

86   Joan Sangster, "Doing Two Jobs: The Wage-Earning Mother, 1945-70," in Joy Parr (ed.), *A Diversity of Women: Ontario, 1945-1980* (Toronto: University of Toronto Press, 1995), 98-99.

87   Owram, *Born at the Right Time,* 251.

88   Veila Ercole, *Chatelaine*, November 1945, 38-39.

89   Byrne Hope Sanders, *Chatelaine*, November 1947, 2.

90   Byrne Hope Sanders, *Chatelaine*, April 1948, 2.

91   Byrne Hope Sanders, *Chatelaine*, July 1950, 3.

92   Prentice et al., *Canadian Women: A History*, 352.

93   Lotta Dempsey, *Chatelaine*, January 1947, 13.

94   Roland Wild, *Chatelaine*, April 1948, 5.

95   Ibid.

96   Lotta Dempsey, *Chatelaine*, February 1948, 26.

97   Ibid., 27.

98   Rosemary Boxer, *Chatelaine*, May 1955, 22.

99   In 1951, five years after the three wartime women's auxiliaries disbanded, "women were again recruited into military auxiliaries during the early phases of the Cold War and Canada's participation in the United Nations' 'police action' in Korea in 1950." By 1952 the air force had 3,133 women, in 1954 the navy had 1,307 and that same year the army had 349. Keshen, *Saints, Sinners, and Soldiers*, 192.

100   Mac Reynolds, *Chatelaine*, March 1953, 23.

101   D.L. Hayden, *Chatelaine*, May 1953, 3. The responses, however, were short and obscure in comparison to the original article.

102   Bland, "Henrietta the Homemaker, and 'Rosie the Riveter.'"

Chapter Six

Prescribing the "Ideal": Women, Nationalism and World Peace

What the Woman Citizen Should Know

Canadian Annual Review of Value to Every Citizen

...THAT the Canadian Annual Review, which was formerly edited and compiled by J. Castell Hopkins and which is so indispensable to all persons who wish to be well informed regarding contemporary history in Canada, has just been issued for 1927-28. It is now ably prepared by Mrs. J. Castell Hopkins and continues to be in great demand by business men, politicians, historians, librarians and all citizens interested in the progress of the Dominion from year to year.

Anne Anderson Perry
Chatelaine, November 1928[1]

Tell Us About England

Does everyone over there want to come to Canada, believing it to be the best place in the world? "Canada and Canadians lack artistic values. They are smug. They think their country has everything, but I couldn't live there. I would miss things that really matter to me – the ballet, art galleries, the theatre, intelligent conversation that isn't always superficial."

Margaret Ecker Francis
Chatelaine, September 1950[2]

197

Lipstick and High Heels:

In 1930, the Right Honourable Arthur Meighen, former Prime Minister of Canada, delivered an address before the World Alliance for International Friendship in Washington. *Chatelaine* published a transcript of the speech in January 1931. H. Napier Moore explained that the former Prime Minister's talk was "worthy of earnest study by every Canadian woman [and] every Canadian man." His reasoning was that many European dignitaries "were convinced in their own minds that some spark ultimately would set Europe ablaze once more." Thus, Canadians should be aware of the problems facing world peace and how they could best contribute to the continuation of global harmony.[3]

Meighen's speech highlighted the need to maintain world peace. He stated, "Civilization has to end war, or war will end civilization." Advanced technologies and the development of air and sea battlefields made war an unpalatable option for the former Canadian Prime Minister. "War has lost its efficacy," he began, continuing, "it never can bring victory again: it can only bring defeat and despair for both conquerors and conquered; it can leave nothing behind but victors in reaction and vanquished in revolution, and all alike impoverished." War had become pointless according to Meighen: "War once served a human purpose; it can now of its very nature serve such a purpose no longer; it solves no problem; it affords no security; it offers no prizes to the victor." The outbreak of another European war needed to be prevented at all cost. The only way Meighen saw this happening was if the American government and population fully committed to the cause. To his American listeners Meighen commented, "…Such an organization cannot be brought about without the United States." He appealed to his audience, "believing as I do that destiny hangs on the American nation coming to accept it, I dare to implore you not to lightly cast those simple words aside." According to Meighen the fate of world peace rested with the Americans.[4]

Meighen's speech underscores two fundamental themes and concerns that wove their way through *Chatelaine* in the 1930s, 1940s, and 1950s: national identity and world peace. Throughout this nearly thirty-year period Canadians struggled to define themselves as they lay politically and culturally suspended between their British motherland and their southern neighbour. Without severing their British ties, increasingly, as Meighen's speech suggests, Canadians turned to the United States for solutions. Nonetheless, some Canadians continued to independently campaign for world peace and many did not abandon the ideal of creating a Canadian culture distinct from that of their southern neighbour and their British motherland.

But, as the contrast between the two epigraphs suggests, between the 1920s and the 1950s something changed. The 1950 critique was correct regarding the images of modern Canadian womanhood presented in *Chatelaine*. In the 1920s and early 1930s, *Chatelaine*'s modern woman actively engaged in the public sphere to promote national pride and world peace. By the late 1930s, the images of modern Canadian middle-class womanhood presented in *Chatelaine* became closely associated with the private sphere. Women now fought for peace and the spreading of national pride directly as wives, mothers and homemakers. In *Chatelaine*, at the same time that the democratic way of life appeared to be under direct attack, the commitment to creating a national identity through the development of Canadian arts and literature was replaced by an emphasis on representing the ideal middle-class nuclear family. This is not surprising considering the concomitant changes in attitudes towards the importance for modern Canadian women of marriage and motherhood.

As has been discussed, *Chatelaine*'s modern woman of the 1920s and 1930s wore many hats. One that was particularly important to the magazine's readers and its contributors was that of peacemaker. Through this role women were also defenders of the nation. Although Canadian foreign and defence policies in the 1920s and 1930s largely suggested an isolationist stance,[5] some Canadians were active in international affairs. Of particular importance to *Chatelaine* was the work that Canadian women were doing in support of world peace. As Thomas P. Socknat remarks, Canadian women's commitment towards peace remained high in the interwar years.[6] *Chatelaine* continuously took it for granted that women were naturally interested in and had a particular affinity for this work.[7] This was one area where it was also assumed that middle-class women could and should enter the male dominated domain of the public sphere in pursuit of maternal feminist goals with little or no concern about challenging gender norms. For example, in the May 1930 editorial, titled "The Problems of Peace and How Women Can Meet Them," editor Byrne Hope Sanders encouraged women to educate themselves on political issues and to then form opinions that could be shared with others in their communities. While suggesting that men and women should work together to achieve world peace, she hinted that women would enjoy greater success. Sanders stated that, "Women will work for something, with methods that are out of the ordinary, for causes which many men will not publicly avow … and women will accomplish their purpose."[8] She observed that men would not openly admit to fighting for world peace for two reasons: first, the success rate was dubious at best; and second, the fight for peace might have a de-masculinizing effect – women were far "less afraid than men of being thought silly."[9]

The early images of strong, capable women in pursuit of world peace in *Chatelaine* were coupled with a simultaneous emphasis of the femininity of such women. Competence and femininity were clearly not in competition. In describing one of the great British female peace advocates of the time, Kathleen Courtney, a woman who had been active in the suffrage movements of the early twentieth century and who had since devoted much of her time working for world peace through various peace organizations and by giving speeches to women's clubs, Sanders noted in 1930 that she was a "womanly woman." This comment likely meant that Courtney had some strong feminine qualities. Continuing with her description Sanders wrote, "She is gracious; gentle; soft-voiced. But so powerful is her earnestness, her idealism, her common sense, and sense of humor ... that she has, perhaps, done more than any other single woman for the cause of world peace."[10]

Throughout the 1920s and into the 1930s, *Chatelaine* was writing for and about strong capable middle-class women who were concerned with peace without denying their femininity. For example, in August 1932 *Chatelaine* ran a story about Winnifred Kydd, one of three Canadian delegates to the Disarmament Conference in Geneva and the only full-time woman delegate from the British Empire. The article applauded Miss Kydd's university education in political science and political economy. It was also noted that although a self-declared "Utopian visionary," Miss Kydd's analysis of the conference was firmly rooted in reality. Miss Kydd acknowledged that world peace – hindered as it was by the diversity of global cultures – would be a long time in the making. She nonetheless reached out to Canadian women to join the long fight for peace. On the subject she stated, "It is an educational process in which every woman must take an untiring interest."[11] While Miss Kydd did want all women to fight for peace, she was likely appealing to middle-class, educated women. Readers were also reminded that Miss Kydd was a woman. "She has shining red-gold hair and blue eyes that can crinkle easily with laughter ... she is slim and tall..." the opening paragraph of the article detailed.[12] Even more noticeable were Miss Kydd's age – she was still in her twenties – and her single status. According to the article, delegates of the Disarmament Conference had remarked that Miss Kidd must have been at school during the Great War. However, they had also told her that, "you represent the coming generation. You and your classmates will inherit what we are trying to do over here. You represent a young country, and we greet your enthusiasm and your viewpoint. It is right that you are here!"[13] Young or old, single or married, Canadian women were expected to be concerned with world peace and to actively pursue this goal in their communities and beyond. Moreover, there was an implicit connection made between Canadian women and their distinctly female ability – possibly vocation – to raise a young nation to be peace-minded.[14]

In the early 1930s, *Chatelaine* directly encouraged women to extend their energies beyond hearth and home in the pursuit of world peace and nation building. *Chatelaine* considered these ideal roles in which women could and should partake in the public sphere. This was considered particularly relevant in 1933/34 as fascist and Nazi governments gained power in Europe. The January 1934 editorial proposed a challenge for all Canadian women. It began, "It is no longer true that Woman's place is only in the home."[15] Echoing a maternal feminist rhetoric, it claimed that there was "much work to be done [outside of the home] that only women can do."[16] Heading the list was women's collective ability to stop war. The editorial declared: "An intelligent, understanding womanhood must educate the coming generation to be peace-minded." A connection was made between the traditional roles of women as educators and nurturers, and world peace. Women were believed to possess innate qualities that inextricably linked them to these positions but the magazine did not deny that women would have to work hard to achieve their objectives. In March 1934, a guest editor reminded readers that true patriotism was not just "flag-waving." She wrote, it "is studying and endeavouring to understand the problems of our great empire and its international relations."[17] Canada's connection to the "empire" was explicit here. A year later, editor Byrne Hope Sanders placed these views in a national context. She wrote that, "Women have the responsibility in their hands for peaceful homes and the building of a courageous and gallant youth. ...It is one to demand the best that any woman can bring – an intelligent, informed, understanding interest."[18] Women were the "mothers" of the nation, a role that became even more prominent during the Second World War. As mothers of the nation, they were expected to focus their energies in the pursuit of world peace, because, as the January 1935 editorial stated, "Theirs is the real agony when a man marches the glory (?) road."[19]

Increasingly, as time eroded the vivid memories of the Great War and fascism and Nazism continued to spread through Europe, women of all ages were reminded by the magazine that it was their responsibility to assure that the young men of the day would not again choose war over peace. An article that appeared in September 1935, entitled "Can Youth Win the Peace," was optimistic in its outlook. The author concluded that young Canadians would not choose to fight if a war broke out in Europe. In justification of the human loss of the First World War she wrote, "If modern youth has realized, as I believe it has, that to live for one's country can be a finer type of patriotism than to die for it, then the youth of my generation will not, after all, have laid down the best of its life in vain."[20] The author linked women's positions as mothers with the political will of a nation. According to this article, Canadian women, and women in the rest of the British Empire and the United States, had done a good job of "raising" their countries' youth and instilling in them the virtues of peace, something that meshed well with Canada's largely isolationist stance.

While *Chatelaine* expected women to spread national pride and work for peace, it recognized, as have many historians since, that war, while it often strengthens the first objective, directly challenges the second, particularly for mothers. During the Great War, pacifist women in Canada and throughout most of the British Empire, had been confronted by hostile responses from both sexes. In the post-World War One period, women returned to the position of peace advocates. Their role remained tempered, however. Veronica Strong-Boag notes, "In a fundamentally middle-class peace movement only the very brave demanded an end both to armed conflict and to privilege."[21] Generally, pacifist groups did not want to break down barriers of class, race and ethnicity. Nonetheless, Canadian women continued to express their sex's traditional abhorrence of war and "predisposition" to be peace-minded. They were confident in their ability to create a better world.[22] By the late 1930s, however, this confidence was being questioned. In large part, this was undoubtedly a reflection of the changing international situation. As Strong-Boag notes of the Canadian situation during the late 1930s, "...although many citizens had their awareness of world issues raised, female activists in the Dominion, as elsewhere, found their methods an inadequate response to the dilemma of the times. They depended on levels of receptivity, tolerance and common sense which were all too rare."[23] Thomas P. Socknat would have concurred with Stroag-Boag's assessments. Regarding the international challenges of the late 1930s, Socknat remarks: "...the liberal democracy that had seemed the route to world peace was increasingly in need of defence – ultimately, it would be argued, by armed resistance. Socially radical pacifists would find it difficult to evade the approaching crisis."[24] By the late 1930s, even pacifists were beginning to realize that war, ironically, might be the best guarantor of democratic peace.

As far as *Chatelaine* was concerned, Italy's invasion of Ethiopia in 1935, the Spanish Civil War that began the next year and Hitler's expansionist ambitions for Germany, were all reasons to believe that peace was indeed being seriously threatened. Particularly alarming was the idea that democratic freedoms might be at risk with the rise of Hitler's Germany. As early as 1936, *Chatelaine* pondered the Canadian response to another world war precipitated by German aggression.

As the fear of another European war was spreading, *Chatelaine* began to slowly disengage women from the central role of "peacekeepers." An article entitled "Will the Church Say Fight?" appeared in September 1936. The article published several responses from leading Canadian divines regarding the role that the Church should take should the British Empire be involved in another war. The replies were mixed. However, according to almost every religious affiliate who was quoted, the churches' role in matters of peace and war was to instil the virtues of peace within their congregations. The article stated that "the Church's greatest task is not to defend the nation by war, but against the war spirit; to disarm the human mind of fear, hate, jealousy, and to abolish the social and economic evils which foster the war-spirit."[25]

As war approached, the images of women upholding peace began to fade in *Chatelaine*. The now seemingly impossible job was transferred to other agencies, notably the Church. Within a month of the September 1936 article, *Chatelaine* published an article titled "Is Feminism Declining?" The apparent failure of women to uphold the peace seemed to be the driving force behind this article. *Chatelaine* chronicled the views of Canada's second woman senator, Iva Fallis. The senator observed that women had "the greatest potential force for good to be found in this country." But she cautioned that "the great majority of women are still not sufficiently interested to sacrifice time and effort toward the achievement of the desired result."[26] The senator concluded that, "When we believe enough in our mission, something will happen. Upon the way we, today, fulfill the duties of the higher citizenship to which we have been called, hangs the fate of women in the next generation."[27] True or not, the article explicitly connected the declining interest of women to "fulfill the duties of higher citizenship" with an ebbing of feminism. The author further reminded readers – hopefully all future maternal feminists who would be actively engaged in the fight for peace – that Canada's four women senators were still feminine. She noted,

"I remembered that I must write a story some day about the charm and attractive appearance of Canada's four women parliamentarians; each in her way, smart, pleasant, interesting, good-looking."[28]

By 1937 *Chatelaine* was convinced that another world war was likely. The magazine now clearly no longer championed women's fight for peace. Instead, the magazine was filled with images of women accepting the losses incurred by the First World War. An article titled "Sound of Trumpets" appeared in November 1937. The subtitle of the article asked, in respect to the fallen soldiers of the Great War, "Did they die in vain?" It promised that the upcoming short fiction piece would provide "an unforgettable answer" to the question. The story's protagonist was an elderly British woman who had lost her three sons during the First World War. When anyone asked the woman about her loss she recited lines which she had apparently rehearsed repeatedly, often without sentiment: "It was a bit hard. But they gave their lives, and we gave them, that men might be free, that democracy might not pass from the earth, that the world might know peace."[29] Later she was captured confessing to a close friend that she occasionally felt that her sons had died in vain. However, in the last scene, at a Remembrance Day ceremony, the elderly woman stated with conviction, "Men will be free and democracy will not pass from the earth, and the world will know peace."[30] The reader was left with the feeling that through the events of the story the woman had realized the importance of the sacrifices that she and her sons had made during the Great War. However, unlike the article that had appeared in 1935, this short story suggested that young men were once again willing to go to war. Removed from the vivacity of the 1920s, this new generation apparently considered global conflict a possible option. Importantly, this story helped to show *Chatelaine*'s mainly women readers how this action would not necessarily negate the sacrifices their mothers had made during the Great War.

The acceptance of sending sons off to war was not made without lament. By 1937, *Chatelaine* was publishing material that underscored the dichotomy of women raising the nation for peace and yet facing the realities that another European war could place upon them. The poem "He Was Not Made For War," published in November 1937, illustrated the struggle that women in the late 1930s faced. It read in part:

> He was not made for war, this lad of mine. ...
> I've taught him kindliness and love for man. ...
> And oh, his heart! His heart was made for holding
> All the young dreaming that youth belong – ...
> Waiting fulfilment. Oh God! It was made
> Eager, insistent, for living...for living..!
> Never for halting a bullet or blade.
> And so, he does not know
> The hidden barb; the prodding of a sore –
> My mind's torment when people talk of war.[31]

Canadian men and women, according to *Chatelaine*, were clearly emotionally unprepared for another war. At the same time, the poem also suggested that some at least partially accepted what *Chatelaine* increasingly thought to be inevitable.

By 1938, articles in *Chatelaine* began to focus on what Canadian women could do for any future war effort. In January 1938, for example, *Chatelaine* published an article titled "Women at War," written by Canadian Lieutenant-Colonel (LCol) Fraser Hunter. LCol Hunter began by describing the heroic actions of twentieth century women around the world who had fought in defence of their homes. "Can Canadian women pooh-pooh altogether the idea that such a destiny could await them?" he asked. The LCol did not think that they could. He challenged the assumption that military training would automatically degrade the moral integrity of women. He wrote, "If she wants to a girl can find as much trouble in her ordinary life as she could in the army." Indeed, he continued, "Women may often make bad mothers, but they also make good lawyers, doctors – perhaps warriors." Such questioning of what many considered innate differences between the genders was unusual. Hunter was careful not to push his analysis too far, however. The participation of women that the author proposed remained within the purview of home defence. He also appealed to women to fight for peace. But he pointed out that war might be one of the ultimate means to secure peace. "...Wishing for peace, praying for peace, hoping for peace, can never keep peace, for you can never get peace by mooing like cows at passing soldiers. If you wish peace you must fight for it."[32] The LCol's message was unclear. On one hand he defended gender equality in modern warfare – or at least some version of it. At the same time, however, he relegated women's interest to the defence of the home and children and thereby confirmed their presence in the private sphere. Interestingly, in the LCol's article, women were associated with being young mothers with young children. He was not connecting women to the role of mothers of potential soldiers.

While the message of the January article may have been mixed, the published responses a couple of months later were almost universal: Canadian women were prepared to take an active part in the defence of their homes. The rationale was, "that as women had claimed so many of men's privileges, they should not balk at the idea of fighting for those privileges."[33] Notably, no distinction was drawn between home defence and overseas service. Women did not want war. However, as one respondent wrote, in March 1938, "If peace and prosperity are to come through war, then it would seem that the sooner it were over the better."[34] According to *Chatelaine*, Canadian women were prepared to support their men should their nation enter into a European war and they were ready to defend their homes if directly threatened.

Importantly, within *Chatelaine*, women supported the war effort as mothers and the magazine encouraged their full support. The assumptions made in *Chatelaine* reflect some theories behind women's peace movements in Canada. It has been argued that women, as mothers, had and have a natural desire to preserve peace and have a special role in peace education.[35] However, as Janice Williamson and Deborah Gorham suggest, this type of argument is easily undermined, "because," they write, "Women's opposition to war on behalf of their sons can quickly become women's support of the 'war effort' when those sons become soldiers."[36] It was not until towards the end of the war that the topic of peace resurfaced in *Chatelaine*. Clearly this was going to be a "new" fight for peace.

Before the end of the war women's collective power was explicitly re-harnessed for the new fight for peace. In February 1944, *Chatelaine* published an article titled, "Women Can Win the Peace." This article, however, was not nearly as optimistic as earlier articles had been about women's ability to uphold peace. While it acknowledged that collectively women could win the peace, it suggested that they could do so because they were for the most part housewives and "The housewife is, in a sense, a member of a great semi-leisure class, a class that has some leisure to do the things that must be done if we are to have a better world – the things that women best can to."[37] Men were apparently too preoccupied with other endeavours that included "selfish objectives" to entangle themselves in the fight for peace. The association of men to the public sphere and women to the private sphere also meant that women were again expected to fight for peace from the home.

During the Cold War, *Chatelaine* continued to focus on world peace. As mothers, women were expected to be particularly interested in this topic. In July 1947, Isabel Lebourdais remarked that "The anguish of mothers the world over who have given their sons to war could raise such a cry as would drown out all other sounds on earth." Yet she noted that "each mother weeps alone." She described how, "Each woman who bears a male child suffers the torturing question: which war will he be ready for? And no voice is raised to save her, to say 'this ghastly waste must stop!'" Lebourdais clearly saw the prevention of another war as a woman's responsibility, particularly if she was a mother. But she remained saddened by the lack of collective action that mothers were taking to assure world peace. She concluded, "Love your little boy, mother. ... No voices are raised to declare that no mother's son shall be torn from his school games and driven into the slaughter business again. ... why are there no voices raised to cry aloud that no victory under heaven is worth the price?"[38]

In a July 1948 article entitled, "Nine Ways to Stop Wars," Canadian men and women were encouraged to raise their children with love and leniency so that they would grow into peace abiding adults. The author, however, clearly prioritized the woman's responsibility, as a mother, in raising her offspring to be peace-minded. "Grown-up children have always engaged in wars," wrote Dr. Brock Chisholm. He continued, "women carry the major responsibility for the development of the character of children, therefore we cannot avoid the conclusion that women are at least as, and probably more, responsible for wars than men." He concluded, "The vital question is whether women, in their own homes, their own communities and schools, and in the polling booths, are capable of answering the challenge, and in doing so saving the race from destruction."[39]

Chatelaine now no longer portrayed women as leaders in the peace process. Instead, as wives and mothers they supported their husbands efforts for peace from their suburban homes and were expected to raise their children to be peace abiding. An article called "Atom Town ...There's No Place Like It," published in August 1949, again illustrates this point.[40] Atom Town was a place for young people. It was a place where everyone had financial security. There were "no slums, no unemployment, no private property, and no in-laws." And it boasted the highest birth rate in Canada. In the mornings the men were bussed off to the nuclear fission plant and, until their return in the evening, Atom Town was a village of women and children. The women were assured that their men were working in the plant to guarantee peace and not for war. As one of the scientists, who was a man, a husband and a father said, "We already know how to be destructive with this power. What we are after is putting it to (good) use." With this assurance, the women were left to enjoy each other's company, their children and to shop. One female resident explained, "People really live in Deep River. In the city they don't know what they want, or where they're going. It's the simplicity we like here."[41] Indeed, women were being distanced from the "fight" for peace in *Chatelaine*. The modern woman of the 1950s was resolutely a wife and mother.

Chatelaine's preoccupation with women's abilities to promote peace were intimately tied to the implicit, and at times explicit, encouragement of its readers to promote national pride. From the beginning, *Chatelaine* was a Canadian women's magazine. *Chatelaine* stressed the importance of establishing a distinct national culture. *Chatelaine* encouraged women, like J. Castell Hopkins in her role as editor of the Canadian Annual Review, to enter the public sphere in order to contribute directly to the growth of a "Canadian" culture.[42] Regular columns were devoted to Canadian history and art to help readers develop an appreciation for their country.[43] Women, also seen as mothers of the nation, were additionally encouraged to populate all corners of the vast Canadian landmass.

At least initially, *Chatelaine* tried to fulfil its mandate as a national woman's magazine. British content was nonetheless high, particularly in short stories and noticeably in the immediate pre-World War Two period. In May 1939, for example, an entire issue was dedicated to the visit by King George VI and Queen Elizabeth, "Canada's King and Queen."[44] During its first decade, while *Chatelaine* tried to help develop a unique Canadian culture, this largely meant a culture free from American influence rather than devoid of European content. Yet, the magazine, like Arthur Meighen, also recognized that the United States was socially and politically powerful and its close geographic proximity to Canada made it culturally attractive. Anti-Americanism in *Chatelaine* was mixed: while *Chatelaine* lobbied for restrictions on American periodicals,[45] it was happy enough to regularly feature articles about Hollywood movies and stars.[46]

From the time of its infancy, however, *Chatelaine* was coping with what authors John Herd Thompson and Allen Seager have coined the "cultural conundrum."[47] As Thompson and Seager explain, the interwar years awakened amongst middle-class intellectuals a desire to establish a distinctly Canadian culture that manifested itself in national musical and literary projects and the popularization of Canadian artists like the Group of Seven. The movement, however, was beset by a major irony: the attempts to develop a national culture were rarely novel or solely Canadian in origin. Moreover, British and American cultural influences remained high. More alarming, however, was "the fear that their struggle to define and proclaim a cultural identity might be of consuming uninterest [sic] to the great majority of Canadians."[48]

Chatelaine was born at the height of this intellectual movement. Examining how the magazine dealt with issues of national identity adds the dimension of gender to the conundrum of culture. Interestingly, the images of Canadian womanhood presented in *Chatelaine* became distanced with this struggle at around the same time that the movement itself dissolved because of the war, only to resurface in the postwar period with the increasing availability of American consumer goods.[49]

In the 1920s and 1930s, *Chatelaine* did assume that women played an active role in raising Canada's youth and the development of the country. Initially, *Chatelaine* was particularly interested in portraying women literally populating the young dominion and inhabiting remote locations. True to its 1928 pledge, the magazine, at least in its early years, tried to be national in scope. *Chatelaine* also highlighted women's responsibilities in assuring cultural sovereignty – something that in the 1930s largely meant cultural independence from the United States.

To help spread *Chatelaine's* message, within a few months of its inaugural launch, the magazine began to be sold by subscription. What is remarkable, as *Chatelaine* noted in July 1928, was that "the permanent direct sales staff will be composed entirely of women of the best type and who will be assured of a splendid welcome wherever they may call." The rationale was "that a woman's magazine should be presented to our Canadian woman by members of her own sex who are familiar with the problems that confront her."[50] By becoming a sales manager for *Chatelaine*, each "chatelaine" could help spread the magazine's nationalistic message as a participant in the public sphere.

Chatelaine recognized and paid tribute to those women who helped to spread national pride and populate remote areas.[51] For example, the September 1930 editorial described a young woman with "bobbed hair" waiting for groceries to be delivered by boat to a small hamlet in British Columbia. Having picked up her groceries, the editor described how, "She staggered with her parcels to her canoe. Picked up her small son by his shirt and braces, much as if he had been a puppy, dropped him casually on top of the bundles, and started paddling strongly off...."[52] This type of female independence was connected with the development of the nation yet was likely somewhat exceptional. *Chatelaine* felt that all women could relate to the scene, however, because it was obvious that the young woman was also a mother. Motherhood in this case did not tie this young woman to her home, or seem to have limited her in any way, but it most probably, in some form, directed her interests. It also placed this young woman – even if she challenged traditional ideas about womanhood by the subtle connections drawn to the 1920s stereotype of the flapper – in the symbolic position of mother to the nation.

Contributors also took pride in Canadian women extending their purview beyond the national border. The following was noted in *Chatelaine* in the March 1929 column of "What the Woman Citizen Should Know": "Canadian Woman Chosen for Important U.S. Position: THAT a Canadian woman, Mrs. E.J. Woodhouse is the active director of the recently proposed Women's Institute of Professional Relations with headquarters at North Carolina College." It was clear that Mrs. Woodhouse was an educated woman and presumably from either the middle or upper class. The announcement explained that Mrs. Woodhouse would be running "A program for developing new professional and business activities for women, linked with establishment of a clearing house of information by the American Association of University Women."[53]

But, while *Chatelaine* applauded Canadian women who extended their influence into the United States, the magazine was generally less likely to rejoice when the border traffic reversed directions, particularly if Canadian culture appeared to be threatened. The debates concerning the taxes on periodicals that had been going on since the early 1930s were an aggravating issue for *Chatelaine*'s publishers. The 1 January 1936 Bill that made American periodicals duty and tax free while simultaneously leaving Canadian periodicals burdened with high taxes and duties on materials did not escape notice.[54] In March 1936 under the caption "You and Your Magazines" *Chatelaine*'s publishers asked the following: "Did you ever realize how important a part Canadian magazines play in your life?" The article continued, "Did you ever think what your outlook would be without them? Or consider how much you learn from their pages about Canadian life and thought; about our country's men and women, our social ideals, our national problems?" The next question truly revealed the magazine's mission: "Without Canadian magazines, what would foster within the younger generations that all powerful necessity – national consciousness?"[55] This theme was revisited the next month under the caption "Foreign Ideas Fostered." The column read in part, "Foreign ideas and ideals, furthering foreign interests may be best for foreign peoples but they may not be best for Canadians. The spread of Canadian ideas and ideals is vital to Canadian welfare and progress. But, foreign ideas and ideals are fostered in Canada by giving foreign periodicals preference over Canadian periodicals ..."[56] It was clear that in this case "foreign" was synonymous with "American" and that US ideas were not solicited.

European and American influences in the magazine, however, were undeniable. This was especially true in the areas of fashion and entertainment. For example, in January 1930 *Chatelaine* published "A Letter from Paris." The news item reported the latest fashion trends: long skirts were in; so too were hats.[57] By March 1930 a letter by Ellen Mackie in New York would apparently provide the definitive answers for women's wardrobe problems. Mackie remarked that "Talk of panic in the stock market, the rise and fall of governments, world wars! All are mere episodes compared to the pandemonium caused by the raising of a beltline and the lowering of a hem." She noted of the gravity of the situation, "The problem as to how she shall vote pales before the momentous question whether or not she will cover her legs with twenty-five yards of flat crepe." Mackie noted that Paris predicted a return to long skirts, but she also encouraged women not to blindly follow trends. She wrote, "the really smart woman will always conform the fashions to her own individuality, rather than let the modes make a caricature of her...."[58] Canadian middle-class women were expected to apply the same insight in respect to other cultural influences, particularly from Great Britain and the United States.

Perhaps the area where American influence was most noticeable in *Chatelaine* was in reports about motion pictures. For example, the regular column "Movie Gossip" in March 1934 began "The other day I was in New York. Naturally I went movie hunting – not for the shows that would be in Canadian theatres in a week or so, but for such as would probably never come our way."[59] Canada's second-class status in the film industry was apparent. More interesting, however, was the fact that the film industry was also an example of the cultural conundrum that taunted Canadians stuck between European influences and American ones'. As war approached the British made gains in this tug-o-war. "Are British Movies Outshining Hollywood?" queried the cover of the March 1939 issue of *Chatelaine*. The latest view according to author Mary Lowrey Ross was that British movies were "the worst in the world." She also noted that in the past "Considerable effort was made to popularize these films with Canadian audiences, but the attempt came to very little. Movie houses which announced a policy of all-English programs soon discovered that for the impatient moviegoers patriotism wasn't enough." Canadians apparently were "ready to make a reasonable sacrifice for the Mother Country, but they wouldn't sit through two hours of its film entertainment." But, according to the article, the British film industry was undeniably improving. Speaking of the screen adaptation of his play "Pygmalion" British playwright George Bernard Shaw remarked that, "the really good thing about it is that when you have seen these on the screen – and if you like them – all the American films will become much more like my films. And that will be a splendid thing for America." Canadians, however, would remain caught in the middle. As consumers they would be able to cast their vote for either industry. Ross speculated that British films would win Canada's vote. She concluded, "the chances are that Mr. Shaw is right. He usually is."[60]

While it may have done little for the British film industry, war and fear of war served to strengthen the British imperial connection in the magazine, particularly the association of king to country. For example, in May 1937 *Chatelaine* ran an article about the upcoming coronation;[61] the May 1939 issue was billed as a collector's edition, dedicated to King George VI and Queen Elizabeth;[62] and September 1939's copy had an article about the King's mother, Queen Mary of England.[63] *Chatelaine's* middle-class readership was clearly of British descent. One reader had even stated in October 1936, "I have no sympathy with a spineless pacifism that forgets our Canadian obligations to the Motherland."[64] There is no doubt that *Chatelaine* supported the war effort in part through an historical association with the British Empire while simultaneously underscoring the "Canadian-ness" of the magazine.

With war in 1939, *Chatelaine's* readership was encouraged to be patriotic to all the Allied forces and middle-class Canadians' British heritage became more pronounced. *Chatelaine*, however, no longer presumed that women would partake in public forums to debate Canadian cultural sovereignty like they had in the 1930s. This change lasted well into the 1950s.

World War Two both changed how the magazine defined cultural sovereignty and how women engaged in this debate, but it did little to solve the "cultural conundrum" that has shaped twentieth century understandings of Canadian culture. Throughout World War Two, while it was recognized in *Chatelaine* that Canadian mothers had sent their sons – and in some cases daughters – off to Europe and the South Pacific, for the most part the mother figure of the war years was young and so were her children. When mentioned, soldiers were generally seen as husbands and fathers. Images of women that appeared in *Chatelaine*, such as the November 1943 advertisement for Canada Corn Starch that appealed in bold writing to "Canada's Housoldiers [sic]" helped to uphold the idea that in this magazine at least, women were first and foremost mothers and homemakers. The advertisement read in part: "Canadian mothers and wives – Canada's Housoldier, [sic] are backing up the 'food for fitness' urge by following Canada's Official Food Rules – so that Canadians may become an even more healthy and hardy people."[65]   It is likely that most women were following these rules after a full day of war work. As chapter five shows, war work did not fundamentally challenge the myth in *Chatelaine* that women's primary position was in the home. Indeed, it seems to have helped perpetuate it and to strengthen the ties between motherhood and national prosperity, and reaffirmed women's position in the private sphere while marginalizing women's contributions to the public sphere. Noticeably, *Chatelaine* was directing its message to "Canadian" women.

Most patriotic jobs that *Chatelaine* suggested women could do to support the nation at war stressed women's position in the private sphere and their membership in the British Empire.   For instance, in a December 1940 article *Chatelaine* headlined: "An Urgent Call for Help!" "Will you knit for the courageous women of England?" *Chatelaine* asked. The article explained, "An urgent call for help in making woollen comforts for them has been sent out to the women of Canada by the Women's War Work Committee of the Canadian Red Cross." The women of the British Auxiliary Territorial Services "were standing side by side with the men of the fighting forces," and needed the support of their overseas sisters.[66] Canadian women were also urged to send packages to the Allied men directly involved in the war overseas. A March 1942 article in *Chatelaine* noted, "If you made friends with New Zealand or Australian Air Force Lads training in Canada under the Empire Air Training Scheme, the regulations laid down for sending them gifts in Britain are exactly the same as those for Canadian personnel – in fact, for any Dominion troops here."[67]

Even for Canadian women who obviously left the private sphere of hearth and home to contribute to the national war effort in uniform, beyond emphasizing their national origin, *Chatelaine* described them in ways that underscored traditional women's work such as cooking, mending and nurturing. Readers were encouraged to be proud of these women because they were Canadian and because they were obviously still feminine. For example, in November 1943 *Chatelaine* described the lives of several Canadian Airwomen stationed in Great Britain. It was noted that, "the WD officers and airwomen have a chance to know one another as they chat over sewing kits and ironing boards, and finish off with cocoa and a singsong before 'lights out.'" Writing to beaus was another favourite pastime for these Canadian women.[68]

Chatelaine reminded women that the Canadian men overseas were not immune to the charms of British women. British war brides were to be welcomed to Canada and *Chatelaine* readers were encouraged to educate them on how to become good "Canadian" wives. In May 1943, Mollie McGee asked *Chatelaine*'s readers to greet the "10,000 British Brides" with open arms. McGee noted that, "Canadian soldiers are excellent publicity agents, and their ten thousand wives are as keen about Canada as their fathers and mothers were one or two generations back, when Canada was taking the best from Britain." She also partially quoted a letter that explained how eager British brides were to learn about their new home. "I know you won't tell anyone how afraid I am that I will not be as clever as the Canadian girls I will meet," the letter began. It continued, "but can you give me a little advice on what I should read. I'll study while the baby is asleep."[69]

Chatelaine suggested that women, in addition to being proud of the Canadian men overseas, should also recognize that some of them, as mothers, were instrumental in forming Canadian manhood, past, present and future. A September 1944 article by Wallace Reyburn about the

Italian campaign noted that "The superiority in men is something that boils down to the fighting qualities and the character of the individual soldier. Especially character. If there is one important discovery I have made, after a year in Italy with the Canadian troops, it is that the Canadian fighting man can stack up against any other soldier in the world." Reyburn continued, "he has the stability of character which remains with him on and off duty, and I believe it is a possession that traces directly back to the homes and family life of their Dominion. It's something the women folk especially the mothers and wives who wait, can be proud of." Certainly, during the war, one of the main ways that *Chatelaine* encouraged women to spread national pride was through their roles as wives and mothers and performing their duties in the private sphere.

In the post-World War Two period, Canadian nationalism remained an important topic in *Chatelaine*. The magazine cautioned its readers about what might happen if women failed to promote national pride within the "citizens" of Canada – a category of citizenship that had just emerged in the immediate postwar period. In July 1946, a story described "Why Canadians Leave Home." The article explained that "the Canadian is developing an international mind. ...people are becoming more and more convinced that the boundary line doesn't matter."[70] It was up to every man, woman and child to help change what the author considered to be a grave situation. One woman who was interviewed for the story suggested that the problem had deep roots. She explained that: "The Canadian people are so busy guarding themselves from the economic pressure of the United States and from England that they don't build up a personality of their own."[71] She blamed women for this predicament and claimed that they had failed to instil national pride among their children. But there was no mention of women entering the public sphere to contribute to the promotion of Canadian art and literature like there had been in the early 1930s.

Canadian nationalism in *Chatelaine* in the postwar period was different from what it had been during the interwar years.[72] By the 1950s, *Chatelaine* was accustomed to publishing debates between American and Canadian wives concerning who provided best for their husbands and children. Arguably, as the British woman remarked in the epigraph to this chapter, conversations chronicled in *Chatelaine* about Canada's place in the world seemed to be quite "superficial."[73]

After World War Two, it was clear in *Chatelaine*, as elsewhere in Canadian society, that it was "Americanization" that posed the most direct threat to a Canadian cultural identity. For example, a July 1956 article asked the questions: "Do we really dislike the Americans? Do we have to sneer at our neighbors to show that we're good Canadians?"[74] The author did not think that such behaviour was necessary. She quoted one American woman's explanation as to why some Canadian women felt the need to do so, however: "It's because they are nationally immature, still afraid of the States and fighting the war of 1812. It is because they cling to certain vestiges of colonialism to bolster their Canadian ego instead of looking to their country today for their pride, the glory of achievement."[75] The author surmised that Canadians should embrace the maturity of their country and harbour no ill feelings towards their southern neighbours.

According to *Chatelaine*, women could now help spread national pride by being good Canadian wives; when national pride appeared to be lacking, they could be criticized for not being good wives. In March 1952, two American wives wrote the article, "Canadian Women are Suckers." They told Canadian readers that "You are suckers about men in general and husbands in particular because you let them live in another world, a masculine world where there is no place for you."[76] The authors loosely compared this conjugal behaviour with Canada's international position vis-à-vis the United States and Great Britain.

They wrote: "Domestically as well as socially you are victims of your unsuccessful compromise. Again you are trying to take a middle path between the European concept of separate domestic duties and the American share-the-work plan."[77] The implication was that if women had more influence over their husbands, then Canada would be a stronger and more independent nation and perhaps have a cultural identity of its own.

The March 1952 article received much feedback from readers. Canadians defended their virtues as wives and denied that Canada lacked a distinct culture. One respondent wrote: "I like Americans. I'm just fed up with the ones who want to build a little America everywhere they hang their hats. The atmosphere we live in is the atmosphere of Canada 1952 and that's the way it should be. Canadians are people, doggone it, and they don't want to be a carbon copy of any other nation on earth!"[78] However, as historians Robert Bothwell, Ian Drummond and John English note of Canada in the post-World War Two period, "its residents resembled the Americans with who they had such close connections."[79] The editors of *Chatelaine* also assumed that there was an American cultural influence in Canada and they tried to curb it by promoting Canadian homes and families.

The 1950s, particularly because of the Cold War, provided a rich forum in which to underscore the quality of life available in Canada. Interestingly, however, it was Canada's democratic lifestyle and consumer culture that were considered appealing; *Chatelaine* no longer overtly promoted a distinct Canadian culture.[80] The belligerence in Korea in the 1950s created an opportune comparison. In 1953, a recent Canadian visitor to Korea wrote: "After five weeks in Korea … I came away wondering just how long I would stay cheerful if my homeland were transformed, as theirs has been, into a hell-hole of horrors."[81] The author, Theresa A. Potter, described seeing a five-year-old boy traipsing through rubble in high-heeled women's shoes, (any shoes were considered better than none), a five-year-old girl who weighed a mere ten pounds, and an orphan with stumps for feet. Compared to life in Korea, life in Canada was ideal in multiple ways, particularly, as this article demonstrated, as an environment in which to raise children.

During the Cold War, *Chatelaine* also underscored the traditional gender relationships that were expected to exist in Canadian middle-class families. Men worked, women stayed home and raised the children, and the state, through social welfare programmes, assured the stability of the ideal family. This was expected to be particularly appealing to women from Eastern-Bloc countries. For example, in March 1954 *Chatelaine* published an article about Mrs. Gouzenko, wife of Russian exile Igor Gouzenko who in 1945 had provided the Canadian government with documents proving the existence of a Soviet spy ring. Following a discussion about Mrs. Gouzenko's appearance – it was determined that she did not have thick legs and a bulky figure, stereotypical of many Russian women, and that she dressed particularly well for the women of her country – the interviewer asked Mrs. Gouzenko if she liked living in Canada. She did. Mrs. Gouzenko stated that, "Canada was not like Russia. They do not shoot people here just for a charge. ..."[82] Canada was a democracy and citizenship had rights. Consumer culture was also another privilege that middle-class Canadian citizens enjoyed. According to the author, Mrs. Gouzenko "liked Canada the first time she saw it. She liked the food in the big stores and on display in the magazines. She liked the pattern of Canadian family life."[83] In essence, *Chatelaine* underscored the fact that Mrs. Gouzenko liked the traditional gender roles that women played in Canada – wives, mothers and homemakers – and how some Canadian communities had developed suburbs and shopping malls to facilitate these gendered divisions.

Despite the complex and changing ways that Canadian national identity was represented from 1928 to 1956, *Chatelaine* did not see the topic of national identity as a paradox. In its first decade, the magazine promoted Canadian fare and encouraged women to take an active role in developing a national spirit. That white, Anglo-Saxon, middle-class, English Canadians – *Chatelaine's* intended audience – remained connected and concerned with their motherland was not denied in the magazine or seen to directly challenge Canadian identity. That British and American influences remained in areas that Canada had not yet developed, such as women's fashions and the motion picture industry, was not seen as a problem. However, when foreign influences were in danger of superseding Canadian products, such as the tax on periodicals, then these foreign influences were to be fought. *Chatelaine* encouraged women to spread national pride without denying their British heritage or their geographic proximity to the United States. In retrospect, that may appear as a somewhat paradoxical way to establish a national identity, but in *Chatelaine* in the 1920s and 1930s it was normal. So too was the strengthening of British ties in the magazine once whispers of war swept across the Atlantic in 1936/37. When war did come in 1939 and women were repositioned to the private sphere in *Chatelaine* and expected to spread national pride from their positions as wives, mothers and homemakers, a change also occurred in how *Chatelaine* dealt with the topic of national identity. Canadian identity now became associated with the fight for democracy and the search for distinct cultural icons was halted. During the Cold War, democratic freedoms, including a consumer culture, began to help define Canadian citizenship within the magazine. According to *Chatelaine*, women in their roles as suburban housewives and mothers personified some of the advantages of Canadian citizenship, which led to a cultural identity in the magazine that was based on the ideal middle-class nuclear family. While the topic of cultural identity in *Chatelaine* was undeniably complex, in the 1930s, 1940s and 1950s it was unlikely viewed as a conundrum.

The issues of world peace and the need to develop a "Canadian" consciousness were inextricably linked in the pages of *Chatelaine* between 1928 and 1956. Modern Canadian women were expected to be concerned with both of these issues. How women were to address these topics certainly fluctuated over time. As the central understanding of modern Canadian womanhood and her roles as wife, mother, homemaker shifted, so too did her relationship to the peace movement and to promoting a distinct Canadian national identity. When democratic peace appeared to be directly at risk starting in 1936/37, women were increasingly expected to fight for each cause from within the private sphere of hearth and home and to support the war effort of 1939 to 1945 as good Canadian wives, mothers and homemakers. As Francois Thebaud chronicles, English and French women during the Great War had faced similar pressures.[84] In the postwar years, amidst a continued threat to the democratic way of life, *Chatelaine* continued to be concerned with spreading national pride and peace. Clearly women were no longer leaders in these endeavours, however. Now, as wives and mothers, they provided support to their husbands.

Endnotes

1   Anne Anderson Perry, *Chatelaine*, November 1928, 54–55.

2   British hairdresser cited by Margaret Ecker Francis, *Chatelaine*, September 1950, 5.

3   H. Napier Moore, *Chatelaine*, January 1931, 13.

4   Arthur Meighen, *Chatelaine*, January 1931, 13-14.

5   Canadian political autonomy from Great Britain was achieved by degrees culminating with the Treaty of Westminister in 1931. For example, Prime Minister W.L. Mackenzie King abolished the system of peerage in Canada in 1919. H.V. Nelles, *A Little History of Canada* (Don Mills: Oxford University Press, 2004), 181. King also refused to participate in the Chanak crisis of 1922, was influential in insisting that the word "autonomous" appear in the Balfour Report of 1926, the precursor to the 1931 Statute of Westminister. Thompson

CHAPTER SIX

and Seager, *Canada 1922-1939*, 42-43, 48-49. As an autonomous nation, up until 1937, the Canadian government largely ignored international incidents such as the 1931 Japanese invasion of Manchuria, Italy's 1935 invasion of Ethiopia and the Spanish Civil War, 1936-39. Nelles, *A Little History of Canada*, 179-180. By the end of the 1930s, however, the rise of fascism and nazism in Europe was becoming impossible to deny and Canada started to rebuild her defences. J.L. Granatstein, *Canada's Army: Waging War and Keeping the Peace* (Toronto: University of Toronto Press, 2002), 171-174. Informed by the experiences of the Great War, belligerence was still to be avoided at all cost, and Prime Minister W.L. Mackenzie King assured Canadian citizens that participation in another European war would not be taken lightly and would be a parliamentary decision. In 1938, however, the Prime Minister had already recorded in his diary that being at Britain's side in future belligerence "was a self-evident national duty." Cited in Thompson and Seager, *Canada 1922-1939*, 315-316.

6   Thomas P. Socknat, "For Peace and Freedom: Canadian Feminists and the Interwar Peace Campaign," in Janice Williamson and Deborah Gorham (eds.), *Up and Doing: Canadian Women and Peace* (Toronto: the Women's Press, 1989), 66-92.

7   Some historians claim that the gendered divisions associating men with war and women with peace have deep roots. Historian Ruth Roach Pierson describes the male exclusivity of the armed services as resting on "the division of labour by sex that relegated women to nurture, men to combat, women to the creation and preservation of life, men, when necessary, to its destruction." Ruth Roach Pierson, *"They're Still Women After All": The Second World War and Canadian Womanhood* (Toronto: MaClelland and Stewart Limited, 1986), 129. Janice Williamson and Deborah Gorham, editors of *Up and Doing Canadian Women and Peace*, also remark that, "women are by their very nature more likely than men to support peace...." Janice Williamson and Deborah Gorham, (eds.) *Up and Doing Canadian Women and Peace*, 29. (It should be noted that Williamson and Gorham also point out that women often fought for peace through male organized and dominated peace groups.) Indeed, social welfare and peace were some of the central issues put forth by Canadian maternal feminists in their twentieth century suffrage campaigns. As Nellie McClung, one of Canada's most famous maternal feminists, remarked in 1916, "When the hand that rocks the cradle rules the world, it will be a safer, cleaner world for the occupant of the cradle." Cited in Thompson and Seager, *Canada 1922-1939*, 70.

8   Byrne Hope Sanders, *Chatelaine*, May 1930, 16.

9   Ibid.

10   Ibid.

11   Byrne Hope Sanders, *Chatelaine*, August 1932, 42.

12   Ibid., 26

13   Ibid.

14   For more about Winnifred Kydd see N.E.S. Griffith, *The Splendid Vision: Centennial History of the National Council of Women of Canada, 1893-1993* (Ottawa: Carleton University Press, Inc. 1993), 181-209. About the Disarmament Conference, Thomas P. Socknat notes that "The enthusiastic response of Canadian women to the disarmament declarations suggests that disarmament had become one of the major international issues of the day." Thomas P. Socknat, *Witness Against War: Pacifism in Canada, 1900–1945* (Toronto: University of Toronto Press, 1987), 129.

15   Byrne Hope Sanders, *Chatelaine*, January 1934, 1.

16   Ibid.

17   Mrs. James Ince, *Chatelaine*, March 1934, 2.

18   Byrne Hope Sanders, *Chatelaine*, November 1934, 2.

19   Byrne Hope Sanders, *Chatelaine*, January 1935, 16.

20   Vera Britain, *Chatelaine*, September 1935, 26.

21   Veronica Strong-Boag, "Peace-making Women: Canada 1919-1939," in Ruth Roach Pierson (ed.), *Women and Peace: Theoretical, Historical and Practical Perspectives* (London: Croom Helm, 1987), 171.

22   Strong-Boag, "Peace-making Women," 172.

23   Ibid., 185.

24   Socknat, *Witness Against War*, 161.

25   *Chatelaine*, September 1936, 11.

26   Lotta Dempsey, *Chatelaine*, November 1936, 4.

27   Ibid., 48. It should be remembered that just a few years earlier *Chatelaine* had been written as though all women were interested in, and willing to take an active part in, the peace process.

28   Ibid., 4.

29   Leslie Gordon Barnard, *Chatelaine*, November 1937, 15.

30   Ibid., 53.

31   Maude Broomhall Sabine, *Chatelaine*, November 1937, 31.

32   Fraser Hunter, *Chatelaine*, January 1938, 10-11.

33   *Chatelaine*, March 1938, 10-11.

34   Ibid.,10. At least some Canadian women also felt that they were prepared for war. An Ottawa resident wrote: "Women in Canada are more fully trained for war today than any of those much-photographed, uniformed amazons in other countries. Today finds a mobilized force of experienced, intelligent

women, who have been successfully fighting their own battles in every field of commerce for the past twenty years." Ibid. A Calgarian responded, "Certainly the women of Canada should be organized to fight, if need be, for their lives and the protection of their homes." Ibid., 11.

35   Williamson and Gorham, *Up and Doing,* 31.

36   Ibid. It should be noted that this quote was in direct reference to the First World War.

37   Clare Boothe Luce, *Chatelaine*, February 1944, 6.

38   Isabel LeBourdais, *Chatelaine,* July 1947, 23, 49.

39   Brock Chisholm, *Chatelaine,* July 1948, 36-37.

40   The similarities between this real life spot in Deep River, Ontario and the fictional town of Stepford in Ira Levin's 1972 novel *Stepford Wives* are eerie.

41   Maria Parlow French, *Chatelaine,* August 1949, 16, 35, 34.

42   Anne Anderson Perry, *Chatelaine*, November 1928, 54-55.

43   During its first few years *Chatelaine* ran a column called "Art" that regularly featured Canadian artists, and one titled "Educational" that promoted Canadian history. The columns only lasted into 1931, but Canadian historical and artistic contributions remained high for several more years.

44   *Chatelaine*, May 1939, 10-12.

45   Canadian National Newspapers and Periodicals Association, *Chatelaine*, April 1936, 100.

46   "Movie Gossip," or "At the Movies" as it was sometimes called was renamed "As Hollywood Likes it," in May 1934, then "My Hollywood Diary" in July 1934 and appeared on a semi-regular basis thereafter with direct reference to Hollywood.

47   See for example, Thompson and Seager, *Canada 1922-1939,* 158-192; John Herd Thompson, "Canada's Quest for Cultural Sovereignty: Protection, Promotion and Popular Culture," in R. Douglas Francis and Donald B. Smith, (eds.), *Readings in Canadian History: Post Confederation* (Toronto: Harcourt Brace & Company, 1994), 508-521; and Nancy Christie and Michael Gauvreau, (ed.), *Cultures of Citizenship in Post-war Canada, 1940-1955* (Montreal: McGill-Queen's University Press, 2003).

48   Thompson and Seager, *Canada 1922-1939*, 158-192, quote, 175.

49   As Doug Owram notes of Canadian popular culture in the 1950s, "Like radio before it, and mass magazines before that, television extended the cultural influence of the United States." Doug Owram, *Born At The Right Time: A History of the Baby Boom Generation* (Toronto: University of Toronto Press, 1996), 92.

50   *Chatelaine*, July 1928, 46.

51   Canada in the 1920s and 1930s was a predominantly white Anglo-Saxon community with European roots. With a population of roughly 8.8 million people, 60 per cent of the people according to the 1921 census lived in the two central provinces, Ontario and Quebec. Urban dwellers slightly outnumbered rural inhabitants and the cities continued to expand. For the middle classes, the nuclear family was the cornerstone of Canadian society and Christian religion provided guidelines on proper moral and ethical behaviour. Thompson and Seager, *Canada 1922-1939*, 3, 5, 8. Restrictive, and arguably racist, immigration laws assured that these trends would continue throughout the interwar years. Valerie Knowles, *Strangers at Our Gates: Canadian Immigration and Immigration Policy, 1540-1997* (Toronto: Dundurn Press, 1997), 99-124. By 1931 the population of Canada had risen to just over ten million people. M.C. Urguhart and K.A.H. Buckly (eds.), *Historical Statistics of Canada* (Toronto, 1965), 14; *Canadian Statistical Review*, 1971, 1982; and *Canadian Social Trends* (Summer, 1992), reprinted in J.L. Finlay and D.N. Sprague, *The Structure of Canadian History,* 6th Edition (Scarborough: Prentice Hall Allyn and Bacon Canada, 2000), 582.

52   Byrne Hope Sanders, *Chatelaine*, September 1930, 16.

53   *Chatelaine*, March 1929, 39.

54   *Chatelaine*, March 1936, 63. For a brief discussion on Prime Minister King's treatment of tariffs regarding periodicals in the mid and late 1930s see Fraser Sutherland, *The Monthly Epic: A History of Canadian Magazines, 1799-1989* (Markham: Fitzhenry & Whiteside, 1989), 115-116. According to Mary Vipond, "Within a period of five years, Canadian government policy had managed first to create and then to break the custom of publishing foreign magazines in Canada, without having much effect on the circulation of foreign periodicals in the country." Mary Vipond cited in Ibid., 116.

55   The Publishers of *Chatelaine*, *Chatelaine*, March 1936, 90.

56   Canadian National Newspapers and Periodicals Association, *Chatelaine*, April 1936, 100.

57   *Chatelaine*, January 1930, 12-13.

58   Ellen Mackie, *Chatelaine*, March 1930, 19.

59   Elizabeth Hope, *Chatelaine*, March 1934, 16.

60   Mary Lowrey Ross, *Chatelaine*, March 1939, 10, 40.

61   Mollie McGee, *Chatelaine*, May 1937, 12-13.

62   *Chatelaine*, May 1939.

63   Mollie McGee, *Chatelaine*, September 1939, 16.

64   *Chatelaine*, October 1936, 84.

65   *Chatelaine*, November 1943, 71.

66   *Chatelaine*, December 1940, 16.

67   Wallace M. Reyburn, *Chatelaine*, March 1942, 16.

68   *Chatelaine*, November 1943, 67.

69   Mollie McGee, *Chatelaine*, May 1943, 22-23, 28.

70   Liz Gardner, *Chatelaine*, July 1946, 71.

71   Ibid., 11.

72   So too was the population. By 1941 the population was eleven and a half million and by 1951 it had increased to fourteen million. With the postwar "baby boom," by 1961 Canada had over eighteen million inhabitants. Finlay and Sprague, *The Structure of Canadian History*, 582.

73   British hairdresser cited in Margaret Ecker Francis, *Chatelaine*, September 1950, 5.

74   Phyllis Lee Peterson, *Chatelaine*, July 1956, 9.

75   Ibid., 59-60.

76   *Chatelaine*, March 1952, 9.

77   Ibid., 75.

78   Mrs. L. H. Achenson, *Chatelaine*, May 1952, 3.

79   Robert Bothwell, Ian Drummond and John English, *Canada Since 1945: Power, Politics, and Provincialism*, Revised Edition (Toronto: University of Toronto Press, 1989), 92. Nancy Christie and Michael Gauvreau question this assumption of Canadian and American cultural similarity. They suggest that between 1940 and 1955 the Canadian economy more closely resembles that of Germany, Britain and France. "American modernisation," according to Christie and Gauvrey, was delayed in reaching these nations. Christie and Gauvreau, *Cultures of Citizenship*, 4-6.

80   Vincent Massey reported similar findings in 1951 when he published his report on the Royal Commission on National Development in the Arts, Letters and Sciences. "In the aftermath of the Massey Commission Report" writes Valerie Korinek, "There was a heightened sense of the importance attached to creating, promoting, and popularising 'Canadian culture.'" Korinek was discussing Doris Anderson's tenure as editor of *Chatelaine* in the 1960s. Korinek, *Roughing It In the Suburbs*, 49.

81   Theresa A. Potter, *Chatelaine*, July 1953, 17.

82   John Clare, *Chatelaine*, March 1954, 68.

83   Ibid., 69.

84   Francois Thebaud, "Work, Gender, and Identity in Peace And War France, 1890 – 1930," in Billie Melman (ed.), *Borderlines: Gender and Identity in War and Peace* (New York: Routledge, Inc. 1998), 409.

Chapter Seven

Conclusions:
Revisiting *Chatelaine*'s Modern Woman

Husband: "What's a woman want with plans of her own …
when she's got a home and a man …"
Wife: "Anybody that's any good likes to have plans of their
own. … Even if it's ever so little it teaches us [women] – just
like it does the men …"

Mary Shannon

Chatelaine, October 1928[1]

In 1928 *Chatelaine* published an article by Mary Shannon that claimed
in its subtitle to be "a story of the age-old bond of womanhood." The
story was about Mary, her husband Daniel, their son Stuart and his
beautiful fiancée Ruth. Mary had spent her adult life subordinated to
her husband. Daniel worked the land for a living and had become
consumed with building a dyke. His considerable efforts were fruitless
and all the family's assets – most of which had come from Mary's father
– had been eaten up in the process. Daniel was oblivious to his
obsession. Mary feared that their son was heading down the same path.
When she reminded him that Ruth wanted to set up a chicken coup
Stuart asked, "What's she want with things of her own anyhow? What's
mine is hers isn't it?" Mary feared for Ruth. Ruth would be giving up
her job as a schoolteacher to be a full-time wife. "Why this child
had no idea of the life before her," Mary reflected. She explained,
"This sudden, hasty courtship! A love-match, of course, but. …" She

contemplated the results of marriage for Ruth, "This glowing young thing subdued, protesting, despairing, shriveled heart and soul to a bare kitchen with its endless dishes and washing and baking!" Mary was determined to help Ruth avoid the life that she had led. In an exceptional act of defiance she stood up to her husband and recited her long list of objections as to how he had controlled their destiny – in her opinion, largely for worse. Their son overheard their debate and vowed not to be like his father. Daniel, now rejected by his only offspring, took solace in the fact that Mary, despite her oratorical defiance, continued to stand by him. Ruth re-entered the picture as the family theatrics subdued. "I want to help get supper," Ruth announced. Her reason, "I must learn about – well, about what Stuart likes especially, you know." Mary considered this a wonderful request now that she had assured a "happy" marriage between her son and the schoolteacher. And, "With hands clasped in the age-old bond of womanhood, they went across the spring decked pasture to the old house."[2]

Wife, mother, homemaker, wage-earner, nation builder, peace advocate – who was *Chatelaine*'s modern woman? *Lipstick and High Heels* presents a patchwork of stories, both real and imaginary, that were published in the pages of *Chatelaine* from its inception in 1928 to 1956. As a collection, these images provide insight into who *Chatelaine*'s modern woman of the depression, the war years and the postwar period was. She was not a singular composite – like Ruth, she was at once many things and her image changed with time and, like Mary, women of an older generation often helped to define modern womanhood. Several threads, however, managed to weave their way throughout connecting *Chatelaine*'s modern pre-World War Two woman with her postwar counterpart and served to both reflect and shape assumptions about middle-class Canadian womanhood. These threads represent the continuities that existed in *Chatelaine*'s modern woman, although their expression was often more symbolic of discontinuities.

Each chapter of *Lipstick and High Heels* explores one of these threads. Nearly every issue of *Chatelaine* that was examined covered all of these topics. Interestingly, while these categories provide prisms through which to study *Chatelaine*'s modern woman, the results are kaleidoscopic. What is clear is that the war – and indeed the fear of war – did have a fundamental and long lasting effect on how *Chatelaine* portrayed modern Canadian womanhood.

Of most importance to this book is the fact that it is undeniable that *Chatelaine*'s modern woman was transformed at the same time that the magazine started to project serious concerns about another European war, circa 1936/37. At this time the very survival of democracy appeared to be threatened – a fear that continued into the Cold War.

In the diverse roles of women – as wives, mothers, homemakers, wage-earners, nation builders and peace advocates – there were two major changes that occurred in *Chatelaine* from 1928 to 1956. Motherhood and femininity – each important components of womanhood in *Chatelaine* from 1928 to 1956 – increased in value for *Chatelaine*'s modern woman in the immediate pre-war period. These changes were long-lasting and they often situated women in the private sphere, generally to the exclusion of the public sphere, although a woman's femininity could sometimes help legitimate her paid employment.

The increased status of motherhood and the emphasis placed on femininity indicate areas that previous researchers have used to measure effects of war on gender relationships. An increase in the pervasiveness of either image has usually been used to argue that war had a negative impact on women's social positions. Conversely, the absence of these categories in analyses of wartime participation and women's postwar status has led some to claim that war is "liberating" for women. Much of this research, however, assumes that motherhood and femininity are largely incompatible with feminism.

Lipstick and High Heels rejects the idea that the feminine mother is by mere virtue of these attributes not a "liberated" woman. Interestingly, however, there are parallels that suggest that the heightened attention associated with motherhood and femininity in *Chatelaine* has, to some degree, been associated with a re-negotiation of the gender relationship in which the man is seen to profit. While it is important not to assume that emphases on motherhood and femininity automatically subordinate women to men, in *Chatelaine* these emphases were generally combined with an absence of other, perhaps more relevant, information such as the work that women were performing. Arguably, these absences can be used to suggest that many of these images are largely incompatible with liberal feminist beliefs. Notably, however, they are not so far removed from the maternal feminism that was popular in the 1930s, 1940s and 1950s. While Jeffrey A. Keshen is correct in his claim that feminism and femininity are not necessarily in opposition, it is important to realize that this statement does not mean that they will never be in opposition.[3] This examination of *Chatelaine* magazine during the thirty years surrounding the Second World War illustrates this point; it was only in the late 1930s, that the feminine, competent woman was replaced by the "lovely," feminine wife/mother figure.

Lipstick and High Heels returns the debate on gender, war and society to Ruth Roach Pierson and supports her claim that the Second World War ultimately had a feminizing effect on images of Canadian womanhood even if women were temporarily accepted into the workforce between 1939 and 1945.[4] The Second World War – and, indeed, even the fear of war beginning in 1936/37 – was a watershed for images of women in *Chatelaine*. Like Cynthia L. White does in the British context,[5] *Lipstick and High Heels* shows how images of women in *Chatelaine* became more "traditional" as war approached, a change that proved long lasting.

In a way, however, this book also supports Margaret R. Higonnet and Patrice L.-R. Higonnnet's model of a double helix.[6] Like Alison Prentice, Paula Bourne, Gail Cuthbert Brandt, Beth Light, Wendy Mitchinson, and Naomi Black argue in "The Bren Gun Girl and the Housewife Heroine," *Lipstick and High Heels* shows how the war perpetuated the image of women in support of men.[7] It also agrees with M. Susan Bland's findings on the images of women in advertisements published in *Maclean's* magazine during the 1940s. Bland argues that these images were more illustrative of continuities than discontinuities and that the women in the advertisements had overtly feminine qualities.[8]

Importantly, however, *Lipstick and High Heels* also shows that when viewed within the broader time frame of 1928 to 1956, what has previously been categorized as wartime continuities in gendered representations are actually markedly different than those that existed in the late 1920s and early 1930s. The double helix model only applies in the case of *Chatelaine* if the analysis begins in the immediate pre-war period, circa 1936/37. Certainly, as this work shows, there is much value in exploring the relationships of gender, war and society within a broader time frame. Indeed, each chapter of *Lipstick and High Heels* supports the argument that the war, and, more importantly, the threat of war, was a watershed moment for women and men and the relationships between the sexes that were portrayed in *Chatelaine*.

In chapter three, *Chatelaine's* modern wife started out confidently choosing a husband at her leisure for emotional and/or economic reasons. If the marriage was not successful, then divorce was a socially acceptable option. With an expressed threat of war in 1936/37, husbands became a "needed" commodity. Women were encouraged to act as feminine as possible in order to "catch" a man. The change to *Chatelaine's* modern wife is apparent. However, the important difference between

Lipstick and High Heels:

Chatelaine's pre-World War Two wife and her wartime counterpart was not that the latter was perhaps more feminine, it was that she was no longer complete on her own – she needed a husband. In the postwar period, women did not lament the application of beauty products or other feminine rituals. Instead, the images in *Chatelaine* suggest that single women were frustrated with the search for a man and some women, who were now expected to stay married at all costs, felt trapped in their conjugal binds.

Changes to *Chatelaine*'s modern mother followed a similar pattern. *Chatelaine* always assumed that women married to have children. But at first the magazine did not suggest that women were naturally good at this task or that motherhood would be their sole occupation – recreation and working for wages provided viable alternatives. With the Second World War, however, motherhood increased in social value and paradox-ically, given the pervasiveness of the image of working women in the magazine, women were expected to be even more devoted to their off-spring. This carried into the postwar period. It was not motherhood, however, that caused some women to question their happiness. According to *Chatelaine*, women were discouraged by the fact that motherhood and homemaking were expected to be their only pursuits. The heightened importance of motherhood alone did not confine women; it was some of the other associated social implications that were put on them that did.

The major change for *Chatelaine*'s working woman was that the war years created new criteria to evaluate her work ability. Generally, productivity was exchanged for femininity in the workplace. Additionally, *Chatelaine* suggested that the main reason that women worked – outside of directly contributing to the war effort – was to "catch" a husband. It was generally accepted that women would leave the business world when they became wives. Certainly, *Chatelaine*'s working wife, especially if she was a mother, presented unique challenges to gender norms in the magazine. In these cases, feminine qualities were often exaggerated.

Another transformation that occurred in *Chatelaine* in the immediate pre-World War Two period is that women were increasingly connected with the private sphere of hearth and home, largely to the exclusion of the more male dominated arenas of politics and economics. Chapter six shows how these developments affected *Chatelaine*'s images of women as peace advocates and nation builders. Advocating peace and nation building, always central concerns for *Chatelaine*'s modern woman, were placed aside after World War Two as many women now no longer took active roles in these processes but instead supported their husbands' work.

To return now to the question of who *Chatelaine*'s modern woman was, one must conclude that she remains largely an enigma, yet she nonetheless had some defining characteristics. By grouping the chapters thematically, *Lipstick and High Heels* shows how *Chatelaine*'s modern woman had diverse roles – she was a wife, mother, homemaker, wage-earner, nation builder and peace advocate. Interestingly, while she was all of these things, there was also much overlap between these spheres. For example, the wage-earning mother usually had a strong national consciousness, she was often concerned with peace and she undoubtedly took care of the home. And she was also resolutely middle-class. Teasing out these differences in each chapter has allowed for changes and continuities to be observed individually in each of these areas and collectively. While *Chatelaine*'s modern woman did evolve as a whole, the chapters show that the changes were somewhat unique in each area. Of most importance to *Lipstick and High Heels* is the fact that generally these transformations occurred in the late 1930s and were coupled with an expressed fear in *Chatelaine* of another European war and a growing perception that the survival of democracy might be in peril.

In fact, *Lipstick and High Heels* builds a strong case for the argument that the war did affect images of women in *Chatelaine* and, more importantly, fear of war seems to have initiated these changes. War was not an agent of "liberation" in respect to how *Chatelaine* portrayed modern Canadian womanhood; despite the growing involvement of women in the public sphere during the wartime emergency, the images that were published in *Chatelaine* of modern Canadian womanhood from 1939 to 1945 were more traditional than those of the previous decade.

Endnotes

1   Mary Shannon, *Chatelaine*, October 1928, 59.

2   Ibid., 20-21, 57-60.

3   Jeffrey A. Keshen, *Saints, Sinners, and Soldiers: Canada's Second World War* (Vancouver: UBC Press, 2004), 151.

4   Ruth Roach Pierson, *They're Still Women After All: The Second World War and Canadian Womanhood* (Toronto: MaClelland and Stewart Limited, 1986).

5   Cynthia L. White, *Women's Magazines, 1693 – 1968* (London: Michael Joseph, Ltd., 1970).

6   Margaret R. Higonnet and Patrice L.-R. Higonnet, "The Double Helix," in Margaret Randolph Higonnet, Jane Jenson, Sonya Michel and Margaret Collins Weitz, (eds.), *Behind the Lines: Gender and the Two World Wars* (New Haven: Yale University Press, 1987), 31-47.

7   Alison Prentice, P. Bourne, G.C. Brandt, B. Light, W. Mitchinson and N. Black, "The Bren Gun Girl and the Housewife Heroine," in R. Douglas Francis and Donald B. Smith, *Readings in Canadian History: Post-Confederation*, 3rd edition (Toronto: Holt, Rinehart and Winston of Canada, Limited), 440-462.

8   M. Susan Bland, "Henrietta the Homemaker, and 'Rosie the Riveter': Images of Women in Advertising in *Maclean's* Magazine, 1939-1950," *Atlantis*, 8 (1983), 61-86.

Bibliography

Primary Source

Chatelaine, 1928 – 1956

Secondary Sources: Books, Chapters and Articles

Aitken, Margaret and Byrne Hope Sanders. *Hey Ma! I Did It.* Toronto: Clarke, Irwin & Company Limited, 1953.

Alonso, Harriet Hyman. *Peace as a Woman's Issue: A History of the U.S. Movement for World Peace and Women's Rights.* Syracuse: Syracuse University Press, 1993.

Anderson, Doris. *Rebel Daughter: An Autobiography.* Toronto: Key Porter, 1996.

Arnold, Gladys. *One Woman's War.* Halifax: Goodread Biographies, 1988.

Axelrod, Paul. *Making a Middle Class: Student Life in English Canada During the Thirties.* Montreal & Kingston: McGill-Queen's University Press, 1990.

Baillargeon, Denyse. "'If You Had No Money, You Had No Trouble, Did You?': Montreal Working-Class Housewives during the Great Depression," in Wendy Mitchinson, Alison Prentice, Paula Bourne, Gail Cuthbert Brandt, Beth Light and Naomi Black, (eds.). *Canadian Women: A Reader.* Toronto: Harcourt Brace Canada, 1996.

Barrell, Joan and Brian Braithwaite. *The Business of Women's Magazines.* 2nd edition. London: Kogan Page, 1988.

Beddoe, Deidre. *Back to Home and Duty: Women Between the Wars, 1918 – 1939.* London: Pandora Press, 1989.

Berg, Alison. *Mothering the Race: Women's Narratives of Reproduction, 1890–1930.* University of Illinois Press, 2002.

Bland, M. Susan. "Henrietta the Homemaker, and 'Rosie the Riveter': Images of Women in Advertising in *Maclean's* Magazine, 1939-1950." *Atlantis* 8 (1983): 61-86.

Bothwell, Robert, Ian Drummond and John English. *Canada Since 1945: Power, Politics, and Provincialism.* Revised Edition. Toronto: University of Toronto Press, 1989.

Bowlby, Rachel. "'The Problem with No Name': Rereading Friedan's The Feminine Mystique." *Feminist Review* 27 (September 1987): 611-75.

Brandt, Gail Cuthbert. "Postmodern Patchwork: Some Recent Trends in the Writing of Women's History in Canada." *Canadian Historical Association* 9 (1998): 441-470.

Braybon, Gail. "Winners or Losers: Women's Symbolic Role in the War Story," in Grayzel, Susan S., (ed.). *Women's Identities at War: Gender, Motherhood, and Politics in Britain and France During the First World War.* Chapel Hill: the University of North Carolina Press, 1999: 86-112.

Braybon, Gail, (ed.). *Evidence, History and the Great War: Historians and the Impact of 1914-1918.* New York: Berghahn Books, 2003.

Brock, Peter and Thomas P. Socknat, (eds.). *Challenge to Mars: Essays on Pacifism From 1918 to 1945.* Toronto: University of Toronto Press, 1999.

Bruce, Jean. *Back the Attack: Canadian Women During the Second World War.* Toronto: Macmillan, 1985.

Christie, Nancy and Michael Gauvreau, (eds.). *Cultures of Citizenship in Post-war Canada, 1940-1955.* Montreal: McGill-Queen's University Press, 2003.

Comacchio, Cynthia. "'A Postscript for Father': Defining a New Fatherhood in Interwar Canada." *The Canadian Historical Review* 78 (1997): 385-408.

Condell, Diana and Jean Liddiard. *Working for Victory?: Images of Women in the First World War, 1914-1918.* London: Routledge, 1987.

Cook, Ramsay. *Canada: A Modern Study.* Toronto: Clarke, Irwin, 1971.

Cuordileone, K.A. *Manhood and American Political Culture in the Cold War.* New York: Routledge, 2005.

Currie, Dawn H. *Girl Talk: Adolescent Magazines and Their Readers.* Toronto: University of Toronto Press, 1999.

De Groot, Gerald J. "'I Love the Scent of Cordite in Your Hair': Gender Dynamics in Mixed Anti-Aircraft Batteries During the Second World War." *History* 82 (1997): 73-92.

Dempsey, Lotta. *No Life for a Lady.* Don Mills: Musson Book Company, 1976.

De Pauw, Linda Grant. *Battle Cries and Lullabies: Women in War from Prehistory to the Present.* Norman: University of Oklahoma Press, 1998.

Dewar, Jane. *True Canadian War Stories.* Toronto: Lester and Orpen Denny's Limited, 1986.

Dreisziger, N.F., (ed.). *Mobilization for Total War: The Canadian, American and British Experiences, 1914-1918, 1939-1945.* Waterloo: Wilfred Laurier University Press, 1981.

Dummitt, Chris. "Finding a Place for Father: Selling the Barbecue in Postwar Canada." *Journal of the Canadian Historical Association* 9 (1998): 209-222.

Edgerton, Robert B. *Warrior Women: The Amazons of Dahomey and the Nature of War.* Boulder: Westview Press, 2000.

BIBLIOGRAPHY

Finlay, J.L. and D.N. Sprague. *The Structure of Canadian History.* 6th edition. Scarborough: Prentice Hall Allyn and Bacon Canada, 2000.

Fraser, Sylvia, (ed.). *A Woman's Place: Seventy Years in the lives of Canadian Women.* Toronto: Key Porter Books, 1977.

Freeman, Jo. *Women: A Feminist Perspective.* 3rd edition. Palo Alto: Mayfield Publishing Company, 1984.

Friedan, Betty. *The Feminine Mystique.* New York: Bantam Doubleday Dell, 1963.

Geise, L. Ann. "The Female Role in Middle Class Women's Magazines from 1955 to 1976: A Content Analysis of Nonfiction." *Sex Roles* 5 (1979), 51-62

Gidney, Catherine. "Under the President's Gaze: Sexuality and Morality at a Canadian University During the Second World War," in Cynthia R. Comacchio and Elizabeth Jane Errington, (eds.). *People, Places and Times, Readings in Canadian History: Volume 2: Post-Confederation.* Toronto: Thomson Nelson, 2006: 232-244.

Gleason, Mona. *Normalizing the Ideal: Psychology, Schooling, and the Family in Postwar Canada.* Toronto: University of Toronto Press, 1999.

Goldstein, Joshua S. *War and Gender: How Gender Shapes the War System and Vice Versa.* Cambridge: New York : Cambridge University Press, 2001.

Golz, Annalee. "The Canadian Family and the State in Postwar Period." *Left History* 1,2 (1993): 9-49.

Gorham, Deborah. *The Victorian Girl and the Feminine Ideal.* Bloomington: Indiana University Press, 1982.

Gossage, Carolyn. *Greatcoats and Glamour Boots.* Toronto: Dundurn Press, 1991.

Granatstein, J.L. *Canada's Army: Waging War and Keeping the Peace.* Toronto: University of Toronto Press, 2002.

Grant, George. *Lament for a Nation: the Defeat of Canadian Nationalism.* Toronto: McClelland and Stewart Limited, 1965.

Grayzel, Susan S., (ed.). *Women's Identities at War: Gender, Motherhood, and Politics in Britain and France During the First World War.* Chapel Hill: the University of North Carolina Press, 1999.

-- -- -- "Liberating Women? Examining Gender, Morality and Sexuality in First World War Britain and France," in Grayzel, Susan S., (eds.) *Women's Identities at War: Gender, Motherhood, and Politics in Britain and France During the First World War.* Chapel Hill: the University of North Carolina Press, 1999: 119-126.

Griffiths, Naomi Elizabeth Saundaus. *The Splendid Vision: Centennnial History of the National Council of Women of Canada: 1893-1993.* Ottawa: Carleton University Press, 1993.

Gubar, Susan. "'This Is My Rifle, This Is My Gun': World War Two and the Blitz on Women," in Margaret Randolph Higonnet, Jane Jenson, Sonya Michel and Margaret Collins Weitz, (eds.). *Behind the Lines: Gender and the Two World Wars.* New Haven: Yale University Press, 1987: 227-259.

Hacker, Barton C. "Women and Military Institutions in Early Modern Europe: A Reconnaissance." *Signs: Journal of Women in Culture and Society* 6 (1981): 643 -671.

Higonnet, Margaret and Patrice Higonnet. "The Double Helix," in Margaret Randolph Higonnet, Jane Jenson, Sonya Michel and Margaret Collins Weitz, (eds.). *Behind the Lines: Gender and the Two World Wars.* New Haven: Yale University Press, 1987: 31-47.

Hobbs, Margaret. "Equality and Difference: Feminism and the Defence of Women Workers during the Great Depression," in Wendy

Mitchinson, Paula Bourne, Alison Prentice, Gail Cuthbert Brandt, Beth Light and Naomi Black, (eds.). *Canadian Women: A Reader.* Toronto: Harcourt Brace & Company, 1996: 212-232.

Hobbs, Margaret and Ruth Roach Pierson. "'A Kitchen that Wastes No Steps...' Gender, Class and the Home Improvement Plan, 1936-1940." *Histoire Sociale/Social History* 21 (1988): 9-37.

Honey, Maureen. *Creating Rosie the Riveter: Class, Gender, and Propaganda During World War II.* Amherst: University of Massachusetts Press, 1984.

Houlihan, Inez. *The Image of Women in Chatelaine Editorials: March 1928 – September 1977.* MA Thesis, OISE, University of Toronto, 1984.

Iacovetta, Franca and Mariana Valderde, (eds.). *Gender Conflicts: New Essays in Women's History.* Toronto: University of Toronto Press, 1992.

Kealy, Linda and Joan Sangster. *Beyond the Vote: Canadian Women and Politics.* Toronto: University of Toronto Press, 1989.

Keshen, Jeffrey A. *Saints, Sinners, and Soldiers: Canada's Second World War.* Vancouver: UBC Press, 2004.

-- -- -- "Revisiting Canada's Civilian Women." *Histoire Sociale/Social History* 30 (1997): 239-66.

-- -- -- *War and Propaganda and Censorship During Canada's Great War.* Edmonton: The University of Alberta Press, 1996.

Kessler-Harris, Alice. *Women Have Always Worked: An Historical Overview.* Old Wesbury: The Feminist Press, 1981.

Kirkham, Pat. "Beauty and Duty: Keeping Up the (Home) Front," in Pat Kirkham and David Thoms, (eds.). *War and Culture: Social Changes and Changing Experience in World War Two.* London: Lawrence & Wishart, 1995: 13-28.

Klein, Yvonne. *Beyond the Home Front: Women's Autobiographical Writing of the Two World Wars.* New York: New York University Press, 1997.

Knowles, Valerie. *Strangers at Our Gates: Canadian Immigration and Immigration Policy, 1540-1997.* Toronto: Dundurn Press, 1997.

Korinek, Valerie J. "'Don't Let Your Girlfriends Ruin Your Marriage': Lesbian Imagery in *Chatelaine* Magazine, 1950-1969," in Cynthia R. Comacchio and Elizabeth Jane Errington, (eds.). *People, Places and Times, Readings in Canadian History*, Volume 2: Post-Confederation. Toronto: Thomson Nelson, 2006: 245-264.

-- -- -- *Roughing it in the Suburbs: Reading Chatelaine Magazine in the Fifties and Sixties.* Toronto, University of Toronto Press, 2000.

Levesque, Andree. *Making and Breaking the Rules : Women in Quebec 1919-1939.* Toronto: McClelland and Stewart, 1994.

Ladouceur, Barbara and Phyllis Spence, (eds.). *Blackouts to Bright Lights: Canadian War Bride Stories.* Vancouver: Ronsdale Press, 1995.

Latta, Ruth, (ed.). *The Memory of all That.* Burnstown: the General Store Publishing House Inc., 1992.

Light, Beth and Ruth Roach Pierson, (eds.). *No Easy Road: Women in Canada, 1920s to 1960s: Documents in Canadian Women's History.* Volume 3. Toronto: New Hogtown Press, 1990.

Luxton, Meg, Harriet Rosenberg, and Sedef Arat Koc, (eds.). *Through the Kitchen Window: The Politics of Home and Family.* Toronto: Garamond Press, 1990.

Marwick, Arthur. *The Home Front: The British and the Second World War.* London: Thames and Hudson, 1976.

-- -- -- *War and Social Change in the Twentieth Century: A Comparative Study of Britain, France, Germany, Russia and the United States.* London: The Macmillan Press Ltd., 1974.

BIBLIOGRAPHY

Mathews-Kline, Yvonne. "How They Saw Us: Images of Women in National Film Board Films of the 1940s and 1950s." *Atlantis* 14 (spring 1979): 20-33.

McCracken, Ellen. *Decoding Women's Magazines: From Mademoiselle to Ms.* London: Macmillan, 1993.

McLaren Angus and Alrene Tigar McLaren. *The Bedroom and the State.* Toronto: McClelland and Stewart Limited, 1986.

Meyerowitz, Joanne. "Beyond the Feminine Mystique: A Reassessment of Postwar Mass Culture, 1946 – 1958," in Joanne Meyerowitz, (ed.). *Not June Cleaver: Women and Gender in Postwar America, 1945-1960.* Philadelphia: Temple University Press, 1994: 229-262 .

Michel, Sonya. "American Women and the Discourse of Democratic Family in World War II," in Margaret Randolph Higonnet, Jane Jenson, Sonya Michel and Margaret Collins Weitz, (eds.). *Behind the Lines: Gender and the Two World Wars.* New Haven: Yale University Press, 1987: 154-167.

Modell John and Duane Steffey, "Waging War and Marriage: Military Service and Family Formation, 1940-1950." *Journal of Family History* 13 (1988): 195-218.

Mitchinson, Wendy. "The WCTU: 'For God, Home and Native Land': A Study in Nineteenth-Century Feminism," in Linda Kealey, (ed.). *A Not Unreasonable Claim: Women and Reform in Canada, 1800s-1920s.* Toronto: The Women's Educational Press, 1979: 151-168.

Molyneaux, Heather. *The Representation of Women in Chatelaine Magazine Advertisements.* M.A. Thesis, The University of New Brunswick, 2002.

Morton, Desmond. *Understanding Canadian Defence.* Toronto: Penguin Canada, 2003.

Nicholson, Mavis. *What Did You Do in the War, Mummy?: Women in World War Two.* London: Chatto & Windus, 1995.

Nelles, H.V. *A Little History of Canada*. Don Mills: Oxford University Press, 2004.

Nourie, Alan and Barabra Nourie, (eds.). *American Mass Market Magazines*. New York: Greenwood Press, 1990.

Ohmann, Richard. *Making and Selling Culture*. Hanover, NH: Wesleyan University Press, 1996.

Owram, Doug. *Born At The Right Time: A History of the Baby Boom Generation*. Toronto: University of Toronto Press, 1996.

Palmer, Brian D. *Working-Class Experience: Rethinking the History of Canadian Labour, 1800-1991*. Toronto: McClelland & Stewart Inc., 1992.

Parr, Joy, (ed.). *A Diversity of Women: Ontario, 1945-1980*. Toronto: University of Toronto Press, 1995.

Pierson, Ruth Roach. "Gender and the Unemployment Insurance Debates in Canada, 1934 – 1940," in A.D. Gilbert, C.M. Wallace and R.M. Bray, (eds.). *Reappraisals in Canadian History: Post Confederation*. Scarborough: Prentice Hall Canada Inc., 1992: 336-367.

-- -- -- *Women and Peace*. London: Croom Helm, 1987.

-- -- -- *They're Still Women After All: The Second World War and Canadian Womanhood*. Toronto: McClelland and Stewart Limited, 1986.

-- -- -- *Canadian Women and the Second World War*. Ottawa: The Canadian Historical Association, 1983.

Pilkington, Gwendoline M. *Time Remembered: A Woman's Story of World War II*. Burnstown: the General Store Publishing House Inc., 1993.

Porter, Ann. "Women and Income Security in the Postwar Period: The Case of Unemployment Insurance, 1945-1962," in Wendy Mitchinson, Alison Prentice, Paula Bourne, Gail Cuthbert Brandt,

BIBLIOGRAPHY

Beth Light, and Naomi Black, (eds.). *Canadian Women: A Reader.* Toronto: Harcourt Brace & Company, Canada, 1996: 322-351.

Prentice, Alison, Paula Bourne, Gail Cuthbert Brandt, Beth Light, Wendy Mitchinson and Naomi Black. "The Bren Gun Girl and the Housewife Heroine," in R. Douglas Francis and Donald B. Smith, (eds.). *Readings in Canadian History: Post-Confederation.* 3rd edition. Toronto: Holt, Rinehart and Winston of Canada, Limited: 440-462.

Prentice, Alison, Paula Bourne, Gail Cuthbert Brandt, Beth Light, Wendy Mitchinson and Naomi Black. *Canadian Women: A History.* Toronto: Harcourt Brace Jovanovich, 1996.

Reed, David. *The Popular Magazine in Britain and the United States, 1880 – 1960.* Toronto: University of Toronto Press, 1997.

Riley, Denise. "Some Peculiarities of Social Policy Concerning Women in Wartime and Postwar Britain," in Margaret Randolph Higonnet, Jane Jenson, Sonya Michel and Margaret Collins Weitz, (eds.). *Behind the Lines: Gender and the Two World Wars.* New Haven: Yale University Press, 1987: 260-271.

Roman, Leslie G., and Linda K. Christian-Smith, (eds.). *Becoming Feminine: The Politics of Popular Culture.* London: Falmer Press, 1988.

Rubinstein, David. *Before the Suffragettes: Women's Emancipation in the 1890s.* New York: St. Martin's Press, 1986.

Rupp, Leila J. *Mobilizing Women for War: German and American Propaganda, 1939-1945.* Princeton: Princeton University Press, 1978.

Rutherdale, Robert. "Fatherhood, Masculinity, and the Good Life During Canada's Baby Boom, 1945-1965." *Journal of Family History* 24 (1999): 351-373.

Russell, Peter, (ed.). *Nationalism in Canada.* Toronto: McGraw-Hill, 1966.

Rymell, Heather. "Images of Women in the Magazines of the 30s and 40s." *Canadian Woman Studies* 3 (1981): 96-9.

Sangster, Joan. "Doing Two Jobs: The Wage-Earning Mother, 1945-70," in Joy Parr, (ed.). *A Diversity of Women: Ontario, 1945-1980*. Toronto: University of Toronto Press, 1995: 98-134.

Scanlon, Jennifer. *Inarticulate Longings: The Ladies' Home Journal, Gender, and the Promises of Consumer Culture*. London: Routledge, 1995.

Schwartz, Mildred A. *Public Opinion and Canadian Identity*. Berkeley: University of California Press, 1967.

Sentek, Jennifer, M. *"Women at War": Recruiting Images of the CWAR 1942-1945*. M.A. Thesis, Royal Military College of Canada, June 1997.

Smith, Harold L. "The Effect of War on the Status of Women," in Harold L. Smith, (ed.). *War and Social Change: British Society in the Second World War*. Manchester: Manchester University Press, 1986: 208-229.

Snell, James, G. *In the Shadow of the Law: Divorce in Canada, 1900 – 1939*. Toronto: University of Toronto Press, 1991.

Socknat, Thomas P. "For Peace and Freedom: Canadian Feminists and the Interwar Peace Campaign," in Janice Williamson and Deborah Gorham, (eds.). *Up and Doing: Canadian Women and Peace*. Toronto: The Women's Press, 1989: 66-88.

-- -- -- *Witness Against War: Pacifism in Canada, 1900 – 1945*. Toronto: University of Toronto Press, 1987.

Srigley, Katrina. "In case you hadn't noticed!' Race, Ethnicity, and Women's Wage-Earning in a Depression-Era City." *Labour/ Le Travail* 55 (2005): 69-105.

Strong-Boag, Veronica. "'Their Side of the Story': Women's Voices form Ontario Suburbs, 1945-1960," in Joy Parr, (ed.). *A Diversity of Women: Ontario, 1945-1980.* Toronto: University of Toronto Press, 1995: 46-74.

-- -- -- "Canada's Wage-Earning Wives and the Construction of the Middle Class, 1945- 1960." *Journal of Canadian Studies* 29 (Fall 1994): 5-25.

-- -- -- *"Janey Canuck": Women in Canada, 1919-1939.* Ottawa: The Canadian Historical Association, 1994.

-- -- -- "Intruders in the Nursery: Childcare Professionals Reshape the Years One to Five," in Joy Parr (ed.). *Childhood and Family in Canadian History.* Toronto: McClelland and Stewart Limited, 1982: 160-178.

-- -- -- "Home Dreams: Women and the Suburban Experiment in Canada, 1945 – 1960." *Canadian Historical Review* 72 (1991): 471-504.

-- -- -- *The New Day Recalled.* Toronto: Copp Clark Pitman Ltd., 1988.

-- -- -- "Peace-making Women: Canada 1919-1939," in Ruth Roach Pierson, (ed.). *Women and Peace: Theoretical, Historical and Practical Perspectives.* London: Croom Helm, 1987: 170-191.

Strong-Boag, Veronica and A.C. Fellman. *Rethinking Canada: the Promise of Women's History.* Toronto: Copp Clark Pitman Ltd., 1991.

Summerfield, Penny. "Gender and War in the Twentieth Century." *The International History Review* 19 (1997): 4-15.

-- -- -- *Women Workers in the Second World War: Production and Patriarchy in Conflict.* London: Croom Helm, 1984.

Sutherland, Fraser. *The Monthly Epic: A History of Canadian Magazines.* Markham: Fitzhenry & Whiteside, 1989.

Swerdlow, Amy. *Women Strike for Peace: Traditional Motherhood and Radical Politics in the 1960s.* Chicago: University of Chicago Press, 1993.

Thebaud, Francois. "Work, Gender, and Identity in Peace and War France, 1890 – 1930," in Billie Melman, (ed.). *Borderlines: Gender and Identity in War and Peace.* New York: Routledge, Inc. 1998: 397-421.

Thom, Maryé. *Inside Ms.: 25 Years of the Magazine and the Feminist Movement.* New York: Henry Holt, 1997.

Thompson, John Herald and Allen Seager. *Canada 1922-1939: Decades of Discord.* Toronto: McClelland and Stewart Limited, 1985.

Thompson, John Herald. "Canada's Quest for Cultural Sovereignty: Protection, Promotion and Popular Culture," in R. Douglas Francis and Donald B. Smith, (eds.), *Readings in Canadian History: Post Confederation.* Toronto: Harcourt Brace & Company, 1994: 508-521.

Thorn, Deborah. "Making Spectaculars: Museums and How We Remember Gender in Wartime," in Gail Braybon, (ed.). *Evidence, History and the Great War: Historians and the Impact of 1914–1918.* New York: Berghahn Books, 2003.

Trofimenkoff, Susan Mann and Alison Prentice, (eds.). *The Neglected Majority: Essays in Canadian Women's History.* Toronto: McClelland and Stewart Limited, 1977.

Tuchman, Gaye, Arlene Kaplan Daniels and James Benet, (eds.). *Hearth and Home: Images of Women in the Mass Media.* New York: Oxford University Press, 1978.

Valverde, Marianna. "'When the Mother of the Race Is Free': Race, Reproduction, and Sexuality in First-Wave Feminism," in Franca Iacovetta and Mariana Valverde, (eds.). *Gender Conflicts: New Essays in Women's History.* Toronto: University of Toronto Press, 1992: 3-26.

-- -- -- *The Age of Light, Soap, and Water: Moral Reform in English Canada, 1885-1925.* Toronto: McClelland & Stewart Inc., 1991.

BIBLIOGRAPHY

Vance, Jonathan F. *Death So Noble: Memory, Meaning and the First World War.* Vancouver: University of British Columbia Press, 1997.

Vipond, Mary. "The Image of Women in Mass Circulation Magazines in the 1920s," in Susan Mann Trofimenkiff and Alison Prentice, (eds.). *The Neglected Majority: Essays in Canadian Women's History.* Toronto: McClelland & Stewart, 1977: 116-124.

-- -- -- *The Mass Media in Canada.* Toronto: James Lorimer, 1989.

White, Cynthia L. *Women's Magazines, 1693 – 1968.* London: Michael Joseph, Ltd., 1970.

Wicks, Ben. *Promise You'll Take Care of My Daughter.* Toronto: Stoddart Publishing co. Limited, 1992.

Williamson Janice and Deborah Gorham, (eds.). *Up and Doing Canadian Women and Peace.* Toronto: Women's Press, 1989.

Wilson, Susannah Jane Foster. *The Relationship Between Mass Media Content and Social Change in Canada: An Examination of the Image of Women in Mass Circulating Canadian Magazines 1930-1970.* Ph.D. Dissertation: University of Toronto, 1977.

Winship, Janice. *Inside Women's Magazines.* London: Pandora, 1987.

Wright, Gordon. *The Ordeal of Total War.* New York: Harper and Row, Publishers, 1968.

Wolf, Naomi. *The Beauty Myth: How Images of Beauty Are Used Against Women.* New York: William Morrow and Company, Inc., 1991.

About the Author

Emily Spencer has a Ph.D. and Master of Arts in War Studies from the Royal Military College of Canada (RMC) and a Bachelor's degree in Psychology from Dalhousie University. Dr. Spencer is currently employed as a Research Officer with the Canadian Forces Leadership Institute where she focuses on the applicability of cultural intelligence to current Canadian Forces deployments and counter-insurgency, as well as leadership issues. Additionally, she works as an Adjunct-Assistant Professor with the History Department at RMC. Dr. Spencer has taught Canadian history and Canadian military history to both cadets and regular force officers. Moreover, Dr. Spencer has given numerous keynote addresses in the areas of cultural intelligence, counter-insurgency as well as war and society. She has a number of publications in the same fields.

Index

Houlihan, Inez **35** *endnotes*, 52, 53, **60** *endnotes*, **62** *endnotes*, **244** *biblio.*

Housekeeper 88, 117, 119, 120

Housekeeping 100, 117, 120, 122, 187

Housewife 2, 5, 10, 14, 18, 20-23, **32** *endnotes*, **33** *endnotes*, **35** *endnotes*, 49, 50, 59, 87, 90, 91, 100, 102, 115, 118-121, **150** *endnotes*, 183, 190, **194** *endnotes*, 209, 235, **238** *endnotes*, **248** *biblio.*

Husband 4, 6, 11, 15, 20, 41-43, 53, 58, 65-69, 71, 73-76, 79, 81, 86-91, 93, 95, 97-105, **106-109** *endnotes*, **111** *endnotes*, 115-117, 119, 120, 124, 130-133, 135. 136, 138, 142-144, 146-148, 157, 158, 162, 163, 165, 168, 169, 171, 181, 182, 185, 188, **192** *endnotes*, 210, 211, 217, 221, 222, 225, 231, 232, 235-237

Imperialism 39

Job 2, 12, 15, 18, 21, 25, 42, 47, 48, 50, 51, 53, 58, 59, **60** *endnotes*, **63** *endnotes*, 69-71, 73, 79, 83, 84, 89, 90, 95, 100, **106** *endnotes*, **110** *endnotes*, 120-123, 127, 128, 130, 136, 138, 139, 142, 156-160, 163-171, 173, 175-178, 182, 185, 186, 188, 203, 205, 231

Keshen, Jeffrey A. 9, 11, 12, **28-31** *endnotes*, **62** *endnotes*, 81, **109** *endnotes*, **111** *endnotes*, 141, **153** *endnotes*, 175, 178, 184, **193-195** *endnotes*, **238** *endnotes*, **244** *biblio.*

Kessler-Harris, Alice 163, **191** *endnotes*, **244** *biblio.*

Klein, Yvonne 11, **30** *endnotes*, **151** *endnotes*, **245** *biblio.*

Knowles, Valerie 55, **63** *endnotes*, **229** *endnotes*, **245** *biblio.*

Korinek, Valerie 22, 24, **28** *endnotes*, **29** *endnotes*, **34** *endnotes*, **35** *endnotes*, 52, 53, 57, 58, **61-63** *endnotes*, **112** *endnotes*, 122, **150** *endnotes*, **230** *endnotes*, **245** *biblio.*

Labour force 12, 15, 106, 163-165, 167-169, 175, 184

Ladies Home Journal 23, **34** *endnotes*

Liberal feminism **33** *endnotes*

Liberation 9, 14, 16, 19, 97, 239

Light, Beth 18, **32** *endnotes*, **61** *endnotes*, **107** *endnotes*, **109** *endnotes*, 125, **150** *endnotes*, 159, 163, 184, 186, **190** *endnotes*, **193** *endnotes*, **194** *endnotes*, 235, **238** *endnotes*, **244** *biblio.*, **245** *biblio.*, **249** *biblio.*

Maclean's 12, 18, **33** *endnotes*, 58, **113** *endnotes*, 183, **194** *endnotes*, 235, **238** *endnotes*, **240** *biblio.*

Maclean Publishing 7, 28, **29** *endnotes*

Macpherson, Mary Etta 38, 48-52, **62** *endnotes*, **63** *endnotes*, 182, 183, **194** *endnotes*

Male 11, 12, 16, 18, 21, 38, 43, 49, 58, **61** *endnotes*, 67, 68, 79, 91, 94, 96-99, 105, **106** *endnotes*, 125, 126, 141, 145, 147, 158, 161, 163, 174, 176, 178, 180, 184, 187, 200, 210, **226** *endnotes*, 237

Matrimony 66, 83, 84, 93, 171

Marital status 158, 164, 172, 187, 189